RECKONING
with
APOCALYPSE

RECKONING
with
APOCALYPSE

Terminal Politics and Christian Hope

DALE AUKERMAN

CROSSROAD • NEW YORK

1993

The Crossroad Publishing Company
370 Lexington Avenue, New York, NY 10017

Copyright © 1993 by Dale Aukerman

Printed in the United States of America

Library of Congress Cataloging-in-Publication Data

Aukerman, Dale.
   Reckoning with apocalypse : terminal politics and Christian hope /
Dale Aukerman.
     p. cm.
   Includes bibliographical references and index.
   ISBN 0-8245-1243-X
   1. End of the world. 2. Church and state—United States.
3. Christianity and politics. 4. Fundamentalism—Controversial
literature. I. Title.
BT876.A85 1993
236'.9—dc20   92-38425
                                       CIP

FOR RUTH
to whom I owe
along with so remarkably much more
her making possible the long writing of this book.

Or will thy all-surprising light
Break at midnight?

Henry Vaughan,
"The Dawning"

Contents

Part III
THE MESSIAH'S TRIUMPH

FOREWORD

Dale Aukerman has the gift of reading our existence biblically. Accordingly, his new book, *Reckoning with Apocalypse*, is a gift to us all who lead lives of quite atheism precisely because we do not know how to make the language of the Bible inscribe our lives into a different reality. I thought his earlier book, *Darkening Valley*, could not be surpassed in its power to help us see theologically what was at stake in the threat of nuclear weapons.

Reckoning with Apocalypse, however, is even more powerful, as now Aukerman helps us see how our current politics is intelligible only as judged by God's lordship. Reminding us that apocalypse is the disclosure of God's truth in Jesus Christ for the consummation of history, Aukerman frees apocalyptic from those who use selected passages of the Bible to forecast this or that happening as well as from those who ignore or demythologize apocalyptic as not crucial for Christian existence.

With a talent that can only be described as poetic, Aukerman reclaims apocalyptic as not just one other aspect of the gospel, but as at the very heart of the good news of God's call to Israel and the Cross and Resurrection of Christ. Accordingly he helps us see that our lives are embedded in forces and powers that can be understood and resisted only to the extent that we understand that as Christians we have been made citizens of a Kingdom of the end times.

Aukerman may well be one of the most important theologians writing in our time. In the future his work will surely be compared to that of Jacques Ellul and John Howard Yoder.

STANLEY HAUERWAS

PREFACE

In 1982 I was with a group vigiling and leafletting outside the Sheraton-Washington Hotel in Washington, D.C., to witness against an arms bazaar being held inside. A prim and very self-assured older woman soon reached the point of informing me that what had been happening in Lebanon with the Israeli invasion was the fulfilment of prophecies in the Bible. She urged me to read the Bible and see for myself. As it happened, just one prophecy was haunting me: "The violence done to Lebanon will overwhelm you" who perpetrate it (Hab. 2:17). There on the street corner and elsewhere at other times I have been perplexed about what to say in response to such appropriation of biblical prophecies, especially when used to justify warmaking. Before and during the U.S.-Iraq War, prophecy specialists of the religious right wielded considerable political influence through their claims on television and radio and in best-selling books that the rise of the "Babylonian" Saddam Hussein and the war with him were all previewed in biblical predictions.

With few exceptions, church people[1] who give emphasis to forecasts about the end of the world are uninvolved in the struggle against the nuclear peril and other threats to human survival. A common attitude is that the predicted horrors are going to come anyway, and Christians must not let themselves be diverted from the all-important task of winning persons to a saving faith in Jesus Christ. Such an outlook typically includes the view that in the rapture of the church Christians from midair will look back down at the nuclear blasts and be filled with joy at God's mercy to them. Outside that arms bazaar an Air Force officer assured me that he had no fear at all of nuclear war because all true Christians are to be taken up from the earth just before the bombs go off. He was a genial fellow and, boarding an Air Force bus, called to me cheerily, "See you at the rapture." Faith of that sort is a formative element in the thinking of many who have a part in the management of the immense U.S. military might.

Two main approaches to biblical eschatology (teaching about the future consummation of history and what leads up to it) predominate within the churches. In the first, one tries to identify biblical passages as forecasts of specific contemporary events in order to predict the future, including the approximate time of the Second Coming of Jesus. The United States and its allies are characteristically viewed as largely aligned with God's righteous purposes. Church folk, dismayed about turmoil around the world, want to see everything as within God's control. Interpreters of prophecy, from television preachers through Hal Lindsey to the Jehovah's Witnesses, speak to this yearning.

In the opposed approach, biblical eschatology is simply ignored or demythologized away from its original intent. First World Christians who are deeply involved in the struggle for peace and justice generally avoid issues of eschatology as a diversion or as the already annexed playground of the religious right. As in the beginnings of the "social gospel" movement, such Christians tend to be "adamant in their opposition to all eschatologies that might justify passive Christian response to societal injustice."[2] If they have any eschatology, it may be hardly more than the faltering affirmation that humanity, assisted by God, will bring to actualization its visions of a better world.

In this book both approaches are seen as misguided. For a Christian reading of contemporary events, biblical eschatology must be reclaimed from the religious right and become as determinative for discipleship now as it was in the early church. This book is an attempt to survey what is against humanity and to discern for current history and the future how Jesus Christ is for humanity. After the foundational first chapter, Part II is weighted more toward the *against*, and Part III, more toward the *for*; but throughout is the encounter of those contrary movements. Christians should not contemplate what they are up against without keeping in view the One who rescues; and they look to the One who saves in terms of what they are saved from.

Jesus said to the Pharisees and Sadducees who came to test him: "You know how to interpret the appearance of the sky, but you cannot interpret the signs of the times" (Mt. 16:3). They could spot a storm arising over the Mediterranean, but not the storm of disaster developing on the political horizon.[3] The irony of that inability is far greater in our time. We are given weather forecasting, hurricane watches, economic indicators, computer projections about what is ahead for anything and everything; yet in the matter of basic societal direction and what that must lead to, there is a tragic lack of discernment, even among those claiming to live by God's word. Jesus' comment had the implication that his disciples were to do what his opponents were failing to do: discern in events around them the indicators of God's impending judgment and salvation. When disciples do that, they heed Jesus' command, "Watch" (Mk. 13:37).

Augustine wrote as the Roman Empire was collapsing. But what looms ahead of us is the collapse, even the end, of human life as we know it. G. C. Berkouwer has commented: "Naturally, Augustine did not pretend to interpret all the secrets of Providence, but he did refuse to leave the events of the day uninterpreted."[4] Looking to the biblical accounts of God's acts in history, one can venture to identify contours of God's acting in our time. "In the path of thy judgments, / O Lord, we wait for thee" (Is. 26:8). That path continues through the centuries. Finding themselves located in it, disciples seek some understanding of the extremity of the current global predicament. How is one to make biblical sense of the preponderant craziness in the world and see contemporary history and its further unfolding in the light of Christ? A critically important test for any theology is whether it has the wherewithal to deal with the prospect of a desolation or end of history brought about by human beings.

This book is written with the United States very much in view as the one remaining superpower in the world. The United States is seen as archetypal, just as in the Bible Babylon or Rome was: The pre-eminent collectivity is not the sole locus of evil but is taken as representing most strikingly the defiance of God regnant in all comparable groupings. A transposition of the issues is appropriate in any other country. The strenuous objection will be made that the picture given is anti-American[5] and far too dark. To be sure, there is in U.S. society and in many of its structures much that is good, much that sustains and enhances human life. The terrible problem is that powers of destruction predominate over all that good, hold it in their embrace, and threaten to undo it totally. So much was good in Jewish society around Jesus, but he saw the forces that were taking it toward cataclysm. He therefore viewed that society very much in terms of those forces. U.S. society and the contemporary world need to be seen in a comparable way. Recognizing their own complicity, Christians in the rich countries, that is, in the imperial powers, need to consider confessionally what these countries are and do in the world.

This book often focuses on views most characteristic of the religious right and the "conservative" range within the churches. But this is done with a recognition that such views are for the most part something like cartoon caricatures of essentially the same beliefs in the mainstream of the churches. God-and-country religion in Christian guise has been around since the Roman emperor Constantine.

As seen in Christian faith, the Lamb that was slain opens the sealed and mysterious scroll of history (Rev. 5–7). His is the Lordship that gives history its meaning, direction, and conclusion. In this perspective the scriptural record of the revelation centered in this One is normative for the understanding of faith and history. This book is meant for any who have interest in considering a Christian view of our imperiled world. My request of Christians who disagree, especially those who most vigorously disagree, is biblically grounded refutation rather than dismissal of the book by misrepresenting it as what it is not.

Jamie Edgerton as advisor, accountability person, and friend has accompanied me through this project with verve and faithfulness, even though he was living in Australia except for brief consultancy trips to the United States. As readers of the manuscript, Burton Blistein, Dale W. Brown, George Hunsinger, Kim McDowell, and (most of all) my daughters Miriam and Maren Aukerman have given substantial assistance with numerous suggestions for its revision. I am grateful to Walter Brueggemann, Jim Wallis, and John Howard Yoder for their counsel with regard to finding a publisher. Justus George Lawler as ever insightful editor has contributed very significantly to the book's final form, and he had the flexibility to accept the chapter "Masada and Golgotha" in spite of some strong disagreements with it.

PART I

"NO OTHER
FOUNDATION"

Chapter 1

GOD'S WORD AND POLITICAL DISCERNMENT

For no other foundation can anyone lay than that which is laid, which is Jesus Christ.

—1 Corinthians 3:11

Together gospel and political application form one circle, one unitary whole.... No periphery without the center!... No center without the periphery!... A circle's center without its periphery is a contradiction in terms. Where Christian doctrine is held while the imperatives of peace and justice are denied, questions arise whether the gospel has been encountered or understood at all. Happily, however, between evangelical truth and social justice we need not choose, for in the unity of the Lordship of Jesus Christ, "there is only one truth and one justice — and no one can serve two masters."

—George Hunsinger[1]

The call of Abraham and the exodus were remembered as acts of God set in the world of nations. The history of Israel and Judah proceeded as very much a part of that wider world. The Hebrew prophets saw God's ruling hand in what was happening internationally around them. They gave graphic descriptions of God's role as sovereign over those events. John on Patmos did the same in the more veiled imagery of the book of Revelation. The events of the life of Jesus were "not done in a corner," as Paul reminded King Agrippa (Acts 26:26). According to the prayer in Acts 4:24–31, the apostolic community in Jerusalem saw the dynamics of the crucifixion of Jesus as international and their struggle, like his, as being on the world stage, with God the chief actor. Jesus looked toward a missionary outreach into all the nations. Acts tells of the beginnings of that, with the claims, demands, and actions of political authorities very much within view.

In our time all who are not personally or ethnically encapsulated are reached to some degree by an unceasing inundation of news

3

from around the planet. Reports about current events in global collage surround people in the technologically more advanced areas. The clashing interrelatedness of this fragmented world dins into the common consciousness. But one finds in the churches little discernment of God as sovereign over these events, little sense of what the prophets saw and declared. As Langdon Gilkey has observed: "It is not so hard to assert the sovereignty of God in our own history — though even this is rare among modern theologians. But it *is* difficult to believe it, and even more difficult for us in our time to know and express reflectively what we mean by it."[2]

This state of affairs led Herbert Butterfield to express the plea:

Nothing is more important for the cause of religion at the present day than that we should recover the sense and consciousness of the Providence of God — a Providence that acts not merely by a species of remote control but as a living thing, operating in all the details of life — working at every moment, visible in every event. Without this you cannot have any serious religion, any real walking with God, any genuine prayer, any authentic fervour and faith.[3]

God, the Cosmos, and History

A question basic to all this and broader than what has to do with history comes into view: What is God's relation to the cosmos and the nearer creation around us? One range of thought, worked out in a variety of ways, tends to identify God with the cosmos or with humanity. All things are seen as parts of God. God is thought of as the immanent creative dynamic in all things, something like the soul in a body. Or "God" is the name given to the reservoir of reason, goodness, love, and harmony that humans carry within themselves and are to be drawing upon.[4] A sense of the divinity inhering in the entities of the cosmos or perhaps seen as especially focused in humans is to draw us into respect and care for them.

Biblical faith, however, knows nothing of any identification of God with the cosmos. Basic to that faith is the clear distinction between God the Creator and the creation. God was before all things. By God's Word all things were brought into being. All the cosmos could vanish away, and God would still be God. Human beings are not manifestations of God. They do not have divinity within themselves, nor does any other creature.

In another mode of thought, God is seen as the One who started things off initially; but from then on, the cosmos has gone along autonomously by its own momentum. One could use the analogy of a scientist who developed and programmed a computerized machine, with the machine then running on its own. We live in a world permeated by a mechanistic understanding of the universe (whether with or without "God"), and that understanding shapes the outlook of us all. Such a view provides the backdrop for attempted human lordship over history and has cleared the way for humans to dominate and exploit the biosphere.

From science comes explanation as to why the sun appears to rise in the morning. The earth has been spinning for more than two billion years, and one further spin brings the sun into sight again. If considered at all in relation to this, God may be thought of as being quite far behind it in the role of the superlative computer programmer. But Jesus said, "Love your enemies and pray for those who persecute you, so that you may be children of your Father who is in heaven; for *he makes his sun rise* on the evil and on the good, and sends rain on the just and on the unjust" (Mt. 5:44–45). Jesus was saying: Each sunrise is God's doing; God is causing that to happen. Jesus, in the Hebraic simplicity of the faith expressed throughout the Bible, woke to see God's sun being brought into view by God. Humans of our time need the same awakening. Jesus' words "he makes his sun rise" have more significance than all that astronomers can discover.

As a university student I heard a memorable lecture by the philosopher Mortimer Adler. What struck me the most was his thesis, not clear to me till then, that everything in creation is being held up moment by moment into existence by God. If for an instant God would withdraw that upholding, the universe would vanish into nothingness. The Creator is the Sustainer. In Emil Brunner's metaphor the creation's "being is like that of a soap bubble which exists only because and as long as it is blown by the blower."[5]

Karl Heim develops the image that each of us is in a prison cell. There is a wall like the wall of a cell between me and other persons. For me the most immediate reality experienced is my own I; and so for each of them, their own I. They have no direct access to that inner I of mine, nor do I to theirs. I can knock on the wall to give expression to myself, as can they. Or if the wall is pictured as pliant thin wax, I or they can make impressions into the wall. The person on the other side may perceive the knocks or the impressions, but these are the communications of an I that remains hidden and mostly inaccessible within the walls of the cell.

However, in Heim's imagery each cell is open at the top, open to God, who totally comprehends the concealed I of each person. And so each is not ultimately isolated and alone.[6] But to go further, if I contemplate my aged dog Babushka, she clearly has some sort of I, a centeredness of being and will, though much more inaccessible to me than that of human friends. Babushka and I each see the bodily actions of the other but can know so little of the other's inner being. And similarly for a sparrow, a toad, a fly.

God "holds in his power the soul of every living thing" (Job 12:10 JB). Heim points to "a wholeness tendency" throughout creation. Each cell, each living thing, has a mysterious wholeness and what can be thought of as an inner will toward that wholeness. But also in the inorganic, in molecules, crystals, snowflakes, stars, galaxies, there is the wholeness tendency. In Heim's view each entity in the cosmos, down to the subatomic, has a hidden inner centering of being and will analogous, however remotely, to our own. Each is held into existence by the Creator. Each smaller entity, from the subatomic, is sustained and coordinated as component into ever larger entities. Each has its line of dependence to God, in whom all lines converge.[7]

This view could easily be dismissed as no more than speculative, were it not that scripture, especially the Hebrew scriptures, points very much in the same direction. Thus a few verses from the Psalms:

> Let the floods clap their hands;
>   let the hills sing for joy together
> before the Lord, for he comes to rule the earth.
>
>   (Ps. 98:8, 9)
>
> Praise him, sun and moon,
>   praise him, all you shining stars! ...
>
> Praise the Lord from the earth
>   you sea monsters and all deeps,
> fire and hail, snow and frost,
>   stormy wind fulfilling his command!
>
> Mountains and all hills,
>   fruit trees and all cedars!
> Beasts and all cattle,
>   creeping things and flying birds!
>
>   (Ps. 148:3, 7–10)

Out of the inner being of other creatures issues a praise of God analogous to praise by humans. They have their chief purpose not in being there for humans but in bringing glory to God. And they typically rest within the will of God as humans, tragically, seldom do.[8]

One should, however, also recognize in the nonhuman natural world rebellious will (Mk. 4:39), skewedness, and provisional "bondage to decay" (Rom. 8:21).

Jesus taught that the Father is with each sparrow in its living and its dying (Mt. 10:29) — so too with every creature — and that the Father gives daily bread, feeds the birds of the air, and clothes the grass of the field (Mt. 6:11, 26, 30). In the faith of the apostolic church the Son is "upholding the universe by his word of power" (Heb. 1:3): That One crucified on Golgotha and risen on the third day is holding into existence and incomprehensible dynamism all galaxies, quasars, black holes. Before God "no creature is hidden, but all are open and laid bare to the eyes of him with whom we have to do" (Heb. 4:13). If God in loving care holds up into existence each entity in the cosmos, if each has its dependence line to God, if God is present with and acting toward every creature, how great should be the wonder, caring, and carefulness with regard to the nonhuman creation and toward human creatures most of all.

That gracious sovereignty envelops history along with the cosmos. In the Hebrew scriptures God's Lordship over creation and God's sovereignty over history are interwoven and complementary. It is God "who stretches out the heavens like a curtain, / and spreads them like a tent to dwell in; / who brings princes to nought, / and makes the rulers of the earth as nothing" (Is. 40:22–23). God is ceaselessly concerned with every entity and aspect of creation. God as all-knowing, all-seeing, all-loving Thou constantly confronts each human being and every human grouping. A parent acts in such varied ways toward a child — affirming, resisting, encouraging, warning, evoking, forgiving; and this mirrors the multiformity of God's acting toward each individual and every grouping, to direct, infuse, confute, transform. One either marvels at the breadth of that providential rule (and this most intimately for one's own life) or does not recognize it.

Persons residing in the lone superpower have two primary options for viewing current history: to see the nation/government/leader as chief actor or to see God as that. What draws the attention is the one exercise of sovereignty or the other. The president is commonly regarded as the one in whom nationally "all things hold together." Especially when a president moves toward war or goes to war with an adversary, most of the populace supposes that this is the acting that really counts. But also those who oppose such actions may be impelled to see them, with dismay, as centrally determinative on the world stage.

To the extent that our gaze is drawn beyond the personal sphere toward the world scene, it is ordinarily filled simply with what draws it. The evening of the U.S. bombing of Libya in the attempt to kill Muammar Khadafi, I watched the news and the shrewd persuasiveness of those who spoke for the Reagan administration. In bed during the night I found my mind reeling with the names of Reagan, Khadafi, Weinberger, Shultz. But then a line and melody of a song from a retreat I had just been in came to me: "Glorify thy name in all the earth." I had been forgetting the name which is above every name (Phil. 2:9), the One who is incomprehensibly mighty beyond all human displays of power. In the night that name of the One who was in sovereign control even over this braggadocio and slaughter of innocents, the One who was with Hannah Khadafi and the others in their dying, more and more displaced those pathetic little names.

Urgently and continuously needed is a biblical calculus of power — a right reckoning of what power is incomparably greater and what power is inferior, along with the discernment that God is mightier not only abstractly and ultimately but also in this present. All of scripture brings to remembrance that God is graciously sovereign over the human family and over the world, through God's word. "Thine, O Lord, is the greatness, and the *power*, and the *glory*, and the victory, and the majesty;... thine is the *kingdom*, O Lord" (1 Chron. 29:11). Jesus said, "You are wrong, because you know neither the scriptures nor the power of God" (Mt. 22:29). Those central correlative aspects of human ignorance underlie most wrongdoing. But Jesus can open eyes to see the incursion of God's Rule, as he and those who bore witness before and after him discerned it. Then one begins to understand what Paul could express only by heaping up synonymous words: "the surpassing greatness of his power [*dynamis*] over us believers — a power [*energeia*] which operates with the strength [*kratos*] of the might [*ischys*] which he exerted [the verb *energeo*] in raising Christ from the dead" (Eph. 1:19–20 Moffatt). Still more than anywhere else God acted with all power in Jesus and his rising. Of that power Paul S. Minear has written: "To biblical writers the living God is always a holy Presence. This Presence makes himself known not so much as a constant spiritual stratosphere, but as an awesome, invasive power. This power moves in the direction and with the momentum of invincible purpose, which all historical vitalities, whether of evil or good, are constrained to serve."[9]

God's Word to the Nations Now

The Hebrew prophets offered revealed commentary on what for them was the present and the future. There is in these days no prophet with such commissioning and authority. The canon is closed. It might seem that in this regard humans are rather in the dark. Church constituencies are inclined to assume such a situation and not to find in scripture God's word as decisive now for national and international affairs as it was originally. Or they give itching ears to whoever can engagingly identify biblical passages as specific forecasts of present and future international developments.

In a story Jesus told, Abraham says to the rich man who was pleading that Lazarus be sent back from the dead to warn his five brothers: "They have Moses and the prophets; let them hear them" (Lk. 16:29). Christians, the churches, and the nations have (access to) Moses, the prophets, and Jesus Christ. It is the common experience of Christians that words of Jesus spoken to specific persons and recorded in the Gospels become his present communication to them. Each person in those stories represented and expressed aspects of who each human being is. In the oneness of humanity all humans were with those who met Jesus. Through interacting with that quite limited number of people in Palestine, Jesus entered into encounter with the rest. In his ministry he found the right words for each person and occasion. Under his present Lordship any saying of his from narrative or from teaching can come as just the right word to those open to receive it or to those not open.

The writings of the Hebrew prophets (and all of scripture) are to be approached with much the same understanding. Each prophet sought to declare God's message to Israel and, secondarily, to other nations. But those nations and times represented all nations and times, and thus the nations of our time. A perspective that Gerhard von Rad described for the later prophetic period should still be held to:

> It was never presumed that the prophet's oracles were addressed to one set of people and one only, and were thereafter to be wrapped in their rolls and deposited among the records. There must have been people who never forgot that a prophet's teaching always remained relevant for a coming day and generation, and who themselves played their part in making it appear relevant.[10]

Jesus did not so much speak God's word to the nations in the manner of the prophets. He came as God's Word to Israel/Judah and all the nations. In his life, teaching, death, and vindication he completed the message of the prophets (Mt. 5:17). What the prophets proclaimed was confirmed and explicated by Jesus. And unless Jesus is seen in close relation to God's word through the prophets to the nations, the understanding of who Jesus was and is remains delimited.

Jesus drew upon the prophetic tradition and recast it. In this he did supremely what successive prophets had done. The issue of violent use of power was a most crucial one for the reshaping that Jesus carried out through his teaching and his way of living and dying. The prophets by and large recognized that full trust in Yahweh precluded resort to violence and war. The main point in the earlier Hebrew battle stories was that the people of Yahweh were not to rely at all on military might and valor but were to have complete trust in him for deliverance — a point totally opposed to the prevailing outlook in every country with regard to the military. Jesus fulfilled that motif. He met his enemies in total dependence on God's faithfulness to act; he rejected all resort to violence under the guise of mediating God's triumphal intervention; and through that utter dependence God won the victory. Jesus gave with utter clarity God's imperative against violence and did that by living out motifs in the prophets, especially in the Servant passages of Second Isaiah. As Lord of scripture he transmuted whatever in the Torah and the prophets might have seemed to support the use of violence.[11]

The book of Revelation recasts the message of the Hebrew prophets and thus affirms it as God's continuing word to his people and to the nations. John did not focus on specific current or impending events to interpret them as the prophets had done but sought to make known how all of history is centered in, and mastered by, God's acting in Jesus Christ.[12] John, more than the earlier prophets, points to motifs that run throughout history and reach climactic immensity at the End (as *telos*, goal, consummation).[13] "Now write what you see, what *is* and what is to take place hereafter" (1:19). John sees, behind the veil of the visible, God in heaven acting into events on earth. Revelation makes clear that the tumult of the nations and things political should for disciples be very much within view. But the tumult must not dominate their perception, just as it does not dominate in Revelation.

God's word through the prophets was mainly addressed not to individuals in their private sphere but to Israel and Judah corporately and to the other nations. It was at times actually sent to Gentile rulers, though there are only marginal indications of this. Jeremiah passed on messages from Yahweh to visiting emissaries of the nations addressed: "Thus the Lord said to me:... 'Send word to the king of Edom, the king of Moab, the king of the sons of Ammon, the king of Tyre, and the king of Sidon by the hand of the envoys who have come to Jerusalem to Zedekiah king of Judah'" (Jer. 27:2–3). Ludwig Köhler maintains for the messages at the beginning of the book of Amos: "No prophet speaks into the air. The only reasonable explanation is that there were representatives of these neighbouring peoples there present at the festival of Jahweh in Bethel."[14]

The parts of scripture that were especially intended as God's word to nations should be looked to as that now. God has not left present-day nations without his word but gives it in Jesus and the scripture centered in him. By and large the church has privatized the Bible and the coming of Jesus. But beyond the individual and personal, these are for the larger groupings, for the nations as nations, and for human beings as participants in them. Jesus came as "a light to the nations" (Is. 49:6, quoted in Acts 13:47 and 26:23), "a light for revelation to the Gentiles [the non-Israelite nations]" as collective groupings, not just as multiplicities of individuals. Jesus is "the very [chief corner] stone which the builders rejected" (Mk. 12:10) — the builders of that and nearly every other society. "The world knew him not... his own people received him not" (Jn. 1:10, 11); it is not most of all as solitary individuals but as collective masses that humans reject him.

Hebrew prophecies gave warning or promise in specific historical situations, such as the rise of the Neo-Babylonian Empire. Calamities were preceded by warnings from God. Such warnings constitute much of scripture and have great relevance to current world affairs. Now as in that long-ago time God's word catches up the disregarded warning in unfolding developments. In that convergence the Lord of history corners peoples and leaders: Either obey or see what will follow if you do not.

Throughout the proclamation of the prophets and into that of Jesus were the three dimensions: "Because... therefore... unless." Because of immense wickedness, a corresponding destruction is coming, unless people repent. Often the "unless" remained unexpressed; the popular commitment to a course in defiance of God was seen as so strong that continuation into cataclysm seemed virtually certain. Later prophets, especially Jeremiah and Ezekiel, took up and restated for Judah and the nations of their time the "because" and "therefore," the warrant and the threat, announced by earlier prophets. Jesus warned the Jewish people around him that the course they were following would bring upon them destruction by the Romans unless they turned to the contrary course he was of-

fering them as the faithfulness required by God. In this preaching,
Jesus was prophet and brought to consummate expression God's
pleas through the earlier prophets. He cried out against wickedness,
especially that of the religious elite. Jesus saw himself as prophet
in continuity with those prophets: "Nevertheless I must go on my
way today and tomorrow and the day following; for it cannot be
that a prophet should perish away from Jerusalem" (Lk. 13:33). His
call to Israel as a whole was his call in like manner to every nation;
for his followers were to transmit it to the people of every nation
(Mt. 28:19–20).

God's word continues to resound toward the nations. Where the
biblical "because" can be currently discerned in the affairs of presumed peoples of God and of nations without this formulation of
the claim, the "therefore" is imminent. Each prophecy was, for the
specific historical situation, a statement about God's way of dealing
with the nations. God still deals in the same way. God's warnings
still hold. "Behold, I am bringing upon this city . . . all the evil that I
have pronounced against it, because they have stiffened their neck,
refusing to hear my words" (Jer. 19:15). What God requires has been
set before all humanity in God's revelation to Israel and in Jesus.
What God allows to come as consequence of wickedness has also
been made clear, especially in the prophets. The motifs of judgment
on human rebellion, of casting down the mighty and rescuing the
lowly, of later punishment coming upon those who have been instruments of judgment, of remnant and return, are as determinative
in contemporary world affairs as they were in the ancient biblical
Middle East.

Disciples of Jesus stand in a line of witness continuing that of the
Hebrew prophets: "for in the same way they persecuted the prophets
who were before you" (Mt. 5:12 NRSV). Like the prophets, disciples
identify the dominating forms of collective wickedness. Only so can
they resist that dominion pressing upon *them*. However, prophetic
identification of what in a society is defiance of God can have its
basis only in God's self-disclosure to Israel and in Jesus and not in
ideology (adherence to ideas).

The Focal Disputation

A disputation motif runs through the Gospels. Again and again
Jesus' adversaries tried to get the better of him with a question, usually masking an accusation: about plucking grain or healing on the

sabbath, about his disciples' not washing their hands before meals, about divorce, about the basis for his authority, about paying the tax to Caesar, about the resurrection of the dead. Each time Jesus overpowered them and their intended point with his answer. His adversaries could not outwit him in disputation, even on what they chose as ensnaring rabbinic terrain. Trying to discredit him, they were themselves discredited. When he silenced the Sadducees, the Pharisees made still another attempt (Mt. 22:34–35). But after Jesus' rabbinic question about David's son and Lord, "no one was able to answer him a word, nor from that day did any one dare to ask him any more questions" (Mt. 22:46).

Soon, however, in a very different situation, that of a hearing and trial directed toward a death sentence, his enemies assailed him with accusations and questions. "But Jesus was silent" (Mt. 26:63). "He made no answer" (Mt. 27:12). The climax of their side of the disputation was a prosecution that succeeded in having him executed. They finished their verbal challenges to him as he hung on the cross (Mk. 15:29–32 and parallels). The culmination of Jesus' side of the disputation, his concluding answer, was twofold: silence while being "led to the slaughter" (Is. 53:7; Acts 8:32), that is, his absorbing the assault of interrogation, torture, and execution; and his rising from death to be exalted at the right hand of God. In the unity of both, Jesus completely outdid his adversaries.

Though little recognized, this disputation has continued through history, especially in the countries of Christendom. All that is not with Christ has come as questioning set against Christ. That questioning has been explicit in counterclaims by various philosophers and anti-Christian governments or implicit in rejection of the way of Christ under the guise of allegiance to him. (Dostoyevsky's treatment of that rejection in "The Legend of the Grand Inquisitor" is cast as disputation, met by silence and the kiss of the One meant for execution.[15]) Contrary systems rise and decline. Counterpositions are brilliantly presented. And yet, for any who have discerning ears, "There has never been anybody who has spoken like him" (Jn. 7:46 JB). No one else ever saw so deeply and truly into the human situation or spoke with such authority. No one else ever communicated such a sense of the grounding of all that he did and said in God's constant guidance. No one else ever expressed so well in teaching and life what right human living is. No one has ever outdone him in the unending struggle about what is true. More radically than anyone else in history Jesus called into question prevailing assumptions that generally shape individuals and societies. In his self-understanding he lived not out of innate genius and masterful insight but out of God's acting in him.

Yet, more than his outcomprehending and outteaching others, Jesus outdied them, died, as no other, a death for all. He did more by going into the total silence of death than by all his answers to adversarial questions. God gave, in the resurrection, the supreme answer to all that Jesus had left unanswered in the trial and in his dying. And so it is for everything in life that seems without answer.

This disputation, this adversarial questioning of Jesus' questioning, is to be seen as central to the contemporary world. Jesus and his movement were a momentous threat to the Jewish (and Roman) religious-political power structure of his time. They continue to be that to the power structures of our time. Far more than any other perspective or approach, what Jesus taught and lived contradicts the characteristic ways in which power is exercised from within those structures. Subservient religion in its assigned role as sanctifier of those structures works to eliminate that threat and contradiction. The dominant interests in most countries have been able to contain and overpower dissent in its various ranges. They seem to succeed in this even with God's dissent, God's No in Jesus Christ to most of what they are doing. But they are already outmatched and undone by that supreme dissent.

God's Span over History

What distinguishes the living God of biblical revelation from gods is set forth in Isaiah 46:9–10:

> I am God, and there is none like me,
> declaring the end from the beginning
>   and from ancient times things not yet done,
> saying, "My counsel shall stand,
>   and I will accomplish all my purpose."

What the Lord of history wills is his purpose, which he makes known. As Claus Westermann summarizes, "Yahweh...by his historical word throws a span over events and thereby holds sway over them."[16] That prophetic word does not come simply as prediction of what will happen. As statement of God's sovereign decision about the future, it determines what will happen, though this is in relation to human response to that word.

In the Hebrew Bible and still more fully in Jesus and the apostolic scriptures, God has declared his purpose from beginning to end. The

Word as *the* human being became God's determining span thrown over all of history and thus over the events of our time. Hebrew believers looked back to and recounted mighty acts of Yahweh as basis for their expectation of his continued acting toward them. For such basis disciples look back to and declare, most of all, what God has done in the Messiah. The Word was in the beginning and at the Midpoint and will be the determining content of the End. This Lord in continuity with all that past still speaks and acts. In a friend one meets indirectly all that entered into the shaping of that person. So all that Jesus was and all that shaped him from the story of Israel enters into his risen coming to individuals and to the nations.

God set forth his purpose "in Christ as a plan for the fullness of time, to unite all things in him" (Eph. 1:9–10). Throughout history God acts to accomplish that purpose. As Karl Barth has stated comprehensively: "He wills and works what He has revealed as His will and work in Jesus Christ, His Son.... He wills and works this alone."[17] Because God has put all this before disciples, they have basis for discerning how God is active in what occurs, including events in the world of nations.

Skeptics around Jesus asked for a sign, some clear demonstration of God's power through him. We do much the same when, faced with the vastness of suffering and evil in the world, we want God to act demonstratively to set things right. But the one sign given to this generation is the Son of man (Lk. 11:30). In him most demonstratively God has set, is setting, and will set all things right. Chiefly because disciples see Jesus as God's supreme self-disclosure, they know that God is sovereign over the contemporary world; and chiefly in Jesus they discern the depth and height and contours of that sovereignty.

In Christian perspective, the awesomeness of the present is not constituted primarily by global threats to a sustainable future, but rather by the word of the eternal and almighty God echoing in these days. The central danger is not what enemy groups might do, nor is it that of being killed in nuclear infernos or other terminal catastrophes. The central jeopardy is separation from God. Whatever problems emerge for individuals and nations, the prior and primary problem is in relation — or lack of relation — to God. The One who created the cosmos and humans in it, the One who in the Hebrew story and in Jesus has sought out all deserters, the One on whose scales the multifaceted might of the NATO powers and of all other countries is as specks of dust (Is. 40:15), this One speaks his word of warning and promise now. This word has far greater weight than prospects of imminent catastrophe and far more dynamism than all the frantic efforts of the nations. Beyond intimations of untimely extinction, the word of God "will stand for ever" (Is. 40:8).

According to Ephesians 6:10–20 Christians are to contend against "the world rulers of this present darkness" and for that are to "take the whole armor of God." One weapon in the passage is not completely defensive — "the sword of the Spirit, which is the word of God." A sword is not really a weapon for attack, like spears, bows and arrows, chariots. A sword is for combat at close quarters. "Word" in the Greek text refers to the spoken and written word of God. In standing against the devil, disciples are to do just what Jesus did in the wilderness, rely on God's word and use it as weapon in the combat. This earth is embattled ground, as is each human being. The God of love and light contends with the powers of darkness. The task given Christians is not that of driving the rebel hosts from the field. Even Jesus' triumph has not yet done that. But where by God's strength Christians individually and corporately turn back the incursions of the infernal powers, those powers suffer defeat, defeat that has great significance because it prefigures their imminent collapse.

In Psalm 46:10 (TEV) God says to the nations, "Stop fighting... and know that I am God."[18] The two activities are correlates. To go the way of war preparations and war is not to recognize this God. To cease fighting is a necessary prelude for coming to know God. If the nations do not stop, God will bring about through devastating judgment what the nations have not done in obedience and will stop "wars all over the world" (v. 9). Judgment by nuclear holocaust — breaking the bow, shattering the spear, burning the chariots with fire — could indeed make wars cease around the desolated planet. The prospect of that corroborates God's call to the nations. This command, "Stop fighting... and know that I am God," reached its fullness in Jesus. His life, teaching, death, and rising confirmed it as imperative from God for the community of disciples and, through them, for the nations. The Messianic King, "humble and riding on an ass," does away with the implements of war and commands "peace to the nations." What he will accomplish consummately at the End, he speaks and does in the interim chiefly through that community and through judgments upon the rebel warring nations, for his hidden dominion is already "to the ends of the earth" (Zech. 9:9–10).

PART II

"THE DESOLATING SACRILEGE"

Chapter 2

THE IMMINENCE OF THE END

We can perhaps thus frame the contradiction which life poses: the comfort of the old confession of God's Providence versus the *dread* that rises from the events of our century. Dread has now become the essence and intensification of the unrest and concern latently present in all times.
—G. C. Berkouwer[1]

We must reckon with the end of the whole temporal form of the world as earnestly and as soberly as we reckon with our own death. We must approach every crisis of politics, every social revolution, with the question, What light is thrown on this event by the End?
—Karl Heim[2]

To understand that one may be living, even in terms of calendrical time, shortly before the end of the world has been all along an element in the faith of the apostles, the early church, and those who have come after them. But now, taking into account the prospective end of the world is not something confined mostly to Christians. More and more, secular thinkers and the peoples of the world recognize that the human adventure may soon come to a dismal end. They too consider or dimly sense the prospect, "The end of all things is at hand" (1 Pet. 4:7).

One can sing through "America" any number of times and hardly notice the verse,

> O beautiful for patriot dream
> That sees beyond the years
> Thine alabaster cities gleam
> Undimmed by human tears!

But that earlier visionary optimism is as remote from us as the Egypt of the pharaohs or Periclean Athens. Now hardly anyone holds to that "patriot dream"; hardly anyone supposes that the United States or any other nation can achieve such shalom. Hope earlier had been for transforming the world almost beyond recognition. Now ghastly prospects for transformation have become our dread.

19

"Fear and Foreboding"

In varying degrees of acuteness human beings have always been confronted by darker aspects of uncertainty about the future: Would their personal niche in life and their societal context be preserved? Which threatening possibilities might be actualized? When would one's own death come? Now the uncertainty has been stretched far beyond its former breadth. Will there be a longer human future? Will all (or most) die together and relatively soon? Through the millennia catastrophes have been episodic, delimited — a part of human experience. Now they could become the totality. All have dwelt under the death-shadow (Is. 9:2; Mt. 4:16). Now that ever-impending dominion, rather than remaining slowly sequential, could extinguish all human life together. We are stalked not only by death in its ordinary coming but also (and far more imperiously) by death in its global imminence. What presses upon us is, if not the end of the world, the end of the world as suited for human habitation. The weight of all this in human consciousness around the planet can hardly be assessed.[3]

Luke 21:25–26 gives a prophecy of Jesus that is receiving a more global and striking fulfilment than ever before: "And there will be ... upon the earth distress of nations in perplexity at the roaring of the sea and the waves, men fainting with fear and with foreboding of what is coming on the world." For the Hebrews the sea was the realm of chaos, and its raging was taken as image of the turmoil among the nations (as in Ps. 65:5, 7: "O God of our salvation ... / who dost still the roaring of the seas, / the roaring of their waves, / the tumult of the peoples"). In Jesus' prophecy, words of apprehension are piled one upon the other: "distress ... perplexity ... fainting with fear [which could be translated, "scared to death"] ... foreboding." Throughout history people in one part of the world or another have been overwhelmed by fear of what seemed about to come, or was coming, upon them. But Jesus spoke of fear that would overtake the nations as a whole; and it would have to do with prospects threatening all the world. All peoples would be dominated by a common dread.

There have been regional prefigurings of this: dismay at the collapse of the Roman Empire or at the onward sweep of Muslim, Central Asiatic, or European armies (though not of course dismay among the victors); in Europe around A.D. 1000 panic about the end of the world; terror as the Black Death spread. But never before the twentieth century did globally recognized threats of catastrophe press upon all peoples. Every earlier period after the initial spread of the human race was characterized to a degree by the provincial isolation of diverse geographical segments of the race. In the twentieth century the oneness of history and the interconnectedness of all peoples, discerned by writers of the Hebrew scriptures, became so manifest as to provide the completed context for the all-encompassing dangers and fears that Jesus said were to come.

Fear and foreboding pervade human consciousness in our time. These are to a large extent repressed, as is typically the case with private fears. We are far more comfortable when not afraid, so we seize upon anything that can counter or quiet our fears. We long to be reassured that slow or sudden catastrophic horrors will not come over us.

But the threats to the future are manifold and immense: poisoning of the biosphere, global warming, destruction of the ozone layer, soil loss, deforestation, death of the oceans, desertification, a world population that may double yet again by the middle of the twenty-first century, loss of control over newly created forms of life, AIDS, ever-increasing damage of the human gene pool, the nuclear arsenals. George Wald, Nobel Laureate in Physiology and Medicine, warns that "human life is now threatened as never before, not by one but by many perils, each in itself capable of destroying us, but all interrelated, and all coming upon us together."[4] The impulsions toward species self-destruction running all through history are now meshed with the technological means adequate for bringing an end to the human story or, short of that, for terribly and irremediably blighting any future.

Fear of other countries is the most fateful determinant of the foreign policies of the nations. Diffuse beneath that and feeding into it is the "foreboding of what is coming on the world." The foreboding is often transposed into fear of enemies. Dangers harder to identify are given the name and shape of those easier to identify. "National security" efforts can supposedly hold enemies at bay, even if they cannot be comparably looked to for holding off "what is coming on the world." In fact, fear of enemies constantly feeds into the buildup toward that imminence — this most notably in the global military competition. But in the vicious circle, the nation and its leaders are then still more looked to for holding off whatever looms dark on the horizon.

Periods of greater fear alternate with periods of less fear. The early years of the Reagan administration brought acute and widespread anxiety that nuclear war would come. With the collapse of communist governments throughout Eastern Europe and then in the Soviet Union, most Americans euphorically concluded that the dangers in-

herent in the nuclear arms race were nearly past. Undercurrents of
foreboding persisted, but they were much less directed toward the
threat of nuclear annihilation. Yet as the Iraqi invasion of Kuwait
in August 1990 showed, a time of decreased fearfulness can suddenly be transposed into one in which imminence of a war with vast
consequences looms over the world.

The reduction of tension and hostility between the NATO powers and what had been the Soviet Union is certainly a very positive
development which in itself decreases the danger of nuclear war.
But the world after the collapse of communism throughout the former Warsaw Pact nations is much more unstable than before. The
main post–World War II checks and balances are no longer in place.
Whatever the resolution of the problem of who controls the nuclear
weapons spread across several of the Soviet successor states, the
political instability and volatility in those countries weighs into the
continuing global nuclear peril.

A sense of the inevitability of nuclear war, so widespread in the
early 1980s, has receded; but subservience to weapons and resignation to whatever future they may bring continues. As became
widely known, studies of nuclear winter have indicated that nuclear war could bring the extinction of human life and of all higher
forms of life on this planet.[5] The nuclear threat should not be focused upon to the disregard of other dangers, but neither should it
be ignored as now largely overcome. Nuclear holocaust remains the
greatest threat, towering over the others, and has the most deadly
potential for devastating the planet and quite possibly annihilating
humankind.[6]

The stunning "success" of U.S. and allied military power in the
U.S.-Iraq War came as a strong impetus toward increased reliance by
nations generally on the most sophisticated and powerful weapons
attainable. That war was a lesson in what can happen to a Third
World power trying to acquire nuclear weapons. But part of the lesson could be that only with such weapons does an aspiring Third
World power have some deterrent protection against the sort of destruction inflicted on Iraq. As long as nuclear weapons are so widely
seen as the ultimate means for national projection of power, the lure
to acquire them will remain strong. The breakup of the Soviet Union
and the consequent decrease in military production left tens of thousands of high-level nuclear and "conventional" arms engineers with
the possibility of providing their services to the highest bidder. The
danger that desperate, reckless leaders of lesser powers or of under-
ground groups will use nuclear bombs increases, as does the prospect

of an ultimatum: "We have this nuclear bomb ready to go off, and we have these demands." The detonation of one small nuclear bomb on or at a nuclear power plant could make an area one third the size of former West Germany uninhabitable for a long period.[7]

Albert Einstein likened an ever more powerful technology to an ax in the hands of a maniac.[8] To hold in readiness such vastly lethal technology goes against all sanity, and the likelihood of far greater bursting forth of the maniacal remains with us. The U.S.-Iraq War should have made clear that the threat of maniacal wielding of that ax does not come simply from those seen as adversaries. The end of the Cold War presented the nations of the world with an extraordinary opportunity to move quickly and decisively toward global disarmament — doing away with that ax. Nuclear disarmament will almost certainly not come except as correlated with general disarmament. A complete ban on nuclear testing is the step that could do most to curb the nuclear arms race and set the stage for the turn to disarmament, but the U.S. government has steadfastly opposed such a ban. In spite of the breakup of the Soviet Union, U.S. leaders and populace seem very far from any willingness to turn, in concert with other nations, from reliance on the war system and to dismantle their nuclear and "conventional" weapons. That stance may possibly change but not without the unlikely relinquishment of the collective determination to be *the* superpower in the world. With the decline of the Soviet/Russian threat, the continuous "upgrading" of U.S. (and Western) military "capabilities" has to do more obviously than before with imperial domination of the planet.

Popular thinking about nuclear bombs has always been in the short term. And so it is now. With no hostile superpower in competition with the United States and the West, the world seems a much safer place. It is safer with regard to annihilation resulting from an East-West nuclear exchange. But the accelerated velocity of the historical process, which has brought these extraordinary shifts in power relationships and in who is enemy to whom will certainly continue. Present allies (after being enemies earlier) may in a few years become enemies again. That possibility can be considered especially for Japan and the United States. Increase in hostile attitudes toward Japan could provide grounds for the development of whatever Japanese military deterrent seems needed. And one should not assume that the United States will long continue as the lone superpower or even as a superpower in the world. If the Soviet Union could be brought down so abruptly (apart from nuclear war), so can the United States.

Any decrease in the extent of public fearfulness about nuclear holocaust will remain relatively superficial and short-lived unless the United States and other countries make the decisive turn away from reliance on the military and war and toward "the things that make for peace" (Lk. 19:42). The nuclear peril is less than it was in the early 1980s; but as long as the addiction to those weapons and all weapons continues, that stalking desolation will pursue humanity. Even if worldwide disarmament is achieved, the possibility of quick return to weaponry and nuclear bombs will remain.

For Jonathan Schell in *The Fate of the Earth*, the opposite of "the second death," understood as human extinction, can be summed up like this: "While each of us is mortal, our species is biologically immortal." He draws upon Hannah Arendt's concept of "the common world":

> The common world . . . is made up of all institutions, all cities, nations, and other communities, and all works of fabrication, art, thought, and science, and it survives the death of every individual. It is basic to the common world that it encompasses not only the present but all past and future generations. "The common world is what we enter when we are born and what we leave behind when we die," Arendt writes. . . . "Without this transcendence into a potential earthly immortality, no politics, strictly speaking, no common world, and no public realm is possible."[9]

Schell, in this regard a representative modern thinker, points to what would seem the most fundamental datum: human life in its breadth, continuity, and perpetual amassing. The references to "immortality" and "transcendence" give refined expression to the Promethean expansiveness of the human enterprise.

Schell does not take into account that astrophysical projections about the future of the solar system and the universe make such an assumption about the immortality of our species extremely doubtful quite apart from current technological threats. But millions or even hundreds of thousands of years for the further course of humanity before extinction does provide the appearance of species immortality, seen from the vantage point of a few thousand years of recorded history. Yet a demise so remote would be as all-negating as nuclear or other extinction near ahead.

It is to be noted that human extinction can be contemplated as darkest possibility but would never be experienced as concluding certainty. The very last survivors would have no way of knowing that they were the last. They could not knowledgeably say, "As we now die, the human species comes to an end." Even those dying in a nuclear winter could not know for sure that human extinction was coming. That ending would be unknown except to a transcendent and most intimately involved Observer.

Biblical thought sees human life as the fundamental given, created by God, held up into existence by God, and receiving a future only from God. The Bible does not confirm the common assumption that, though each individual life is terminated by death, the human story goes on without end. Any continuation comes most crucially not through the biological dynamic but as marvel of God's merciful acting. Our species is not to be seen as having in itself the prospect of perpetuity. Humanity on its own produces the opposite prospect.

In scripture what is determinative is not a sense of immanent or achieved stability (as in contrary religions of the time) but of God's imminent judgment and rescue. Prophets and psalmists understood that "all flesh is grass" (Is. 40:6), and this not only in the death of individuals but in the transience of specific nations and in the collapse of the total structure of human presumption. The Bible again and again pictures great evil and catastrophes before the End of history. The prophets speak of terminal cataclysms. Daniel writes of "a time of trouble, such as never has been since there was a nation [Israel] till that time" (12:1). Echoing this, Jesus tells his disciples of many aspects of "great tribulation" (Mt. 24:21) before the End. Rebellion against God comes to its culmination, as does God's judgment upon that rebellion. In the Gospel story this rebellion was centered in the governmental structures and thus in the dominant elites. The book of Revelation gives that picture too for the movement of history to the End. This rebellion drives our world.

The Contrary Apocalypses

Apocalypse and *apocalyptic* have come to be among the most frequently used words for signifying horrors that are too vast for human imagination or language to cope with. Those who understand this use of the words often have at least a vague awareness of their having some connection with the book of Revelation, the Apocalypse.[10] This usage implies that images in that Apocalypse have much relevance for understanding the present and the hauntingly possible future of the world. For the casual reader of Revelation what stands out are the descriptions of cataclysmic woes. The common secular usage fixes upon that impression: *Apocalypse* refers to the impending catastrophic collapse and death throes of much or all of human life

in nuclear war or otherwise. As Hans Schwarz has very simply expressed it: "We live in an apocalyptic age. In a apocalyptic age man
concludes that the end of history is close at hand."[11]

In the apostolic scriptures *apokalypsis* is not a grim, foreboding
word. It means unveiling or disclosure — of God's truth in Jesus, of
specific visions or knowledge, and especially of Jesus Christ in his
glory at the consummation of history. It is the first word in the Greek
text of John's Apocalypse: "A Revelation from Jesus Christ, which
God gave Him so that He might show His servants what must very
soon take place" (Rev. 1:1 Phillips). The Apocalypse is an unveiling
of Jesus' Lordship over the rampages of history on to his triumph
at the End and has its center and meaning in that Lordship, not in
the disasters.

In Jesus God hid himself and disclosed himself. God came into
the human midst veiled in the flesh and life of Jesus of Nazareth. But
for those with eyes opened, to see Jesus was to see the Father (Jn.
14:9). Jesus proclaimed that the world in its disobedience was passing
away and God's Rule to set all things right was breaking in. Now the
risen and coming Lord is hidden behind the veil of the seen. In the
ultimate unveiling, that barrier to sight is to be thrown aside, "and
every eye will see him" (Rev. 1:7). Yet in faith during this time before
the End disciples "see Jesus" (Heb. 2:9). That is the experiential axis
of the Christian life — continuation of the focal disclosure in Jesus
until its consummation.

That disclosure unveils the mystery of iniquity. Earlier Hebrew
"prophecy is essentially a ministry of disclosure, a stripping bare."[12]
In a secondary way John's Apocalypse does have to do with the
unveiling of wickedness and its catastrophic consequences. Human
rebellion, pressing the totality of its claim, lapses still more into manifest chaos. Jesus' life and his death on the cross brought human
hatred of God to its focal and most radical expression. His approach,
as the End draws ever nearer, evokes a sort of global pre-emptive
intensification of the wickedness unveiled at the cross. In Gethsemane Jesus said to the armed band and the representatives of the
power elite, "This is your hour, and the power of darkness" (Lk.
22:53). Again and again through the centuries and in our time the
risen Lord has spoken that concessive word. He has said it especially to the warlords of this world. He will speak it climactically
just before the End.

Jesus told his disciples: "Beware of the leaven of the Pharisees,
which is hypocrisy [pretense of goodness masking concealed evil].
Nothing is covered up that will not be revealed, or hidden that

will not be known" (Lk. 12:1–2). The threat of exposure accompanies each human being. Evil, parasitic on the good, conceals itself. "Satan disguises himself as an angel of light... his servants also disguise themselves as servants of righteousness" (2 Cor. 11:14–15). But the momentum of evil as transgression, the breaking of bounds, impels into boundlessness and thus into unveiling and exposure by God. Sin is "shown to be sin... and sinful beyond measure" (Rom. 7:13).

That unveiling is both current and imminent — as social disintegration, destruction of the environment, devastation and deaths in wars. The masses of the exploited, the hungry, the terrorized are beyond the view of most people in the rich countries. But as populations in the poor countries continue to increase dramatically while food production lags ever further behind, unrest and upheaval become harder to ignore. The buildup of carbon dioxide for the greenhouse effect, the depletion of the ozone layer, and countless pollutants blighting life cannot be seen. Radioactivity from nuclear power plants and from other nuclear sites remains invisible. The killing of plankton in the oceans, which could eventually result in too little oxygen for humans to breath, is out of sight. Yet more and more the consequences of degrading the biosphere present themselves. Weapons of mass destruction are kept hidden. But each of them constitutes a plummet into the abyss of human evil. And within minutes they could bring vast disclosure of that evil.

Looming toward us is utterly desolating apocalypse. But coming to transfigure humanity and history is apocalypse as glorious unveiling of the One who is Light of the world. *Apocalypse* as the end result of terminal politics refers to the darkest possible prospect for the future. Yet in the strange dichotomy of meanings in the word, *apocalypse* refers to the most resplendent future ever conceptualized. Human beings each give themselves to the one apocalypse or the other.

Omnicide?

In the technologically advanced countries a newborn baby's life expectancy is taken to be about seventy years. Yet that projection is imperiled and doubtful. Will the world as we have known it last that long? History may continue for thousands, even millions of years. But there seems to be very little basis for any confidence that it will continue even for several hundred years. Intimations of cataclysm haunt us all.

The extreme uncertainty as to whether individuals or even humankind will have much of a future impels to *carpe diem* self-seeking. Much rock music intimates threat and expresses desire: We don't have long; live as intensely as possible. Feeling themselves abandoned with regard to any meaningfulness for present and future, multitudes live with abandon. Such living, induced in part by the vastness of the threat, feeds into it.

The future can be viewed rather positively if evils in the world are viewed as being progressively overcome through technological advances, global leadership of the rich nations, and the good sense and capability of those who are the ascendant managers of human affairs. But if, to the contrary, one recognizes an apocalypse of evil in our time, a proliferation of violence, lies, oppression, and ruthlessness, and if so much of the power of the rich countries and of the dominant elites (including those in the poor countries) is seen as a central part of all this rather than as countervailing force, it becomes difficult to identify any political prospects or entities sufficient for turning such a world around or even for preventing it from getting worse.

One may look to some worldwide upsurge of human goodness, some beneficent explosion of divinized human capabilities, or to the power of the people in their humaneness winning out and setting things right. Visions of such salvation abound, but they remain peripheral to the dominant exercise of power on this planet. There seems only a slim prospect, if that, for a mustering of human goodness sufficient to avoid global catastrophe.

One test of the biblical message is whether what has been happening in the world tends to corroborate at least negative aspects in its view of history. The present shape of the world is congruent with elements in the biblical view of history that point to cataclysm and judgment and away from humanity's achieving any convincing salvation for itself. In biblical thought history moves toward a climax of human failure and folly.[13] That movement can be discerned all around us, although there is no way of knowing whether it will continue directly to its culmination or will be reversed for one or more periods. A turning back may come. But the limited time given for turning slips away. If the present direction of the nations continues, the End of history under God or, in the atheist view, an end without God presses upon humanity.

No classic philosophy and no other faith has a view of history that forecasts and covers our current global plight. Only in biblical faith is found decisively for the darker side of life what is so generally lacking elsewhere: "a vision of terror and an understanding of evil."[14] A humanist belief in progress dominated modern Western thought well into the twentieth century. (In my boyhood I imbibed it through *The Reader's Digest*.) That belief, in its bourgeois and in its Marxist forms, has collapsed. The constant stream of establishment reassurances has to do chiefly with things not getting worse and with the worst not coming rather than with such progress.

In an article first published in 1941, Rudolf Bultmann wrote: "*The mythical eschatology* is untenable for the simple reason that the parousia [the glorious Coming] of Christ never took place as the New Testament expected. History did not come to an end, and, as every schoolboy knows, it will continue to run its course."[15] Now most schoolboys know all too well what a learned theologian even during World War II evidently did not discern: History may not continue for very long at all; it may soon be brought to an end. For Bultmann and wide circles in the churches, what was taken to be the prevailing modern outlook became the handy criterion for dismissing much in the biblical message. How ironical it is that a part of the modern outlook that Bultmann took as axiomatic for theology was collapsing within his own lifetime and being replaced by a secular apocalypticism as counterpart to biblical eschatology. (The imperative in Romans 12:2, "Do not be conformed to this world," may be more decisively important for theology than for any other dimension of church life.) 2 Peter 3:4 (NRSV) gives a glimpse of scoffers with a favorite question: "Where is the promise of his coming? For ever since our ancestors died, all things continue as they were from the beginning of creation!" In the twentieth century as never before, events have refuted any such assertion.

The recognition that the human future may be completely cut off has emerged from an awareness of political, military, and environmental trends. But throughout the Bible is a prior awareness: that human life, in its full breadth, is terribly threatened by wickedness and folly, by the judgment of God pressing upon these — threatened to the point of imminent destruction. In biblical prophecy there is no clear picture that human beings would develop the means to destroy the world and extinguish human life. But sin, biblically seen, brings on destruction, death, judgment. The worst that human folly can now bring on would be the terminal manifestation of what, in biblical thought, it has always been bringing on. Jesus "knew what was in man" (Jn. 2:25), and that understanding runs through the Bible.

Our current extremity comes as the technological extrapolation of the consequences seen in that view. A Christian understands his or her own death as the wage of sin. The impending death of history is that wage collectively accumulated.

There is so much goodness in people, so much neighborliness, altruism, love, and self-sacrifice. To face the specter of evil in the world is not to see humans as simply bad and corrupt. But in the biblical view any sin and evil are revolt against the Lord of the universe. They must not be, and yet they are. Thus they have horrendous actuality and dynamic. Quantitatively, most people may do more relatively good things than bad things; but the mystery of iniquity is the power of evil to prevail over the good in individuals and, far more, in collectivities. In our time still more than earlier, that mystery overshadows all humanity.

The human species could have vanished just after its creation: "Nevertheless of the tree of the knowledge of good and evil you are not to eat, for on the day you eat of it you shall most surely die" (Gen. 2:17 JB). But God in mercy delayed the full coming of death and made possible the successive generations.

In the time before the flood "the earth was corrupt in God's sight, and the earth was filled with violence" (Gen. 6:11). The salient content of human wrongdoing could best be summed up in that word *violence* then — and now. Violence is the slaughter of vast numbers of human beings in wars of the twentieth century. Violence worldwide is "26,000,000 people in the regular armed forces, another 40,000,000 in military reserves, a stockpile of 51,000 nuclear weapons, 66 countries in the business of peddling arms, 64 national governments under some form of military control — and 16 wars underway."[16] Violence is having more than half the world's scientists and engineers working for the military. Violence is repressive governments holding the masses in subjection by surveillance, terror, torture, and death squads. Violence is sponsorship of such governments by the dominant powers. Violence is forty thousand children dying each day who would not need to die if their simplest needs were given priority over military spending and the acquisition of greater and greater wealth — a holocaust yearly more than double the Holocaust perpetrated by the Nazis. Violence is one-fifth of the human race consuming three-fourths of the earth's economic product and one-fifth receiving 2 percent of that product. Violence is economic arrangements that make the rich richer and the poor poorer. Violence is a homeless man freezing to death on a grate within a block of the White House. Violence is violation of a populace through brainwashing and thought control by the media. Violence is degradation of culture and societal disintegration. Violence is abuse of wives and children, the breaking of covenant, and the collision of personalities in disintegrating marriages. Violence is an estimated twenty-five million abortions each year worldwide. Violence is Faustian genetic manipulation. Violence is deforestation, agriculture as exploitative domination of the land, oil spills, corporate poisoning of our global home. Violence is ever-increasing street crime, drug traffic, rapes, assaults, murders, suicides, prisons, and executions. How small on the scales was all that primordial violence compared to the magnitude of violence around the world in our time.

Yet Genesis 6 states the reality more decisive and awesome than any immensity of violence: God sees it and moves against it. "But Noah found favor in the eyes of the Lord" (Gen. 6:8). The story gives archetypal expression to the understanding that continuing human life on the earth, far from being the natural fundamental prospect, is preserved from destruction only as God in sovereign mercy acts to bring this about. The life of certain human beings and other creatures was preserved from the deluge that swept over that violence. All life was then to continue, not by immanent potentiality, but because of God's covenant with surviving humanity and all living creatures, sealed by the rainbow sign (Gen. 9:12). Religious belief around Israel was grounded in the cycles of nature seen as immutable. But according to Genesis 8–9, permanence does not reside in the processes of nature; rather, God holds back the chaos evoked by human wickedness so that the natural rhythms can proceed. Though the imagination of the human heart would continue to be evil from youth on, God promised never again to move against all life as in the flood (Gen. 8:21). But out of that imagination, in rejection of that covenant, humans can now act against all life.

God had "said to Noah, 'The end of all flesh has come before me [has been decided by me]' "[17] (Gen. 6:13). This intensely ominous Hebrew word *qets*, the end, the cutting off, was also used by some of the prophets to point to the closing eschatological cataclysm or to judgments that prefigure it. They took the term somewhat as we resort to such words as annihilation, holocaust, doom, and extinction to intimate a destruction beyond imagining.

> Then the Lord said to me,
> "The end has come upon my people Israel;
> I will never again pass by them."
> (Amos 8:2, of the Assyrian eradication
> of the Northern Kingdom)

> Our eyes failed, ever watching vainly for help...
> our end drew near; our days were numbered;
>   for our end had come.
>   (Lam. 4:17, 18, of the destruction
>   of Jerusalem by the Babylonians)

> O you who dwell by many waters,
>   rich in treasures,
> your end has come,
>   the thread of your life is cut.
>   (Jer. 51:13, as God's word to Babylon)

This usage is most dramatic in Ezekiel 7: "An end! The end has come upon the four corners of the land. Now the end is upon you. ...Disaster after disaster! Behold it comes. An end has come, the end has come; it has awakened against you. Behold it comes" (vv. 2–3, 5–6). In this passage *end* and *has come* (the prophetic perfect for what has been decided by God and is therefore virtually accomplished) occur again and again, like blows of a hammer, like mighty strokes on a resounding gong. The point of no return has been passed; no prospect remains for a general turning to God that might avert the doom. Under the judging word of God, all that had been cherished, the Jewish "common world," the line of descent from one generation into the next, all is seen as already cut off, demolished, brought to nothing. But more than this, the chosen people of God as the central bearers of his purposes in history are swept away, thus by implication undoing those purposes. That which the mind, formed and nurtured by continuities, cannot take in, is upon them: the cutting off of all continuities, except God's awesome and gracious overruling in human affairs. "Then you will know that I am the Lord" (vv. 4, 9, 27).

Repeatedly in the prophetic writings, overwhelming destruction presses upon Israel/Judah but opens out to take in the other nations. What is coming upon the land (*'arets*) is coming upon the earth (*'arets*). The Babylonians are about to destroy Jerusalem and the Jewish state; but beyond that "all the earth" through defiance of God is threatened with comparable cataclysm. "He will roar mightily against his fold, / and shout, like those who tread grapes, / against all the inhabitants of the earth.... / He is entering into judgment with all flesh" (Jer. 25:30, 31). The cutting off prophesied in Ezekiel 7 took place in the Babylonian destruction of Jerusalem and Judah. Yet any such geographically limited catastrophe turned out to be less than *the* end and was thus an intimation.

All images are too weak to represent cataclysms that may be ahead. But more than any other source, the Bible gives images for glimpsing what is beyond imagining. It is a book of imminent and actual disasters and of God's acting to rescue; it is a book about climactic rescue from final disaster. In the Revised Standard Version Bible the word *destroy* and its other forms occur 542 times, mostly in the Hebrew scriptures. In this dimension the world of the Bible is so evidently closer to our time than that of any other book in the literary and spiritual heritage of humanity.

> Yahweh Sabaoth says this:
> See! The disaster spreads
> from nation to nation,
> a mighty tempest rises
> from the far ends of the world.
> (Jer. 25:32 JB)

They shall not be gathered or buried; they shall be as dung on the surface of the ground. Death shall be preferred to life by all the remnant that remains.
(Jer. 8:2–3 — "The survivors will envy the dead.")

> For the wickedness of those who dwell in it
> the beasts and the birds are swept away.
> (Jer. 12:4)

> I looked on the earth, and lo, it was waste and void;
> and to the heavens, and they had no light. . . .
> I looked, and lo, there was no man,
> and all the birds of the air had fled.
> (Jer. 4:23, 25)

What Jeremiah saw was the end result of the power and the glory of all the kingdoms of the world, which the devil showed and offered to Jesus in the wilderness.

Again and again Hebrew prophecies pictured the sudden overthrow of nations and, at times, of all nations together. The falls of Egypt, Assyria, and Babylon were seen as archetypal. For the twentieth century one can point to the collapse of Tsarist Russia, Nazi Germany, and imperial Japan, the decline of imperial Britain and France, and the breakup of the Soviet Union. In spite of the quite limited geographical knowledge of the time, the vision of the prophets took in all the nations across the continents and through the centuries. Nuclear holocaust would, in line with the most sweeping of those prophecies, bring demolition far more encompassing than anything experienced on earth till now. But so could environmental catastrophes. In the Bible ominous aberrations in nature are foreseen as signs of the End.

Applicable to much biblical prophecy is what C. E. B. Cranfield in *The Gospel according to Saint Mark* states for the eschatological teaching given in Mark 13:

> This discourse is marked throughout by its use of the second person plural imperative. It is in fact exhortation, not ordinary apocalyptic. Its purpose is not to impart esoteric information but to sustain faith and obedience....
>
> The events of history are signs of the End and pointers to the coming Lord.... As our faith recognizes the signs as they occur, we are again and again put in remembrance of our Hope, and our gaze, that is so easily distracted from the Lord who is coming to us, is again and again directed back to him....
>
> In the crises of history the eschatological is foreshadowed. The divine judgements in history are, so to speak, rehearsals of the last judgement, and the successive incarnations of Antichrist are foreshadowings of the last supreme concentration of the rebelliousness of the devil before the End. So for us the fulfilment of these verses is past, present, and future.... The impending judgement on Jerusalem and the events connected with it are for Jesus as it were a transparent object in the foreground through which he sees the last events before the End, which they indeed foreshadow.[18]

Each impending judgment about which the Hebrew prophets gave warning (even a plague of locusts in Joel 2) was in a similar way "a transparent object in the foreground" prefiguring "the last events before the End." For John on Patmos, Rome poised to fall was also "transparent object in the foreground" and image for that aspect of the End. From this perspective contemporary events are stimulus for expectant watching rather than basis (in presumed correlation with biblical prophecies) for forecasts about the future and the calendrical nearness of the End.

However dark the foreground may be, one must not assume that this is about to constitute the end. Even nuclear cataclysm, in present apprehension or in its coming, should not be seen as simply the end. The time approaches when chaotic darkness will be no longer foreshadowing but accompaniment of the End. Since no one can know "that day or that hour" (Mk. 13:32), no one can predict or identify that final shift from penultimate to ultimate until the End itself confirms it. What might sweep over humanity as the seeming culmination would not necessarily be that. If nuclear cataclysm does come, Christians from within that horror should view it as penultimate crescendo of human rebellion and plead still more for the End.

Christians should reckon with the end of the world, not primarily because of nuclear and other perils, but because of biblical revelation about the End, Jesus' command, "Watch" (Mk. 13:37), and his promise that he will appear in splendor to give the world its closure and its rebirth. Christian hope and desire look to the sovereign Lord who rescues at the End and continually before the End. Disciples believe that God in Jesus Christ has moved against all evil to vanquish it, is continuing to do that, and will consummate his triumph. They are to sense the imminence of this acting much more than any imminence of global catastrophe.

Chapter 3

COUNTERFEITS FOR
THE RULE OF GOD

Where the lust for power seizes upon the state as the vehicle on which to ride to hegemonial power among the nations, absolute corruption follows in the wake of this drive for absolute power. For here the use of all mankind as a means is not wished for in hapless imagination but worked for in actual performance.

—Hans J. Morgenthau[1]

According to a motif in Second Isaiah, Yahweh is the only claimant to deity who declares beforehand what will come to pass, and it does. "Who is like me? . . . / Who has announced from of old the things to come?" (Is. 44:7). The sovereignty of Yahweh over history is made known again and again in his declaring through prophets what he will and then does bring to pass.

The historical circumstances that were the context for Second Isaiah would have seemed to offer little evidence for the God of Judah. The nation had been vanquished, much of the population deported, and the national life shattered. Yet in a trial speech in Isaiah 41:21–29, Yahweh challenges the gods of the Babylonian supremacy:

> Tell us the former things, what they are,
> that we may consider them,
> that we may know their outcome;
> or declare to us the things to come.
> (v. 22)

The gods can give no answer. But Yahweh, who has "stirred up one from the north," has declared this beforehand (Is. 41:25–26). He had disclosed himself through "former things" (his earlier acts in history) and their interpretation. He had given warning of the Babylonian destruction of Jerusalem and Judah as his act of judgment. A Jewish return out of exile to the homeland would soon give the latest demonstration in this unfolding sequence. Yahweh's long past with his people was brought into view as he spoke through the prophet into that Babylonian present. Adherents of the gods of Babylon had eyes only for that present and for projecting it into the near future and not for the long sweep of history and its meaning. The people of Yahweh could see the continuity of his action in history, running into their present and on toward the impending salvation now promised them.

Claus Westermann's comment on this passage has much contemporary relevance: "The point at issue is not an idea or concept of deity [polytheism vs. monotheism]. . . . The issue . . . is not divinity *per se*, but Godhead giving evidence of itself in history, divinity that becomes effective as lordship over history."[2] That is still the utterly decisive issue. There is in Western countries relatively little explicit polytheism. The gods over against the God of biblical faith — most notably the nation state, the economic well-being it is seen as providing, and military might as guarantor of both — are not looked to theologically as deities. They are looked to in terms of mastering history. To give one's loyalty to the nation state, especially the lone superpower, is to align oneself with that attempted dominion over history.[3] Thus in the contemporary U.S. religious context, to align oneself with the military might and the superpower role of the nation is not only a rejection of the Lordship of Jesus in the realm of ethics. It is, still more than that, the result of the assumption that human dominion over history to make things come out right must be striven for in its U.S. guise because God's Lordship in Jesus Christ crucified and risen cannot be counted on in the current unfolding of global events.

Ordering the World

God for the Hebrews was Ruler-Judge (*shophet*). God's role as Judge is not to be understood by analogy with judges in modern Western societies: officials charged with deciding, under established legal norms, who is in the right and who is in the wrong. Christians often think of the Last Judgment simply in those terms. In the Hebrew understanding, Yahweh had drawn Israel to himself as covenant partner. The intended wholeness of that relationship to him and of the relationships among the people (and the peoples) and with all of nature was *mishpat* (derived from the same verbal root *shaphat* and inadequately translated as "justice"). *Mishpat* was harmony of interrelationships lived under the gracious ordering sway of this covenant Lord. Any disruption of that wholeness was injustice.

The Hebrews sang: "the Lord...comes to rule [*shaphat*] the earth. / He will judge [*shaphat*] the world with righteousness" (Ps. 98:9, where the RSV gives the same verb in the two lines the roundedness of the double meaning). The Hebrew imperfect tense used in the second line indicates action begun but not yet completed. God was seen as continuously active in human affairs to maintain or, more often, to restore right relationships and as constantly moving against whatever (and whoever) broke away from the coherence and fractured relationships. But all such identifiable action by God came to be understood as leading toward the Day when God as Ruler-Judge would vanquish all resistance, set every relationship right, and draw all creation into glorious harmony under his sway. That fully achieved *mishpat*, that *shalom*, would come only by the consummate saving act of God.

In the common American view, widespread among church people, the United States is looked to as having the world role quite similar to that which the Hebrews recognized as God's: Stability, liberty, justice, peace, and prosperity around the world depend chiefly on the exercise of U.S. power. This outlook has shaped much of American history. John Adams in a letter to Thomas Jefferson on November 13, 1813, expressed it in characteristically messianic terms: "Our pure, virtuous, public spirited, federative republic will last forever, govern the globe, and introduce the perfection of man."[4] Though such optimism as to what the United States can bring about globally is mostly gone, there remains the dogged certainty that the United States must be the world guarantor for everything that has to be preserved and promoted. Even the visionary purposes, vacuous as they have become, are taken up in such themes as "the new world order."

In the later 1960s and the 1970s, U.S. power to direct the course of affairs around the planet was rather obviously declining. The limits of that power became especially evident through the nuclear standoff, the defeat in Vietnam, and the inability to force the release of the hostages in Iran. Frustration with this seeming impotence — the United States as paralyzed giant — became a key factor in U.S. politics. There somehow had to be the adequacy of the power of the good guys as in all those society-molding movie and TV dramas of crime and violence. Lone Ranger, Superman, Knight Rider, Rambo — such are the images that have had a part in shaping the collective view of how the nation should proceed. For a wide range of the population Ronald Reagan and George Bush were successful, through appealing rhetoric and a huge military buildup, in re-establishing the illusion of God-like U.S. power over history. The conquest of Grenada, the bombing of Libya, the invasion of Panama, and, far more, the defeat of Iraq gave the appearance of wielding power decisively against wrong in the world. Most Americans felt exhilaration in being aligned with such moves: Their country had done something and struck an effective, righteous blow against evil. (It has been little recognized that victory in war is as inconclusive morally as was success in duelling.) A member of Congress commented near the end of the U.S.-Iraq War: "The world has learned you can dial 911, and the United States will come to your rescue."[5] But more than policeman, the United States presumes to be prime source and benevolent establisher of order in the world.

During the Cold War the hubris of each side was countered and to a considerable extent kept in check by the other side. Nuclear and "conventional" weapons were kept in readiness to block the adversary but, still more than this, to lord it over history. Each superpower put into question the imperial lordship of the other. The collapse of communism in Eastern Europe in 1989 followed by its collapse in the Soviet Union in 1991 left the United States as unrivaled superpower, freed along with its allies from that restraint. Abruptly and unexpectedly the United States found itself able to play God in the world — most awesomely in the Middle East — without being held somewhat in check by countervailing Soviet power. The nuclear arsenals of the two sides remained, but internal upheaval and economic woes forced the successors to the Soviet leadership into an almost suppliant posture toward the United States and its allies.

Within the United States little remains to hold in check those who wield predominant power — except turns of events that they do not succeed in mastering. The media, by and large, are closely controlled by the vested interests that own them. The country moves still more toward an equivalent of some earlier East European communist governmental arrangements in which there were, for appearances, more than one party but other parties were docile adjuncts of the ruling one. The Congress does not hold the executive branch in check, and the packed courts dutifully play their role in the accelerating curtailment of constitutional rights. In the electoral wasteland, open repression could be blindly voted in as Nazism was in Germany.

Domestically the U.S.-Iraq War was, in a very real way, carried out as a military coup. Not that a government was ousted and replaced. In terms of commitments and identity of interests, the chief powerholders were already in closest coalition with the military. But through the media blitzkrieg during and after the war, those who have that military as their most decisive instrument of power abroad and means of moneymaking at home overwhelmed domestic challengers and consolidated their hold on the country.[6] A successful military coup leaves the military in full control of a country, even if top office-holders are in civilian dress. The junta, however dressed, decides out of its predominantly military mindset what it will allow within the country and undertake elsewhere. As has been the case in many of its client states, rule in the United States centers in one who is a military strong man.

A sign at a peace rally in Lafayette Park across from the White House just after the start of the U.S.-Iraq War read, "American dominion is the new world order." U.S. dominion is impelled by what the ruling elites conceive as their own and the national interest, yet is most skillfully decked out and justified as guarantor of good around the planet. Allegedly moral causes become the overlay for the dominant collective expression of the survival instinct and greed. In his January 29, 1991, State of the Union address, President George Bush declared: "We ... selflessly confront evil for the sake of good in a land so far away. ... We lead the world in facing down a threat to decency and humanity." Much of the world could look to the United States, leading in 110,000 *sorties* (still more sanitized replacement for "bombing *missions*"), to re-establish order in the Middle East.

In cold or hot wars nations take up allegedly righteous causes. A populace is usually quite ready to join in such a cause. So much is wrong in the world. People with significant awareness of the wrong want to see themselves as connected with power set against it. If they are not to despair or intentionally stand with wrong, they are driven to identify and relate to some power seen as at least possibly sufficient against all that is wrong. Manipulative leaders seize upon that need.

The most elemental rationale for military might is the imperative to preserve the nation state from dangers to its security. Held into public view is the threat of ruthless repression by adversaries, of the demise of the all-giving society, and of collective death. People have urgent need for some superior power seen as countering that perceived threat. The nation state as its own guarantor is the most demonstrative claimant to fill that need.

In order to stand against vast wrong and threat, the main alternatives in any country are alignment with the power of the nation or adherence to the *agape*-power of God made known supremely in

Jesus Christ. Confronted by the magnitude of wrongdoing and disorder in the world as defined by the ruling elite, most people count on the power, chiefly the military power, of the nation. When church people too have little sense of God's Rule countering the wrong, alignment with the most obvious claimant to righteous exercise of power is natural, indeed nearly inevitable.

The claimant to right ordering of the world assumes for itself God-like righteousness and exercise of power. What the United States does in this regard, other powers do to the extent they are able. The United States projects its military, economic, and political power into every part of the world to order all nations according to its purposes. The United States has 2,000 military bases and installations abroad for maintaining its hegemony and providing springboards for intervention. Even before the Persian Gulf crisis, 745,000 U.S. military personnel were stationed in other countries or at sea. Iraq had been a U.S. client state to a considerable degree; but after its invasion of Kuwait, it was focused upon and made into the chief deterrent example of what happens to those who challenge U.S. dominion.[7]

The claimant to right ordering of the world seeks to have a God-like omniscience. From 1980 to 1991 the U.S. spy conglomerate quadrupled. By the end of that period the agencies were receiving $35 billion each year. With a budget of more than $5 billion, the CIA has more than 25,000 employees, with additional tens of thousands of "unofficial" workers on its payroll worldwide. Its covert operations in more than fifty countries are an imitation of God's hidden sovereignty over every situation. The Air Force's National Reconnaissance Office, the very existence of which is denied by the government, has a budget of $12 billion to $15 billion a year for collecting satellite data.[8] "He ... sits above the circle of the earth, / and its inhabitants are like grasshoppers" (Is. 40:22).

Martin Hengel writes of Augustus: "The divine ruler became redeemer as well. In 17 B.C., after the horrors of a civil war lasting almost a hundred years, he proclaimed a century of peace. The time of salvation, the Golden Age, appeared to be dawning. The Pax Romana established by Augustus became from then on an essential component of the imperial religious ideology about the state."[9] American ideology about the state and the president has a comparable component. The glory of victory must (in appearance at least) be achieved in peacemaking as well as warmaking. The need for this complementary success was demonstrated by the intense efforts of the Bush administration to sponsor and arrange Middle East peace conferences in the aftermath of the U.S.-Iraq War, though such a con-

ference, agreed to earlier, could have prevented that war by giving
Saddam Hussein a way to save face while withdrawing from Kuwait.
The initiatives of the Bush administration for reductions in nuclear
weapons and military spending served the same need. The imperial
leader must be first in war, first in peace, and first in the trusting
hearts of a voting majority of the populace.

The underside of all this is the economic domination of the poor
countries by the rich countries. Like hapless farmers needing to accept whatever corporate buyers choose to pay, the poor economies
have been devastated by the low prices that managers of the global
system set for raw materials and commodities. Like debtors in the
clutches of moneylenders, impoverished nations are in the grip of
the complex of lending agencies. As was the case in ancient empires,
subjugated provinces struggle to pay the assessed tribute, even if
doing so results in the death of multitudes of children.

Imperial presumption presses its reckless exploitation not only
upon peoples but also (still more ominously) upon the environment
near and far. In this environmental apartheid, other species are the
expendable poorest of the poor. The same arrogance that took the
United States and its allies so needlessly into war in the Middle East
(a war that brought immense damage to the environment) infuses
human domination of the biosphere. Fully ignored is the biblical
understanding of the human proneness individually and collectively
to make terrible mistakes.

The totality of U.S. power is directed toward a global ordering
of relationships — *Pax Americana*. Those who view that projection of
power as generally beneficent tend to justify whatever is done and,
if religious, to see it as main surrogate for God's Rule. But for biblical people this assumed role is clearly a usurpation, an attempted
displacement of the One who rules and judges the world.

Church people who support that usurpation have turned aside
from the biblical understanding of where power really resides: with
God in Jesus Christ. Secretly, though they would deny this, they view
God as paralyzed giant in relation to current history. A standard
charge against Christian pacifism is "We can't be passive, do nothing, be doormats." But implicitly the same charge is brought against
the God of Jesus Christ. These protesters do not see the sovereign
intensity of gracious action and power in Jesus' going to the cross
and rising from the tomb; they do not see it as still moving at the center of the turmoil of history. They do not understand that the human
mastery of history falsely striven for has been given to Jesus of Nazareth. Their political outlook is not shaped by the promise expressed

in Isaiah 42:1 that Yahweh's servant "will bring forth justice to the nations." So often church folk see God as in charge of private piety, of eternal life, and of the history related in the biblical accounts, but hardly as in control of current history — except obliquely as backer of U.S. (or other) hegemony. They give themselves as adherents of the "God" of national power, held preposterously to be the God of Jesus Christ. They may affirm that it is primarily through Jesus crucified and risen that God has met them in their rebellion to turn them from it, but they fail to understand that this is also God's central way of meeting and dealing with the nations. They see the Rule of God in their finding an opportune parking space or getting a salary increase but not in the South African freedom movement or in the suffering of radical Christian communities in Latin America. In concert with avowed non-Christians they look to the nation, not the community of disciples, as the primary bearer of meaning in history. Throughout American history the country has often been characterized as "a light to the nations." The nation supposedly, not God's Messiah (and people), brings fulfilment to Isaiah 42:6 and 49:6.

In Hebrew thought God was not to be alone in striving for *mishpat*. By God's command the covenant community, members within it, and especially its leaders were to live as his agents in securing *mishpat*. The king was often looked to as the central figure for that. This view might seem to support the claim that the United States needs to function as God's primary agent for maintaining order around the world. A great many U.S. church people see their country and its leaders as having this divine mandate, a mandate that would supposedly have a basis in the scriptural motifs just referred to. Preponderance of military power and nuclear weapons are often seen as gift of God to the righteous for this assigned task of preserving order in the world. The United States does hold wider sway around the planet than any earlier imperial power.

A number of biblical passages declared that rulers and governments (ordinarily those of God's covenant community) were to strive for the right ordering of society intended by God. Though the Persian emperor Cyrus did not know the God of the Jews, he was chosen to be instrumental for the Jewish return from exile and the rebuilding of Jerusalem and its Temple. A country like Assyria could be used by God to punish a disobedient people. God gave those limited tasks. But there is not, I believe, any indication in the Bible (except for visions of the coming Messiah) that a government or head of state is to be God's agent in ordering all the world of nations. That is God's domain. (In rule by the Messiah it remains God's domain.) Biblical people are to look to the Lord of history for that, not to the United States, the Western alliance, or even the United Nations. U.S. foreign and military policy has taken on a task never delegated by the God revealed in scripture.

The Soviet counterpart to all this was the unrealized and now widely discredited communist eschatology: The revolution of the proletariat as it proceeded in country after country was to bring in the new day of harmonious order and plenty; the Bolshevik Revolution inaugurated and Soviet power guarded the global good that was in process of becoming. But what was achieved under communist governments remained so pathetically far from the coherent ordering of all things that this ideological anticipation faded, the Soviet-backed regimes across Eastern Europe collapsed, and the Soviet Union itself broke up. In intent the Soviet Union no less than the United States wanted to be in control of history. Its ideology was still more crassly messianic than that prevailing in the United States. Yet throughout the Cold War, in actual projection of power and in the ideology prevailing throughout the populace, the United States proceeded as supposedly God-like ruler-judge of the world far more than did the Soviet Union.

Testing by the Fruits

"You will know them by their fruits" (Mt. 7:20). What does the U.S. ordering of human affairs look like?

•The United States has been involved in master-race repression of Native Americans through hundreds of years; the crushing of Philippine independence with a loss of 300,000 to 600,000 Philippine lives;[10] the overthrow of the democratically elected government of Guatemala as entry into the decades of bloody repression that have followed; abetting the massacre of an estimated 250,000 to one million Indonesians in 1965–66 after the military coup;[11] the overthrow of the Cambodian government of Prince Sikanouk and disruption of the social fabric of the country, followed later by the horrors of Khmer Rouge; sponsorship of the coup that ousted the democratically elected government of Chile, followed by many years of brutal military dictatorship; support for the government of Idi Amin in Uganda (for example, the training of his secret police) as the killing of an estimated 300,000 Ugandans proceeded;[12] support through the second half of the twentieth century for many of the worst client governments and tyrants in the world (for example, the Shah of Iran and

Anastasio Somoza in Nicaragua); the continued military occupation, economic chaos, and repression of dissent after the U.S. invasion of Panama.[13]

•The United States has sponsored "torture on an administrative basis" in a number of countries. For example, the CIA conducted torture seminars for SAVAK, the Gestapo-like secret police of the Shah of Iran.[14]

•In a war to impose the U.S. will on Indochina, 2 million Indochinese were killed, and millions more terrorized, bereaved, wounded, made homeless. The United States "dropped the explosive equivalent of one Nagasaki bomb every week for seven and a half years."[15] U.S. forces sprayed 20 million gallons of Agent Orange on Indochina from 1961 to 1970. (Three parts of dioxin per trillion — one hundred-millionth as much as is found in Agent Orange — will kill 100 percent of chick embryos.) Millions of Vietnamese, Cambodians, and Laotians continue to bear the effects of those defoliation campaigns as do many of the 2.5 million Americans who fought in Indochina.

•One can look at satellite photos of the five hundred oil wells burning in Kuwait with the plumes spreading eastward[16] and consider too that one-fourth of the fragile desert surface of that country was torn up in the war.

•The U.S. national debt rose to $3.7 trillion, mostly because of crazed military spending.

•In the aftermath of the U.S.-Iraq War, two-thirds of all U.S. arms sales and transfers went to the Middle East,[17] already the most militarized region in the Third World.

•The two most profitable businesses internationally are the selling of armaments, followed by the selling of illegal drugs. The United States leads the world in the former; and the U.S. underworld, with involvement by agencies of the U.S. government, leads in the latter.[18] Americans consume 50 percent of the world's cocaine.

•According to UNICEF 100 million children will die unnecessarily from illness and malnutrition in the 1990s. The United States is the leader and chief guarantor of the global system within which those children die. $2.5 billion a year (about what U.S. tobacco companies devote to cigarette advertising), rightly spent, could prevent those deaths.[19] There has not emerged in the United States the political will to shift on behalf of those children any such amount from total military spending 180 times larger than that.[20]

•In the homeland of right order for the world there are more than 8 million unemployed, an estimated 20 million illiterate, 3 million homeless (half of them children), 20 million malnourished, 37 million without adequate health care.[21]

• Within the United States 20 percent of all children grow up in poverty; 15 million children have been abandoned by their fathers; 27 percent of teenagers drop out of school. Parents spend an estimated 40 percent less time with their children than in 1965. The (reported) incidence of child abuse tripled from 1975 to 1991.[22] Among nations of the world the United States ranks twenty-second (from the lowest) in infant mortality rate.

• Overall, every American in 1990 was more than four times more likely to be a victim of violent crime than in 1960. More than 1.8 million Americans are murdered, raped, robbed, or assaulted each year — 23,000 of these murdered. The United States as "the most violent and self-destructive nation on earth" has rates in each type of violent crime far higher than those of other countries. The U.S. rape rate is 26 times higher than in Japan, 23 times higher than in Italy, 8 times higher than in France. The murder rate is 11 times that of Japan, nearly 9 times that of England, and more than 4 times that of Italy. The robbery rate is 150 times higher than in Japan, almost 6 times higher than in England, and 17 times higher than in Italy.[23]

• In the United States an estimated 200 million guns are privately owned. In 1989 handguns were used in 48 percent of all murders (9,000), in 12,000 suicides, and in 1,000 unintentional shootings. Homicide has become the leading cause of death among black males fifteen to thirty-four, with guns figuring in 88 percent of those cases.[24] Yet year after year effective gun control, even for military-type assault weapons, has been blocked by well-financed lobbying.

• From 1970 to 1990 the U.S. prison population tripled to over a million. The United States has a larger proportion of its population behind bars than any other nation with reliable statistics. South Africa is second. Russia is third. Now that South Africa has a moratorium on executions, the United States is the only industrialized Western nation with the death penalty.[25]

• Per capita the United States uses forty-five times more energy than India and pollutes the biosphere forty times as much. Each year U.S. industry generates 1.5 tons of toxic waste for every American and 15 trillion tons of allegedly nonhazardous waste. Each year 80 billion pounds of toxic wastes are dumped into American waters. The United States continues to rely on nuclear power with the vast contamination that this entails.

Can this nation be the chief guarantor of right order in the world?

The darker side of the U.S. present has emerged out of such aspects of the American past as the enslavement of Africans, the glorification of violence and war, scores of military interventions in Latin America, and the exploitative stance toward the wilderness. There is a brighter side. An overview of U.S. contributions to the right ordering of human life could also be put together. But the darker side predominates.

All this is not to set against the prevailing claim of exceptional American virtue the counterclaim of exceptional American wickedness. All (or nearly all) economies, societies, and governments are controlled by elites and are largely shaped by the lust for power and the deforming sway of mammon. By readiness to do lethal violence every nation assumes for itself absolute worth. Nearly all the nations are involved in the world arms trade as suppliers or as buyers. In every nation and in each human being is the drive to wield power over others, to control and use them. All collective domination rising against God's dominion emerges as the massed consolidation of the personal rebellion of individual humans. In this book special attention is given to the United States because at the present time the wrongs that lesser powers do in more limited ways the world's superpower does in a predominating way. Disciples of the One who most of all calls into question those wrongs should be the ones who most of all discern that state of affairs.

Above the Law

The book of Judges closes with the words: "There was no king in Israel at that time. Everyone did whatever he pleased" (21:25 TEV). The lawlessness that then characterized individuals within that society continues among the nations. In spite of rudimentary efforts, the nations of this planet do not proceed in a shared recognition of and subordination to an overarching structure of world order and law. Nor do the nations truly recognize and submit themselves to the One who is Ruler-Judge over all. In the absence of that, military power and resort to war have been the *ultima ratio* for international relations. Within this improvisation, which is older than recorded history, nuclear deterrence emerged as the central and climactic dimension.

James gives the exhortation: "But if you judge the law, you are not a doer of the law but a judge. There is one lawgiver and judge, he who is able to save and to destroy. But who are you that you judge your neighbor?" (4:11–12) Christians are warned not to usurp God's place as giver and arbiter of the law. They are not to presume to be over the law, wielding it against others. They are to discern themselves in jeopardy under God and God's commanding, alongside others.

Although military might, especially in the form of nuclear capabilities, is the prime indicator of international lawlessness, it also constitutes an attempt to lay down the law, the most imposing human law conceivable, for those seen as adversaries. And each nation state that in this fashion presumes to be lawgiver and judge finds itself under the threat of the countervailing "law" set forth by the other side.

In military deterrence generally and most of all in nuclear deterrence there lurks an imitation of God's command in the garden of Eden: "You may freely eat of every tree of the garden; but of the tree of the knowledge of good and evil you shall not eat, for in the day that you eat of it you shall die" (Gen. 2:16–17). Through the Cold War decades the government of each superpower warned the other: "You over there can go about your own affairs; but if you attack us, you shall most surely die." Each side indicated in a general way what would be seen as capital transgression and devoted itself to arrangements for the assuredness and magnitude of the punishment to be inflicted. Though tensions and hostile attitudes have been reduced, those weapons by the thousands remain in place. More than anything else in the dark diversity of sins, nuclear deterrence is a Genesis 3 seizure (and gross distortion) of the role of the God who commands and warns in Genesis 2.

During the Cold War each superpower presumed to be "judge" with the capability "to save and to destroy." Each side was convinced of the necessity, legitimacy, and authority of its deterrent directed against the other side. By and large the deterrent of the other side was perceived not in these terms but mainly as a vast, wicked threat. Those who preside over the "law" impose it on the other side. Contrary to the ways of God in scripture, there is to be mercy only so long as the "law" is obeyed. Transgression or even the appearance of transgression, such as through some computer malfunction, would entail destruction and death in however incomprehensibly extensive a "judgment" choice and chance happen to inflict. The so-called balance of terror has pointed toward a bilateral, substitute last judgment; each "good" side as lawgiver and judge would overwhelm the "bad" side with damnation.

In Hebrew imagery God drove back the primeval chaos and brought into being the created order. But creation could be jeopardized again and again by the onslaughts of chaos from within nature and history: "the mountains shake in the heart of the sea; ... / its waters roar and foam .... / The nations rage, the kingdoms totter" (Ps. 46:2, 3, 6). God, however, could hold back those onslaughts: "God is our refuge and strength.... / He makes wars cease to the end of the earth" (vv. 1, 9).

In Cold War thinking the hostile superpower was viewed as the threatening infernal disorder that would undo all order and goodness. (In the aftermath of the Cold War this role has been pressed upon selected Third World leaders.) The righteous superpower along with its allies holds back the chaos. But the decisive means for doing that is the capability of unleashing immense chaos on the adversary — and on the planet. For the Hebrews the acts of God's ordering Rule that they could discern around them were prelude to the Day when God would again draw all creation fully within that Rule. If continued long enough, military and nuclear deterrence as frantic activity will unleash the primeval chaos within nature to undo the frail, inadequate orderings of nature and human life. Or that undoing could come mainly through ever greater poisoning of the earth. The imperial attempts at a fake world order are so near to bringing on the utter opposite of world order. "You think to defer the day of misfortune, / but you hasten the reign of violence" (Amos 6:3 JB).

"The Abomination of Desolation"

In the apocalyptic teaching found in Mark 13 the warning is given: "But when you see the desolating sacrilege [the abomination of desolation] set up where it ought not to be (let the reader understand), then let those who are in Judea flee to the mountains" (v. 14). In 168 B.C. the Hellenic Syrian ruler Antiochus Epiphanes ("Deity Appearing") desecrated the Temple in Jerusalem by erecting an altar to Zeus upon Yahweh's altar of burnt offering. The detested thing (sacrilege, abomination) appalled and was seen as emptying the Temple of faithful Jews and of Yahweh. The phrase in Daniel 11:31 and 12:11 refers to that desecration. For Jesus that earlier event did not exhaust the meaning of the motif: Something comparable to that sacrilege was impending, and his followers were to be on the look-out for it. In A.D. 40, the Roman emperor Caligula ordered that a statue of himself be erected in the Temple; but Jewish nonviolent resistance, delay by the legate Petronius, and Caligula's death kept this from being done. Before Titus and the Roman legions besieged Jerusalem, the Zealots seized the Temple and made it into a stronghold. "The house of God [was] full of so many abominations ... filled with the feet of those blood-shedding villains."[26] The rebels desecrated what God had designated as central place for his self-manifestation. And the followers of Jesus, having been warned by him, fled from the city. When the Romans in A.D. 70 took the city and destroyed the Temple, they set up their standards in that holy place and offered sacrifices to them.[27]

The motif of "the desolating sacrilege" runs through history and comes to culmination just before the End. When the collectivity, most notably the imperial power and its leader, is given the place of God and sacrificed to accordingly, the sacrilege continues. The designated houses of God and the professed people of God play their part in that displacement. The imperial emblem stands in the sanctuary, as do those who give their allegiance to it. That which attempts to have dominion over history ravages and desolates, and in the sanctuary that desolating wickedness is hallowed. Place and people chosen to make manifest the sovereign grace of God are co-opted by the contrary sovereignty.

But disciples, recognizing the sacrilege, must with utter decisiveness remove themselves from it and flee to the heights away from what desolates and is soon to be desolated.

Related to this motif is Paul's eschatological teaching in 2 Thessalonians 2:1–12: "that day [the glorious Coming of Jesus Christ] will not come, unless the rebellion comes first, and the man of lawlessness is revealed, the son of perdition, who opposes and exalts himself against every so-called god or object of worship, so that he takes his seat in the temple of God, proclaiming himself to be God" (vv. 3–4). In this most perplexing passage Paul writes about the coming (*parousia*) of the final agent of human defiance of God just before the *parousia* of Jesus Christ (vv. 8–9). Paul recognizes that "the mystery of lawlessness is already at work" (v. 7). Every collective rebellion and seizure of the fantasized role of God in the world centers in a leader. The behavior described for Antiochus Epiphanes recurs throughout history: "By his cunning he shall make deceit prosper under his hand, and in his own mind he shall magnify himself" (Dan. 8:25). According to biblical teaching, what has come in Antiochus Epiphanes, Caligula, Nero, Titus, Diocletian, Napoleon, Stalin, Hitler, and countless lesser figures will appear just before the End climactically incarnated in a leader.[28]

Paul's Christian friends in Thessalonika knew from his oral teaching what was restraining that which was to emerge as the final rebel — "you know what is restraining him now" (2 Thess. 2:6). No one can be certain about what Paul was referring to. But the alternations of evil held relatively in check and evil on global rampage continue. Proleptic rebels may claim (if only by implication) to be the chief agent of divine purpose. The final rebel will proclaim "himself to be God." It is hard to imagine such an impostor wielding power over all the world's divisions. But the collapse of the Cold War bi-polarity of the world and the media-mediated global fascination with the "marvels" of the U.S.-Iraq War make the emergence of such a ruler more thinkable.

That rebel "takes his seat in the temple of God" (v. 4). The great falling away from faith, the apostasy (v. 3), provides the religious and political context for the rebel. The interpretation that brings the passage into fullest relevance to the past and the present sees "the temple of God" as the apostatizing church.[29] Since Constantine, rulers in the Western world have made a large part of the church into a sort of sanctifying dome over their dominion and all their undertakings. Present-day mass media have increased the possibilities for such co-opting and control. That final leader will outdo those who went before.

But when disciples pray, "Thy kingdom come, thy will be done on earth, as it is in heaven" (Mt. 6:10), they take up the Hebrew anticipation of God's triumph over all rebellion. This plea, perhaps more than anything else from Jesus or the apostles, expresses the Hebrew understanding of God as Ruler-Judge. Disciples ask that God in these days and on the approaching Day come to draw his creatures out of ruinous division and disorder into his ordering. And they give themselves in the Messianic community, God's emergent *mishpat*, into that coming.

Chapter 4

FALSE PROPHECY

From the least on up to the greatest
    Every one's greedy for gain;
From prophet on up to priest,
    Every one practices fraud.
Yet they treat my people's fracture
    With nostrums, and cry
"It is well! It is well!"
    But it is not well!
Were they shamed by their loathsome behavior?
    No! They neither felt shame
    Nor knew how to blush.
And so — they will fall with the fallen,
    At the time of their doom they'll go down — Yahweh has spoken.
                           —Jeremiah 6:13–14[1]

Do we see how the whole future of mankind depends on the clear distinction between true and false prophecy? May God increase this clarity among us through Jesus Christ.
                           —Hans Walter Wolff[2]

In scripture God is portrayed as ruling the world primarily by his word, his speaking, not by inarticulate application of power. Those who presume to rule the world mimic that speaking. Words upon words mediate that counterfeit exercise of dominion which, grounded as it is in having the preponderance of coercive physical power, expresses itself most characteristically as preponderance of compelling verbal power. The powerholders live out the boast in Psalm 12:4 (JB): "In our tongue lies our strength, / our lips have the advantage; who can master us?" The most decisive domination is that of the imperial speaking, which through the present-day media can be more wide-reaching and pervasive than ever before.

    Over against Jeremiah stood the power elite and the populace of Jerusalem — "they, their kings, their princes, their priests, and their prophets" (2:26). The pronouncements of those speaking for the establishment could be summed up in the words, "Shalom! Shalom! ... It is well!" — the prototypical "positive thinking." What the warning given through Jeremiah identified as rampant greed and dishonest grabbing was generally seen as economic growth. Many were making out well, and they were confident that the country's leadership was getting the better of such problems as there were.

Proclaiming God's word, Jeremiah compared the condition of Judah to that of a shattered limb completely without wholeness or prospect of healing. He used the same word *shebher* for the veiled shatteredness of the apparently thriving society and for the demolition that was about to come upon that people (6:1; 4:6, 20). The largely unrecognized internal ruin was about to become the catastrophic ruin that none would be able to deny. In the imagery of Isaiah 30:13:

> This iniquity shall be to you
>> like a break in a high wall, bulging out, and about to collapse,
>> whose crash (*shebher*) comes suddenly, in an instant.

For Israel/Judah the portentous conflict between true and false prophecy came to its climax in the ministries of Jeremiah and Ezekiel. A rebuke in Ezekiel was similar to that spoken by Jeremiah: "They have misled my people, saying, 'Peace,' when there is no peace; and ... when the people build a wall, these prophets daub it with whitewash" (Ez. 13:10). The wall signified the total collective endeavor to achieve national security and well-being. Shaky and imperiled as that endeavor was, a spate of bland reassurances by favored prophets could make it seem imposing and dependable. The false prophets and the prophets of God were intensely political figures, calling the nation to go in one direction or its opposite. During one period after another, false prophets were the most articulate promoters of a course that led into disaster. "The wall is no more, nor those who daubed it" (Ez. 13:15).

Political False Prophecy

In scripture the chief opposite of trust in God is the individual and collective attitude that human beings achieve life on their own. In line with this, each society commits itself to the manageability of the future. "It is well!" is the primary affirmation of that attitude and effort. The main range of political, economic, and military activity can be understood as structures of salvation accompanied by repetition of that ancient "It is well!" and by whitewashing. In a fashion without comprehensive precedent in earlier human experience, the grim question haunts us: Will there be a future? The direction of nations generally is being set by those who promise, "Follow our lead, especially in national security matters, and we will give you the future." In the United States still more than in other countries, this lead is messianic, for it is the offer of salvation in terms of national ascendancy and involves the destiny of the human race and all the earth. In our time prophecy is the most characteristic and significant function of political leaders. They gain their positions most of all through adeptness in such prophecy and access to the funds needed for trumpeting it.

Political and economic effort amounts in large measure to the building of the tower, the configuration of towers, reaching into the heavens. The multiform ascendancy finds striking spatial expression in rockets, satellites, and shuttle voyages. Collective enterprise has advanced from pyramids to moon landings. From the master builders and from all heights comes the assuring word to the laborers, "Our project is proceeding well." Danger of nuclear annihilation? "Trust us. We'll bring you through." Recession, depression, inflation, economic collapse? "We're on top of things." Destruction of the ozone layer, melting of the polar ice caps, cumulative poisoning of the biosphere? "Don't let alarmists upset you. There have to be trade-offs. Through programs like those of the Environmental Protection Agency, we're looking out for your well-being. We're finding technological answers for whatever problems technology creates." Pesticide residues in foods and throughout the environment, fluoride as severely damaging to health, fallout from the plumes of incinerators and industrial smokestacks? "The amounts involved are too small to pose any threat to the public health." Huge quantities of radioactive and other hazardous wastes? "We'll have it properly stored." In this "utopia of the status quo"[3] the ruling politics is that of the reassuring, controlling word and of the confident management of apocalyptic threats.

When appearances at all allow it, those in political command preen themselves with declarations about how well things are going and claim that as largely their accomplishment. Ronald Reagan as president was a master at this. Opposition candidates cannot simply echo such sentiments. They typically point to certain problems and make a case that they can get the better of those problems so that things will be more nearly all right. "It is well!" for achievement underway or "It will be well!" as promised outcome of changed leadership is what sells politically. Candidates offer superficial remedies and fail to see the deadly sickness of the society. None in the mainstream say sweepingly with Jeremiah, "It is not well!" None really face the internal ruin racking the society and the impending catastrophic ruin.

President Reagan in his initial "Star Wars" speech presented, as he put it, "a vision of the future which offers hope," a vision of an America fully secure because of breakthroughs in ingenious technologies for warding off any Soviet attack. He concluded with the words: "As we cross this threshold, I ask for your prayers and your support. Thank you, good night and God bless you."[4] That promise along with so much in his speeches was prophecy. So was the choice of "Peacekeeper" as the name for a new missile system. (More recently the main rationale for the Strategic Defense Initiative has been that of shielding the United States against nuclear attack by some upstart Third World despot.) A more grandiose false prophecy than the selling of "Star Wars" would be difficult to conceptualize: human titanism, collective achievement of presumed salvation, and, behind it all, structures of greed. But one could also note Walter Mondale's forecast in the second 1984 presidential election debate: "America is forever."[5]

Leaders have acted as prophets when repeating the slogan, "Peace through strength" — that is, avoid nuclear (and other) war through ever greater military power. Most notable among President Reagan's attempts to be Bible teacher of the nation was his justification of enormous military buildup with the first half of a parable of Jesus: "When a strong man armed keepeth his palace, his goods are in peace" (Lk. 11:21 AV). (Many from the religious right have made similar use of the saying.) The president probably had no inkling that "the strong man" in the parable referred to Satan. Jesus then spoke of himself: "When one stronger than he assails him and overcomes him, he takes away his armor in which he trusted, and divides his spoil" (v. 22). To imitate the strong man of the parable is to follow the lead of Satan and to head toward overthrow by the One far stronger.

The economy provides indispensable corroboration for the "It is well!" of the national leadership. The most tangible aspect of the meaning of shalom in the Hebrew scriptures had to do with abundance in the necessities of life — bountiful harvests and multiplying flocks. A U.S. update on that is offered in the constant barrage of media advertising. The average American child by the age of eighteen has watched 325,000 commercials for a total of 2700 hours.[6] Life is said to consist in the abundance of possessions: Buy this, buy that, and you'll find what you are seeking in life. Shopping centers and malls put before us what the media picture: supposed fullness of life from a cornucopia of things. Greed propels the producers; elicited greed impels the consumers. Disquiet within individuals and unrest in the society recede under the commotion of getting and spending. Corporations generally do whatever brings in the most money: too bad if the environment is degraded, the health of workers and consumers is endangered, and poor people in the Third World are left with less than a living wage. "The oppressive system's only future is to maintain its present of affluence."[7] Material prosperity is the opiate of the people — something that communist governments have been far less successful in dispensing. The few get their big slices of the prosperity pie, and many others, their small but gratifying slivers. And the devil take all the hindmost who are crowded away from the table.

How small the distance between such economic arrangements and the manner of the well-to-do in Samaria at the time of Amos:

> Woe to the careless citizens, . . .
> lolling on their ivory divans, . . .
> crooning to the music of the lute, . . .
> lapping wine by the bowlful,
> and using for ointment the best of the oil —
> with never a single thought
> for the bleeding wounds (*shebher*) of the nation.
> (Amos 6:1, 4, 5, 6 Moffatt)

Eat, drink, see that you are entertained; ignore poverty, hunger, oppression, responsibility for vast suffering in the poor countries, the threat of nuclear annihilation. Loll in front of the television (which is on seven hours a day in the average U.S. household),[8] resonate to the din of music, turn from one titillation or sports spectacle to the next, and take all that as the confirmation "It is well!" A most entertaining medley is signal for bowing before the imperial image (Dan. 3:4–5).

Behind greed practiced legally is greed practiced illegally. "Every one practices fraud" (Jer. 6:13) A feature of our time is that again and again government leaders in various countries are shown to be criminals even according to human laws. More than one hundred officials of the Reagan administration left office early because of disclosures of wrongdoing and federal court indictments and convictions. The few who are thus exposed stand in for the many who are not. Influence peddling, bribery, collusions, intimidation, and extortion are the clandestine underside of the society from the highest levels on down.

As at the time of Jeremiah and throughout scripture, the motive power in false prophecy is wolflike rapacity. Vested interests control the government, the media, and the masses. Through pouring money into campaigns, they dominate every major election process. This establishment[9] rewards its promoters. False prophecy, in contrast to true prophecy, is well paid. The building of the lesser (among them the religious) empires flourishes within the larger empire-building.

Government is always by oligarchy. Democracy is distinguished not by a departure from that pattern but by the permission given to question and talk back.[10] Yet the means available for talking back can become quite limited. Herbert Marcuse has given an astute analysis:

> The semi-democratic process works of necessity against radical change because it produces and sustains a popular majority whose opinion is generated by the dominant interests in the *status quo*. As long as this condition prevails, it makes sense to say that the general will is always wrong — wrong inasmuch as it objectively counteracts the possible transformation of society into more humane ways of life. To be sure, the method of persuasion is still open to the minority, but it is fatally reduced by the fact that the leftist minority does not possess the large funds required for equal access to the mass media which speak day and night for the dominant interests.[11]

The vested interests that control the United States and other "semi-democratic" countries become increasingly adept at "craftiness in deceitful wiles" (Eph. 4:14) to maintain a compliant majority. Dictatorship is not needed where the dominant interests can, in this way, dictate. They find it more cost-effective to marginalize dissent than to repress it. Dissenters, especially media dissenters within the stipulated boundaries of discourse, function as part of the charade of democracy supposedly functioning well. To be sure, the media do produce much of value in terms of questioning the status quo and those in power, and the significance of that for the society is considerable. But such questioning is carefully contained and overpowered by the predominant voices that speak continuously for the current structuring of power.

In an overtly totalitarian state, those dependably aligned with the leadership are the ones who suppose they give their adherence freely. In the covert totalitarianism of a "semi-democracy," the proportion of such people tends to be far larger. Noam Chomsky has written: "Propaganda is to democracy what violence is to totalitarianism. The techniques have been honed to a high art, far beyond anything that Orwell dreamt of."[12] With television the sway achieved by the U.S. government over the populace during the U.S.-Iraq War and its immediate aftermath was probably greater than that ever before held over an imperial population.

Wednesday evening of January 16, 1991, and through the night, with the onslaught against Iraq, a phrase from Jeremiah 48:2 kept coming to me: "O Madmen." And also the warning of Jesus in the Sermon on the Mount: "Be on your guard against false prophets; they come to you looking like sheep on the outside, but on the inside they are really like wild wolves" (Mt. 7:15 TEV). In biblical perspective President George Bush's address to the nation about going to war was false prophecy. The president spoke as one confident that he could make history proceed according to his will and forecast: "We have before us the opportunity to forge for ourselves and for future generations a new world order, a world where the rule of law, not the law of the jungle, governs the conduct of nations. When we are successful, and we will be, we have a real chance at this new world order, an order in which a credible United Nations can use its peace-keeping role to fulfill the promise and vision of the U.N.'s founders." Resort to massive obliteration was to lead to a world under the rule of law. The United Nations' sponsorship of a horribly destructive war was to enhance its role as global peacekeeper. The regrettable work of war (actually devastation and slaughter far greater than what had been perpetrated by the Iraqis in Kuwait) was the way to move decisively into a new era of peace. Violence is redemptive. War brings peace.

When President Bush started the ground war, he called the nation to a simultaneous time of prayer and once again presented God as sanctifying sponsor of the American cause: "Tonight, as this coalition of countries seeks to do that which is right and just, I ask only that all of you stop what you were doing and say a prayer for all the coalition forces and especially for our men and women in uniform, who at this very moment are risking their lives for their country and all of us. May God bless and protect each and every one of them, and may God bless the United States of America." More and more the U.S. president, like the Roman Caesars, is *pontifex maximus*, head priest of all.[13]

Whether self-deceived or only deceiving, false prophets are split within themselves. *Hypokrites* in classical Greek meant actor — an etymology especially relevant for the 1980s and beyond. In the Synoptic Gospels hypocrisy refers to "the jarring contradiction between what [the adversaries] say and what they do, between the outward appearance and the inward lack of righteousness."[14] Jesus said to his opponents: "Isaiah prophesied rightly about you hypocrites, as it is written,

> This people honors me with their lips,
>   but their hearts are far from me;
> in vain do they worship me,
>   teaching human precepts as doctrines
>   (Mk. 7:6–7 NRSV).

False prophets take up what seems the reassuring good sense of human assumptions and dismiss the word of God, while claiming to have it. As with Peter when he became false prophet rejecting Jesus' forewarning about his death ("this must not happen to you"), the way they "think is not God's way but man's" (Mt. 16:22–23 JB). They set "realism" against the message of the One through whom all things came to be. Wolflike leaders don the garb of affronted national righteousness, commitment to re-establishing peace, and trust in God. In the West the U.S.-Iraq War was presented and mostly accepted as the main thing going on in the world for a better human future.

A most important adjunct of false prophecy is false witness, the breaking the next to the last of the Ten Commandments. One-to-one or internationally, to bring lying accusations is to strike at the well-being and life of the other. To view another group as an undifferentiated mass under sweeping indictment is to bear false witness. To focus on deplorable actions, with no willingness to take into account complex causes behind them, is to bear false witness. To take the worst happenings and aspects in a society as giving the full picture of what that society is like is to bear false witness. To give a huge amount of attention to wrongs done by the other side and close one's eyes to comparable wrongs done by one's own side is to bear false witness. To regard the lives of those in another ethnic or national group as less valuable than the lives of persons in one's own group is a deduction from false witness. To go to war as the good guys against the bad guys is the consummation of false witness. The opposite of false witness is confession — for oneself and for the country (an imperial nation most of all) within which one lives.

The Hebrew prophets saw that over against God and God's word was not simply the rebel deed but, prior to and underlying that, the rebel word, the lie. "You have forgotten me and trusted in lies" (Jer. 13:25). "They multiply falsehood and violence" (Hos. 12:1). "Woe to those who draw iniquity with cords of falsehood.... Woe to those who call evil good and good evil" (Is. 5:18, 20). (Thucydides, with contrasting Greek restraint, commented: "They altered the accepted usage of words in relation to deeds as they saw fit."[15]) Violence is cloaked in lies — most of all, words and phrases that themselves are lies prior to use in false statements: pacification, humanitarian aid, freedom fighters, "the use of force" to "liberate Kuwait," collateral damage, Operation Just Cause, Operation Desert Shield, low-intensity conflict, counterforce, limited nuclear war. The Persian Gulf conflict brought so dramatically what Christopher Lasch has warned of: "Isolated from criticism and controversy, armed with the most advanced techniques of thought control, armed also with enormous powers of destruction, the modern state can at any moment get almost completely out of control."[16] During the war the American populace, constantly reassured as to the morality of it all, could sip and savor "the wine of violence" (Prov. 4:17).

One of the worst things that occurred in relation to Nazi theory and practice was the acceptance and legitimization of these by the majority in the German churches. But the Nazis found themselves confronted, in contrast, by a Confessing Church. For Christians of the Confessing Church it was clear enough what the main anti-Christian deceptions were. Now too it should be clear to disciples that these are to be found centrally in the politics of the arrogant militarist state. The Thousand-Year Reich was seen, like "the New World Order," as hinging upon world dominion by one nation. In Hitler's Germany Christian witness and evangelism could rightly proceed only by taking into account and coming to grips with the lies and lures ascendant in the society. The same holds currently for the United States and other world powers. Persons cannot be called into discipleship to Jesus Christ unless the forces that most of all draw away from that discipleship are identified and challenged.

The Austrian peasant Franz Jägerstätter was beheaded by the Nazis in 1943 for refusal to enter the German army. The dream he had about National Socialism remains a revealing image for our time:

All of a sudden I saw a beautiful shining railroad train that circled around a mountain. Streams of children — and adults as well — rushed toward the train and could not be held back. I would rather not say how many adults did not join the ride. Then I heard a voice say to me: "This train is going to hell." ... Thus I believe God has shown me most clearly through this dream, or revelation, and has convinced me in my heart how I must answer the question: should I be National Socialist — or Catholic? I would like to call out to everyone who is riding on this train: "Jump out before the train reaches its destination, even if it costs you your life!"[17]

The nations of the earth are being led toward far greater catastrophe than that into which the Nazis took the Germans and the world. The satanic deceptions that press upon people must be countered.

The worst that came upon Germans in World War II was not death in cataclysmic defeat but such death while still in the grip of delusion. Those who see these issues in terms of extreme spiritual jeopardy will take risks in warning people.

In one of his most severe warnings, Jesus said: "Whoever causes one of these little ones who believe in me to sin, it would be better for him to have a great millstone fastened round his neck and to be drowned in the depth of the sea" (Mt. 18:6). In the shadow of that teaching, one can hardly begin to apprehend the vast wickedness perpetrated on television toward children (all others left out of account): the perverting of attitudes about consumption, womanhood, manhood, sexuality, enemies, war, the nation and its role in the world. The average American child watches twelve thousand acts of violence on television each year and by the age of sixteen has viewed the dramatized killing of eighteen thousand human beings.[18] Children are given over into continual molding by violence, most of all in time of war. Presidents model resort to fascinating violence as the way to solve difficult problems. The lure of violence, continuously spread by the media, erupts into practice everywhere across the land. Yet better to be killed earlier in a gruesome way than to become guilty of warping the spirit of one child — or of millions of children.

Religious False Prophecy

In Matthew 7 false prophets are the proponents of the wide and easy way. They hear "these words" of Jesus in the Sermon on the Mount but do not do them (Mt. 7:26). They say, "Lord, Lord," and even prophesy in Jesus' name but proceed in a lawlessness that is the opposite of the will of the Father made known in Jesus. "You will know the false prophets by what they do" (v. 20 TEV). No matter how well covered up, falseness within comes out in deeds. Those who look to the Master are enabled to identify persons and movements that have a message, manner, and results contrary to his. They heed the call of the true Shepherd, not that of impostors (Jn. 10:1–5). They turn from pursuit of death disguised as life.

False prophecy affirms a society and full collaboration in a society structured largely contrary to the way of Jesus given in the Sermon on the Mount, which in turn is fulfilment of the Torah and the prophets. "The false pen of the scribes has made [the Torah of God] into a lie" (Jer. 8:8); by interpretation they had twisted it into its opposite. Later scribes have interpreted away much of the message of Jesus. False

prophecy in the churches persuades multitudes that to be practical
and realistic they can and should disregard much in the Sermon on
the Mount: There has to be nuclear deterrence rather than love of enemies and readiness to suffer persecution; security through military
might rather than through seeking God's Rule; waging war rather
than negotiated settlement and reconciliation; success, affluence, and
financial gain rather than radical sharing with the poor; self-assertion
culminating in world dominance rather than gentleness; promotion
of good in the world through the projection of the military, political, and economic power of the nation rather than through striving
in community to live out the loving power of God. False prophecy
dons the "just war" mantle. It assumes the mode of chaplaincy in the
armed forces. It cancels out much of the call of Jesus but pretends not
to. It provides constant reassurance and justification. False prophecy
orchestrates the nationalist-militarist apostasy in the churches.

With regard to covert wars, military buildup, readiness to incin-
erate hundreds of millions, supposedly cheap invasions, the U.S.
role as leader and defender of the "free world," false prophets in the
churches echo those in the wider society; and that echo is taken by the
society as a most significant affirmation of what is being done. Three
examples of such prophecy can illustrate the predominant support
in the churches for the war with Iraq, though there was also strong
opposition. By spending the evening and night of January 16, 1991,
in the White House and leading a prayer service at Fort Myer the
next morning, Billy Graham gave his highly prized and publicized
blessing to the war. "Robert Schuller of the Crystal Cathedral in California...devoted a televised sermon to Mr. Bush, praising him as
a man now transfigured by prayer, and saying that our glorious en-
deavors in the gulf should be called Operation Desert Prayer."[19] A
guest on "The 700 Club" gave the forecast that the war would bring
a great opportunity for evangelism in the Middle East, a time to con-
vert the Islamic world: "When we have won the victory, there will
be an openness to Americans like never before."[20]

In confirmation of the status quo a few high and many lesser
priests offer a confectioner's gospel — success, happiness, self-
realization, spiritual and material prosperity, investment counseling,
eternal and earthly securities. They take up society's opiate as a prime
part of religion. The popular demand is "Speak to us smooth things"
(Is. 30:10). With celestial sanction "every one's greedy for gain." The
most adept dispensers of this good news become models of attain-
ment. Their easygoing "Peace, peace" to individuals correlates with
an approving "It is well!" to the dominant structures of the society.

"The prophets prophesy falsely, / and the priests rule at their direction; / my people love to have it so, / but what will you do when the end comes?" (Jer. 5:31)

Prophets around Jeremiah could point to the religious reforms under King Josiah; there had been an apparent national revival. Piety was on the rise. People kept saying, "The law of the Lord is with us" (Jer. 8:8), and this was taken as guarantee of God's protection. Much the same view of religious revival is widely held in churches of various countries. What is sought is a spiritual renewal for the nation that would, among other things, revitalize the dominant societal structures. Revival is seen as very much in the national interest.

Interpretations of biblical prophecy that fit well into fervent support for the foreign and military policy of the particular country are a secondary but quite significant part of false prophecy in the churches, mainly those of the religious right. The United States along with its allies was defending God's cause against the Soviet Union identified as the beast. Corroboration in scripture is found for whatever the State of Israel, with U.S. backing, does. The terribly destructive bombing of Iraq was said exultantly to fulfill prophecies against Babylon. Biblical prophecies are read as "a preview of coming thrillers in the cosmic movie theater."[21] The Hebrew prophets cried out against the societal wrongs around them and warned of impending judgment. But instead of seeking contemporary transposition of that, such interpreters pose and confidently solve riddles as to what passages refer to which current events and nations. Totally unlike those prophets, they give sanction to what the ruling elites are doing. "Your prophets? ah, their dreams for you / were false and flattering; / they never made you see your sin, / to save you from captivity" (Lam. 2:14 Moffatt).

An interpretation of prophecy that has had considerable political significance is the widely held belief that true believers will be raptured, caught up from the earth, just as nuclear war brings the horrors of "the great tribulation" for those left behind. Such a "rapture" is the religious counterpart of "Star Wars." In this scenario church folk can evade the way of the cross by siding with militarist nationalism and can then evade the consequences when those come. This view of "the rapture," a standard feature in pop apocalypticism, rests on very questionable exegesis of a few passages and first appeared only in the nineteenth century. If one reads these passages, convinced of a "pretribulation rapture," one can find it there; but the passages themselves would not bring it to mind. The apostolic scriptures teach that those who are God's are to be caught up at the End — this most clearly in 1 Thessalonians 4:13–18. But the idea that

God provides a celestial exit well before the End so that all Christians can escape suffering and persecution runs profoundly counter to how Jesus lived and died and to what he warned would be the typical lot of those who follow him.

Christological False Prophecy

Jesus warned his disciples: "Take heed that no one leads you astray. Many will come in my name, saying, 'I am he!' and they will lead many astray.... False Christs and false prophets will arise and show signs and wonders, to lead astray, if possible, the elect. But take heed; I have told you beforehand" (Mk. 13:5–6, 22–23). In the context of first-century Palestinian Judaism, which was the background for Mark 13, false prophets and false Christs were demagogic political-religious leaders, inciting, most typically, to nationalistic revolt against the Roman Empire. The initial intent of Jesus' warning was that disciples of his not be taken in by such imposters.

Jesus Christ came into the midst of humanity as God's central self-disclosure. The quintessence of all deception and lying is the lure away from him. The most striking expression of this is when someone else claims to be the Messiah, the one who brings salvation. Occasional upstarts through the centuries and some modern cult leaders have done that. But the deception is much broader than such explicit claims and is as manifold as human error.

John wrote:

Who is the liar but he who denies that Jesus is the Christ? This is the antichrist, he who denies the Father and the Son.... Beloved, do not believe every spirit, but test the spirits to see whether they are of God; for many false prophets have gone out into the world. By this you know the Spirit of God: every spirit which confesses that Jesus Christ has come in the flesh is of God, and every spirit which does not confess Jesus is not of God. (1 Jn. 2:22; 4:1–3)

The passages deal with the types of denial of Jesus Christ that were set against the faith of Christians to whom John was writing. But the rigor of the norm holds for the clash of beliefs in every time and setting. The axial negation in the human struggle against God is denial of Jesus as the Christ and incarnate Son of God, rejection of the apostolic message about Jesus (4:6).

"The Word became flesh" (Jn. 1:14) as God's chief initiative toward humanity. Gnostic teachers on the margins of the church later in the first century deprecated matter and the body. They held the docetic view that the divine Christ spirit took the human form of Jesus only as appearance and disguise. In the twentieth century the rejection of Jesus Christ, even in the churches, has come most notably by regarding Jesus as simply the human exemplar of what is really decisive: "the fatherhood of God and the brotherhood of man," the love ethic, nonviolence, revolutionary solidarity with the oppressed, attunement to God, etc. There is no end to the ingenious attempts that seek to exalt Jesus while holding back from the exalted claims made in the apostolic scriptures, initially by Jesus himself. The comment of P. T. Forsyth still applies to a wide range of theological denial: "Most elusive of all is the effort to retain the old passwords, while reducing them to no more than disguises in luminous paint for the subjective processes of a self-saving Humanity."[22]

Warnings against false prophets are given in the Hebrew scriptures, in the Sermon on the Mount and in Mark 13 (with parallels), and in 1 John. A number of times Paul warns against false teachers as when he calls back from "turning to a different gospel — not that there is another gospel, but there are some who trouble you and want to pervert the gospel" (Gal. 1:6–7). Common elements bind together these varied warnings. Ethical, political, and christological denial go together and amount to the same thing. The presumption of knowing better than the giver of the Sermon on the Mount how to live in the world is rejection of his Lordship and of God's coming in Jesus as totally determinative for human living. False prophecy offers a salvation contrary to (though typically in imitation of) that given by the God of biblical revelation. It provides assurance that peace, freedom, well-being, what people want in life, can be had through political resourcefulness, military prowess, violent revolution, the acumen of elites, esoteric knowledge, upright behavior sufficient to satisfy Deity. God is seen, if at all, only as sponsor of the endeavor. Salvation politics, whether of governments or of groups seeking to take political control, continues the messianism of those first-century pretenders, openly or more subtly: "Lo, here! . . . This is the way into what you long for. . . . Here is the leader to bring you through." People look toward some other entity or development, in the way all are called to look toward God's present and coming Rule.

In other facets of modern docetism, it is not recognized that Jesus acted in, and gave response to, an intensely political context with collaborators, Romans, Zealots, and other groups. Much of the ethic of Jesus is held to be supramundane and not really for living out "in the flesh." Direct christological denial turns from the God who saves in Jesus Christ and thus has no ethic or politics centered in this Christ. Derelict theology, whether "liberal" or "conservative," dismembers the body of Christ and abets terminal politics. Theological denial in Germany became a backdrop for the most dramatic political false prophecy in the twentieth century. Paul could summarize the human turn away from God thus: "they exchanged the truth about God for a lie" (Rom. 1:25). That truth and all which proceeds from it is a cohesive whole, an embracing Realm. But the lie also has a measure of cohesion and comes as malignant, encompassing counter-realm.

Paul wrote of the majority of his fellow Jews: "For to this day, when they read the old covenant, that same veil [like the one that covered 'the fading splendor' on Moses' face] remains unlifted, because only through Christ is it taken away" (2 Cor. 3:14). A comparable veil keeps so many church people from understanding those parts of the apostolic scriptures that would bring their militarist-nationalist blindness to an end. "But when one turns to the Lord, the veil is removed" (3:16 NRSV).

The False Prophet of the Apocalypse

In Revelation 13 John sees "a beast rising out of the sea." Another beast (later identified as the "false prophet," Rev. 16:13; 19:20; 20:10) "rose out of the earth; it had two horns like a lamb and it spoke like a dragon. It exercises all the authority of the first beast in its presence, and makes the earth and its inhabitants worship the first beast, whose mortal wound was healed" (13:11–12). It imitates the goodness and innocence of the One who was truly Lamb, but it speaks at times like a dragon. Or in the metaphor of Jesus it is a huge wolf in sheep's clothing. Jacques Ellul comments:

This beast in addition persuades men to raise up the image of the other, the image of the state. It animates this image and gives it the word. Once more, the great weapon of the second beast is the word. It puts its words in the mouth of the state; by it the state speaks, makes itself *known, identified, obeyed*. We are then truly before the extraordinary work of the animation of a dead structure, of a sterile organization, of a mechanism of power, which becomes living and vital presence. That which actually fills all these roles exactly is Propaganda. But we clearly specify, not at all a religious propaganda or bearing upon religious themes: it is precisely political propaganda (which sometimes takes a religious form). And it is an inspired analysis of the situation by John, which distinguishes between the organization of power which is the state, and the animation of this structure by the word of propaganda. On the one side, the sword; on the other, the word. On the one side, severity; on the other, conviction.[23]

This imagery in the Apocalypse brings to culmination the scriptural motif of false prophecy. There such prophecy is seen not mainly as the activity of deluded or deceiving individuals but as a dominating magnitude in history. "And I saw, issuing from the mouth of the dragon [Satan] and from the mouth of the beast and from the mouth of the false prophet, three foul spirits like frogs; for they are demonic spirits" (Rev. 16:13–14). From this trinity emanate the triune plethora of spirits utterly opposite to the Holy Spirit. Pressing upon the peoples of the world, these spirits form attitudes, mind-sets, and the prevailing mentality, in their own anti-Christian likeness. They impel the rulers of the world into revolt against God (v. 14). In this time before the End, these spirits, if not their final manifestation, are abroad in all the earth.

In view for John at that time was the apparatus that drew people into devoted adherence to the Empire and its head. Jewish revolutionaries could present themselves as anti-Roman messiahs. But far more imposing was Rome in its claim to be the arbiter of history and the source of well-being for the world. As nations and empires have taken up Rome's claim, they have developed a comparable apparatus, with signs and wonders, to enthrall the masses. Far oftener than not, churches have assumed a hallowing, exalting, and exonerating role in the apparatus.

In terms of Revelation 13, false prophecy communicates the claim to ultimacy. It is the mouth for the spirit of imperial politics. Lamb and dragon, it espouses freedom, democracy, human rights, development of impoverished nations; and it proceeds with manipulation of electorates, sponsorship of repressive regimes, the widening of the gap between rich and poor, covert wars, "low-cost" military strikes, and weapons of mass annihilation. It thrusts itself into all ears and eyes with unending rituals, flourishes, and technological spectacles. Most notably through use of awesome weapons, the false prophet bedazzles earth's inhabitants by "making fire come down from heaven" (Rev. 13:13). Worship of the beast is evoked by the media, aspects of the educational system, civic routines, the armed forces as mechanisms of indoctrination, war and war propaganda for the mass molding of loyal adherents, the conforming dominion of the economic realm (Rev. 13:16–17), and co-opted religious groupings.

Pop apocalyptists, seeking to decipher biblical prophecy, often warn of impending world government and of one totalitarian world state about to emerge. It is not clear from scripture whether such a monolithic external unification is to come before the End. A configuration of world powers and lesser powers could, to the last, constitute the beast. Across East-West and North-South divisions, the lineaments of the beast have remained basically the same in purpose, bent toward violence, and defiance of God. Mainly through technological developments, the deceptions and perils in our time become global in scope and impinge on all the inhabitants of the earth (Rev. 13:12). Also without a single world state, Satan becomes in more unitary fashion "deceiver of the whole world" (Rev. 12:9).

False prophecy in scripture most often has a political focus. This is especially evident in the passages in Jeremiah and Ezekiel and in the depiction of the false prophet in Revelation 13. The latter makes clear that the culminating deception and jeopardy for the people of God is highly political. Throughout history, much moves toward what is to come climactically just before the End. Therefore the Christian community cannot be simply apolitical. False prophecy can ensnare the churches or many within them into alignment with a beastly status quo. If churches try to be uninvolved or indifferent politically, they remain pathetically vulnerable to the lures of false prophecy. They are shaped decisively either by the news, controlled as it is, and all that comes with it or by the Good News.

Distinguishing True from False

Again and again passages of the Hebrew scriptures that warn against false prophecy deal with how to distinguish between the true and the false. Gerhard von Rad concludes that such ability to distinguish was given to "the person who had true insight into Jahweh's intentions for the time."[24] That might seem to be hardly more than a restatement of the problem. Within Hebrew salvation history, there could be no adequate answer to this question. But in Jesus God's intentions for all time have been made known. He is the truth by which divergent messages are to be tested. Jesus is reported to have said to new Jewish followers: "If you continue in my word, you are truly my disciples, and you will know the truth, and the truth will make you free" (Jn. 8:31–32). The frequently quoted last half of the saying depends on the first half. Only if human beings live as disciples who listen to

Jesus' word are they freed from ensnaring deceptions and know the truth, truth centered in this One who is God come near in human form. He did "no violence," but, giving basis for that, "there was no deceit in his mouth" (Is. 53:9). "Behold, an Israelite indeed, in whom is no guile!" (Jn. 1:47). Through the centuries the cornerstone, the sure foundation, stands firm, in contrast to lies as refuge and falsehood as shelter (Is. 28:15–18).

In Matthew 23 Jesus' warnings to his opponents (note "full of extortion and rapacity," v. 25) conclude with a passage about murder of the prophets. Then Jesus says to the city, "Jerusalem, Jerusalem, killing the prophets and stoning those who are sent to you!" (v. 37). In earlier times true prophets were killed because leaders and people insisted on a contrary course, the one corroborated by the false prophets; and so it was to be with Jesus. His adversaries, unwittingly, were taking this populace toward destruction by Rome: "Behold, your house is forsaken and desolate" (v. 38).

In the Hebrew scriptures false prophets were those who orchestrated the collective movement into disaster. The choice between Jesus and leaders who were pointing the people in the contrary direction was the culmination of the recurring decision by Israel/Judah between true and false prophecy. That choice continues into the present.

Jesus saw false prophets as a grave threat to disciples and the community: "False Christs and false prophets will arise and produce signs and portents to deceive the elect, if that were possible. You therefore must be on your guard" (Mk. 13:22 JB). He urged his followers to be vigilant, discerning, lest they be lured away from their Lord without even knowing it. The ability to identify false prophecy and cope with false prophets is critically important for the church. Part of what is needed is that Christians continually consider where in their own lives false prophecy has gotten hold of them and even made them a mouthpiece. None are free from the taint of deception. Like others, Christians may be in the truth one moment and quite out of it the next. Lies press in from every side, and their gaze may be drawn to other structures of salvation. They try to find at least some of their personal and societal reassurances apart from this Lord.

In the Mark 13 apocalypse, what looms as the chief danger is that of apostasy, falling away from God's Messiah. In the Messianic community that threat should be struggled against more than the nuclear threat or any other. Triumph of God's true word over the lie can emerge within each follower as recapitulation of Jesus' obedience to the Father. Disciples can live in the conviction that, though lies draw multitudes with them, they do not master reality, for this is defined by God's contrary word as history unfolds. And sooner or later this sovereignty over history must shatter the sweet lie "It is well!" and bring in God's shalom.

The opposite of the superficial diagnosis and easy remedy is the cross of Jesus Christ. Far more than Jeremiah, Jesus felt to the utter- most the shatteredness of Judah and of the total human condition. He let himself be smitten by it. "He himself bore our sins in his body on the tree. . . . By his wounds you have been healed" (1 Pet. 2:24). Wounds need healing. Yet his wounds are the source of healing, for in the recovery of that One laid low in death is overflow of healing into all who come to understand how desperately far they and the world are from being well. The Messianic community sees, with Jeremiah, the structures of the status quo in intense conflict with God's will and, because of this, the approach of the day of God's judgment. It cannot for the society chant, "It is well," or dispense nostrums. It offers as only remedy the One wounded unto death.

In spite of all that can and must be said about false prophecy in the churches, God's active, resilient, formative word comes to his people there. Many there are who do not bow to another god. In communist countries the churches were less a department and adjunct of the state than any other grouping, and so they are too in the Western powers. Dissent and resistance in the United States is based more among people of faith than any other constituency. The forecast of Rosemary Radford Ruether will probably be borne out:

> I would foresee that the churches will be a major battleground since, at this point, they are one of the major uncontrolled institutions of international stature. It is for this reason that we can expect to see stepped-up efforts to clothe the hegemonic "order" in the language of religious ethics, to develop further the cadre of "court" theologians and church people willing to sanctify this system of power, and to discredit critical voices from the churches.[25]

Undercover strategists map their campaigns for that battleground.

The Messianic community must seek discernment in relation to politics, must test the political spirits so as to resist temptation, and must strive to set God's true word against the colossus of indoctrina- tion. For example, what should come time and again is that prophets in churches throughout a country speak that word to counter false prophecy emanating from the central government and allied sources, even when it seems "truth has perished . . . they will not listen to you" (Jer. 7:28, 27). There is One "who frustrates the omens of liars" but "confirms the word of his servant" (Is. 44:25, 26). The struggle to live and proclaim God's truth over against false prophecy and not the attempt to transform the world should be the most determinative stance for the political involvement of Christ's people.[26] That happens also to be a goal more within their God-given reach.

Chapter 5

PUBLIC ENEMIES

We must insist that the Christian message is not simply that God is love; it is that God has revealed his love in Jesus Christ, and Jesus Christ is Jesus Christ horribly crucified — there is no other. That is to say, according to the Christian faith, when God discloses himself as love, he does not in the least lead us away from the terrible things which happen in history. He does not say, "Come away from the horror of things and take a look at the daffodils and crocuses in the springtime; let them speak to you of my goodness." On the contrary he leads us right into the very midst of the horror of things, and *meets us there*; he speaks to us out of the heart of the darkness.

—Herbert H. Farmer[1]

We are persecuted in an effort to prevent us from documenting cases [of human rights abuses] and speaking out. They justify our persecution by saying we are collaborators with the guerrillas. The goal is to discredit all independent organizations.... The U.S. embassy doesn't talk to us anymore. The U.S. embassy is in agreement with our destruction. We are a thorn to be eliminated. This month two pickup trucks with armed civilians have come to our offices. Today, we have received anonymous calls threatening us with death.

Herbert Ernesto Anaya, assassinated by a
Salvadoran death squad on October 27, 1987[2]

Extending the Hitler Analogy

Likening Saddam Hussein to Adolf Hitler may have been the single most persuasive argument for going to war against Iraq. Most people agree that Hitler had to be stopped, as indeed he was by the Allies in World War II. Saddam Hussein's treatment of the Kurds inside Iraq was compared to Hitler's treatment of the Jews, and his invasion and annexation of Kuwait, to Hitler's occupation of small countries across Europe. A favorite idea is that Hitler should have been removed from power earlier before he became so strong militarily. Americans and West Europeans were told that in going to war against Saddam Hussein the coalition was seizing the sort of opportunity that had been missed for Hitler. They were not told that the Gross National Product of Iraq was less than 1 percent of that of the United States and about equal to the economic output of Kentucky.[3]

This analogy can be examined in relation to what was the most ghastly horror carried out by the Nazis: the internment and annihilation of six million Jews. Adolf Hitler described how his anti-Semitism developed as he walked the streets of Vienna: "Wherever I went, I began to see Jews, and the more I saw, the more sharply they became distinguished in my eyes from the rest of humanity."[4] Millions of doomed Jews were designated as "enemy," set apart, subjected to dreadful living conditions, and then put to death in the gas chambers. Other "non-Aryan" populations were also distinguished from the rest of humanity and dealt with on that basis.

When more closely scrutinized, warfare throughout history is filled with analogies to Hitler's dealings with the Jews and those conquered populations: Millions are regarded as "enemy" beyond the pale of valued humanity and are subjected to however much violence is regarded as necessary for military victory and political supremacy. From ancient into modern times cities have been besieged. Somewhat like concentration camps during the siege, they often became like extermination camps when captured. Julius Caesar, by his own account, killed huge numbers of people that way in the conquest of Gaul. When the "Christian" Crusaders captured Jerusalem in 1099, they slaughtered seventy thousand Muslim inhabitants, snatched suckling babies from their mothers' breasts and threw them over the walls, herded the surviving Jews into a synagogue and burned them alive. Various Asiatic conquerors and the Iberians in Latin America brought death to millions of people. Any who are of the dominating racial majority in the United States have, to some extent, the distinctive past of ruthless dealings with Native Americans and African Americans. It is estimated that half of those captured in Africa to be made slaves died before they could be sold to American slaveholders.

Again and again the most determinative factor is that the other population is set apart from humanity and given over into what can be inflicted upon them. Later in World War II, the civilian populations of Germany and Japan found themselves very much set apart in that way by their enemies, often in circumstances somewhat comparable to concentration camps, and subject to terror, destruction, and death raining down from the bombers.

The same can be said of the seventeen million civilian Iraqis, half of them children under fifteen, during the U.S.-Iraq War. Iraq became a sort of camp set off from the rest of the world. Domination of the interned population was exerted by an intensity of aerial bombard- ment beyond anything earlier in history. Against Iraqi troops favorite weapons were cluster bombs, each scattering as many as eighteen hundred shrapnel-hurling bomblets, and fuel-air explosives, compa- rable in indiscriminate destructive power to small nuclear bombs.[5] The massacre of millions was not carried out — only of hundreds of thousands — but the traumatizing fear of getting killed by those in control from above came upon many millions as surely as in those Nazi camps.

The German populace knew about the existence of concentration camps but was not told what went on inside them. Good Germans did not want to know. The Jewish enemy was beyond their field of vi- sion. Americans were deluged with information about the bombing of Iraq. But the warriors at the top, whose commands were bring- ing death to so many human beings, were amazingly successful in keeping out of sight the victims on the other side and also the vic- tims on the allied side except when memorial vignettes of the latter were useful in evoking war sentiment. For most Americans the Iraqi multitudes cowering, suffering, dying under those touted "sorties" were completely out of sight.

As the war progressed, more and more Americans were ex- pressing the sentiment, "Nuke them, bomb them to oblivion, get it over with once and for all." A strong case can be made that Hitler proceeded with his worst crimes against humanity because of the constraints of the war. World War II, far from preventing the Holo- caust, evoked it. Throughout history the constraints of war have led repeatedly to similar crimes. If the U.S.-Iraq War had dragged on and brought with it large numbers of American dead and wounded, the attraction toward carrying out a U.S. "final solution" would have grown stronger in the administration and among the public. Because of the crushing coalition victory, that temptation lurks still more for later conflicts: Hi-tech weapons must surely constitute the means for total victory wherever that may be sought.

According to a Greenpeace study, "During the embargo period, the war and its aftermath, the lives of over six million people were directly affected by the war, either being killed, wounded, made refugees, or losing their homes."[6] An eighty-seven-member team that canvassed Iraq in the late summer after the war reported nine hundred thousand malnourished children under five and "unprecedented" levels of anxiety, stress, and abnormal behavior in children of primary school age. According to the report, "Nearly two-thirds of children interviewed believe they will not survive to become adults."[7] The United States and the United Nations saw to it that Iraq remained a desolated concentration camp set off from the rest of the world.

On the Hebrew day of atonement the sins of the people were ritually heaped upon a goat, a scapegoat, before it was driven off into the wilderness (Lev. 16:20–22). *Scapegoat* has become a widely used term, usually without thought as to its biblical origin. All blame for something is put on a person or group. The sins and guilt of the many, not recognized confessionally as on that Hebrew day, are thrust upon the maligned one or many. Hitler made the Jews the primary scapegoat, though other groups were consigned to serve that purpose too. A similar strategy and dynamic can be seen in the United States and other countries. Especially when frustration, anger, and fear are on the rise, these sentiments are directed against minority groups, those on welfare, the homeless, homosexuals, demonstrators, and convicted criminals, especially those on death row.

Hitler himself, titanically guilty as he was, became a scapegoat. Others could feel better about themselves as they chose to see wrongdoing as mainly centered in one man. For the West, Soviet leaders inherited that role. Those who refuse to recognize the enemy within are given enemies without. As the Soviets came to appear less sinister, the managers of U.S. society fixed upon Muammar Khadafi, Manuel Noriega, and then climactically Saddam Hussein, as chief scapegoat. All villainy and wickedness in the world were pictured as mainly incarnate in the Iraqi head of state. And St. George vanquished the dragon.

But we make the world too simple and let ourselves off far too easily when we see evil as largely concentrated in Hitler for one period or in Saddam Hussein for another. The bent toward dominating and destroying other human beings lurks in each of us and in every nation. In occasional private individuals and in some leaders and nations, that bent comes to hold fearful sway. Viewed in terms of the whole of history, Hitler was a towering exemplar, but only one more exemplar, of that. For centuries the Western powers had subjugated other countries and annexed territories not rightfully theirs. That bent can certainly be identified in Saddam Hussein and his mode of exercising power in Iraq and Kuwait. But for decades prior to the launching of the war against Iraq, the projection of U.S. and other Western power around the world was causing far more repression, violence, and suffering than was all Iraqi projection of power.

Though Iraqi forces committed numerous atrocities in Kuwait, most attention was given to reports (later discredited) that Iraqi soldiers had taken premature Kuwaiti babies out of incubators, which were then shipped to Iraq.[8] That did not happen; but what did happen during the three decades 1960–90 was that hundreds of millions of babies and children around the world died because they were deprived of what they needed for life, in a world that was spending $21 trillion of its resources on arms.[9] Most of that amount was spent by the major powers allied against Iraq, including nonbelligerents who voted in the United Nations Security Council for "the use of force." (The Iraqi government did its part toward this deprivation by devoting $46 billion to armaments during the 1980s, nearly all purchased from those major powers.) The fantastically expensive weapons that poured destruction on Iraq and its people had already taken a far higher toll among the poorest of the earth. Coalition bombing cut off electricity for incubators and other life-saving equipment in Iraqi hospitals, but who outside Iraq gave any attention to that?

It may be objected that people in antiwar movements often focus upon the U.S. president as scapegoat in ways quite similar to what is being considered: Evil is seen as having its locus and momentum chiefly in the one leader — Lyndon Johnson, Richard Nixon, Ronald Reagan, George Bush. That inclination must be resisted. Challenging the arrogance of power in a U.S. president may become imperative, but it should not serve as a way of exonerating oneself, one's movement, or the American people. Those who seek to resist horrors contemplated or commanded by a leader should realize that a part of who they have been has entered into the momentum toward those horrors. The realm of deception and violence has some hold on every human being. In the words of Joseph Sittler: "The term 'evil empire' is a description of *all* empires. The internal empire of every person's egocentricity is the template of historical evil."[10]

"Outside the Camp"

At the Midpoint of history One took to himself the equivalent of the lot of the Jews under the Nazis, of the Iraqis under the allied bombers, and of all who have been set beyond the boundary of that part of humanity which is seen as deserving to live. "Jesus also suffered outside the gate in order to sanctify the people through his own blood" (Heb. 13:12). From the time of Moses on, the bodies of the animals sacrificed by the high priest on the day of atonement were burned "outside the camp" (Lev. 16:27). A background image too was the scapegoat of the day of atonement, driven off into the desert. Jesus was cut off from the people, taken beyond the pale of secured habitation, and crucified outside the walls of the supposedly holy city. Jesus let be done to him in fullest measure what throughout history has been done to all who came to be seen as public enemies. His adversaries saw him as a grave threat to them and to the society. They tried to outwit and discredit him. In the end they did what persons in their position have most commonly done: They proceeded to do away with the threat to the status quo. The cross was their way of dealing with an enemy; Jesus made of it his consummate way of facing enemies.

Jesus saw the response and treatment he received as continuation of that given the prophets. Jesus stood in close relation to all before and after him who have been comparable to him in their stance toward a society and in how they have been seen and dealt with by those holding power. He came (and comes) to be united in suffering with every person and group outside the camp, even with those who are more like the two malefactors on that hill than like John and Mary Magdalene at the foot of the cross.

For disciples more is involved than finding themselves cast out of the misguided, murderous city. "Let us go forth to him outside the camp, bearing abuse for him" (Heb. 13:13). Disciples do not occupy the citadel nor even accept its protection. They do not belong there. Disciples are called to go where Jesus went and to bear what he bore. His suffering brought the redemption of the world. Their continuing on the terrain he chose discloses that redemption.

Paul wrote: "We are no more than this world's garbage; we are the scum of the earth to this very moment!" (1 Cor. 4:13 TEV). In classical Greek practice, when a *miasma* or impurity was in the society, it needed to be laid on a *peripsema* ("scum of the earth"), a representative of the people, who was then put to death. *Peripsema* became a term of contempt because condemned criminals or the dregs of society were ordinarily the ones who volunteered to be expiatory victims. Paul and his fellow workers were viewed with contempt by many around them. Jesus had become scum of the earth, and something of that lot was falling upon his followers, whom he had called to live in a way that could cause them to be treated like that.

Leaders like Adolf Hitler and Saddam Hussein and national or ethnic groups like the Jews have been singled out to bear the sins of others. But Jesus alone could do that and willed to do that. When church folk join in the collective identification of a scapegoat, they deny the Gospel about the One without sin who was made "to be sin" (2 Cor. 5:21). There is no need of scapegoats, whether foreign tyrants or death-row prisoners, because Jesus as the one *peripsema* bore the sins of all. Jesus took to himself the totality of the drive within us all to lay our sins on others.[11]

If Jesus had been murdered by a solitary antagonist, his death would have been brought about by the sin of that person. Instead, what came upon Jesus, even in terms of verifiable history, was fully collective. The established elite, drawing with them the Passover populace, brought to pass the execution of this "enemy" of the society and of their power. Roman rule proceeded to do such violence as it was ordinarily perpetrating quite on its own.

Jesus was confronted in the Nazareth synagogue at the beginning of his ministry, not so much by individuals in their unbelief, but rather by the aroused mob that drew individuals into a collective readiness to kill. Throughout the Gospels his confrontations were mainly with representatives of the governing elite and the dominant interest groups. What came upon Jesus was the oligarchic and collective readiness to resort to killing in order to counter a perceived threat to the society. Jesus gave himself over to that readiness, which in its full breadth is the darkest aspect of human history. Most deeply considered, those who crucify, all of us, are the public enemy. But Jesus took what we did not recognize as our place.

The historical form in which evil came upon Jesus at the end of his earthly life should shape the understanding of how "he himself bore our sins in his body on the tree" (1 Pet. 2:24). It is hardly (or not so much) that one's individual sequence of sinning somehow crosses a time gap backward to become part of what Jesus bore in going to his death. Rather, Jesus was killed because the fallenness of human beings finds destructive and lethal collective expression — because history is the way it is. The sin of each human enters into history's being that way and thus into the unitary wickedness that did away with Jesus. "He bore the sins of many," that is, of *all* (Is. 53:12),[12] when at the focal point of history the variegated sins of each and all found culmination in doing away with that "enemy."

That same collective wickedness — machinations of the governing elites, fickleness of the manipulated masses, perverted religion, presumptuous readiness to kill — continues to inflict on incomprehensible numbers of persons something of what was done to Jesus. None (except possibly the youngest) are innocent, none without sin that swells the wickedness. But to be aligned with such victimization and violence (in Latin America, southern Africa, the Middle East, U.S. ghettos, or anywhere) is to stand with the current expressions of that which inflicted torture and death upon Jesus. It is refusal to break with what has been done to Jesus and innumerable others. At stake is not simply the content of the Christian ethic. Either one seeks to break with all violation of others, borne to the fullest by Jesus; or one does not see that break as imperative and does not make it. But without it, how can one stand forgiven with the Savior who for all bore that evil from all?

Subversives

Jesus said to the crowd and his disciples, "If any want to become my followers, let them deny themselves and take up their cross and follow me" (Mk. 8:34 NRSV). In an "adulterous and sinful generation" (v. 38) Jesus quickly came to be seen as dangerous threat to the established order and its avowed righteousness. The cross he spoke of is the hardship and suffering that comes upon any who with him are so regarded. As happened with Jesus, those who stand against the lure of collective violence become prime targets for that violence. Taking up one's cross "is a terrifyingly vivid and ruthless way of saying that discipleship means accepting the death sentence ... to go with Jesus to the execution-ground [rather than] standing with the authorities of the world."[13]

In the Gospels and throughout the apostolic scriptures, persecution is seen as a characteristic circumstance for followers of Jesus. "Love your enemies and pray for those who persecute you" (Mt. 5:44; in the Hebraic parallelism, enemies, primarily, are the persecutors). "You will be hated by all for my name's sake" (Mt. 10:22). "If they persecuted me, they will persecute you" (Jn. 15:20). "Indeed all who desire to live a godly life in Christ Jesus will be persecuted" (2 Tim. 3:12).

Persecutions were also held to be a sign of the approaching End. "Then they will deliver you up to tribulation, and put you to death; and you will be hated by all nations for my name's sake.... And then the end will come" (Mt. 24:9, 14). The apostolic church saw the persecutions it was undergoing as part of that sign. Jesus' death and rising had ushered in the Endtime. Christians under persecution were sharing in the continued sufferings of Jesus in the interim before his Parousia (1 Pet. 4:13). Any persecution is reiteration of what was done to Jesus and is corollary to it as a minute part of what precedes the full revelation of God's triumph already achieved in Jesus' coming, death, and resurrection. The might of Empire is achieved through shedding and threatening to shed the blood of others. But of the Messianic community it is written: "They have conquered him [Satan, the infernal strategist of death] by the blood of the Lamb / and by the word of their testimony, / for they did not cling to life, even in the face of death" (Rev. 12:11 NRSV). The advance of this people comes by witness to the One whose blood was shed by the Empire, witness given in readiness to have their shed blood added to his.

By and large, Christians in the United States and Western Europe are not openly persecuted by their governments. Sometimes church people are a little uneasy when they note the contrast between such a situation and what is regarded as normative in the apostolic scriptures. Generally they have seen persecution as what happens to Christians in communist countries, and the danger that this might come to the United States and other Western countries has been taken as the highest reason for enormous military effort. For half a century many of those engaged in predicting the future, supposedly from biblical prophecy, were forecasting that persecution by the beast in the form of some communist takeover would soon be the lot of believers in what till then had been "the free world."

But most of these speculators and their followers already bow, unaware, to a persecuting beast. Few church people in the imperial powers recognize that persecution of Christians and others, held mostly in abeyance there, has been carried out in many Third World countries under regimes that their governments have maintained in power. Such persecution is an important element in the projection of imperial power around the world. It is carefully kept out of view. As in the Roman Empire, resistance and its suppression come mostly in the provinces. Those who do not go along with the imperial religion are to be slain (Rev. 13:15).

As the chief guarantor of the power structures that are being challenged in many countries, the United States covertly underwrites persecution. It gives support to whatever means are deemed necessary for installing and maintaining regimes compliant with its interests. This is done behind what is often no more than a façade of official expressions of concern for human rights. That Kuwait and Saudi Arabia have tyrannical governments or that telling the Gospel of Jesus is a crime in Saudi Arabia is no problem. The more than seventy-five thousand killed in the Salvadoran civil war, mostly by the U.S.-sponsored regime, is no problem. The genocidal Indonesian repression of the people of East Timor (with an estimated one-third of the population slaughtered) is no problem. The importance of trade with China being what it is, Chinese repression and massacring of Tibetans and of dissidents is no problem.

In the first half of the twentieth century, persecution of Christians and Jews was most notably a Turkish, Soviet, and Nazi endeavor. In the second half of the twentieth century, the exercise of U.S. and other Western power around the world quite certainly brought more suffering, imprisonment, torture, and death to Christians and others than did even the grim and at times monstrous Soviet exercise of power. The Soviets were not more benevolent, but they had less power to project; and dramatic persecution within their domain came more readily under world scrutiny. Even before *glasnost*, it was much less dangerous to be a radical Christian in the Soviet Union or Czechoslovakia than under U.S. client regimes in El Salvador and Guatemala. The genocidal Nazi terror struck God's people of the Mosaic covenant. U.S.-sponsored terror has fallen especially on God's people of the covenant sealed with Jesus' blood.

The dominant tradition of churches in Latin America and in other Third World countries has been that of subservience to the ruling elites. Such churches and newer mission churches with that same attitude enjoy official favor. But in the last half of the twentieth century a contrary church emerged, a church politically and sociologically comparable to the church of the first three centuries in the Roman Empire and to Anabaptist groups in the Reformation. Rather than legitimating the powers that be, this contrary church gives voice and hope to the poor, stands against injustice, and lives out biblical imperatives in challenge to the status quo. In a number of countries the overall threat to the old order is centered in this emergent movement. Intimidation, imprisonment, torture, and death squad killings have been directed especially against Christians.[14] The authorities do not engage in officially declared persecution of Christians. But brutal repression of dissent, which in these countries is inspired most of all by Jesus and the Gospel, amounts to persecution. Those in power move against those whose faith and living constitute a questioning of that power. Through the centuries such questioning has been the chief reason behind persecution. Any followers of Christ who find themselves persecuted take representatively the blows that in their deeper intent are directed against all who would faithfully go with this Lord.[15]

With exotic new religions spreading across the Roman Empire, the Caesars would have given little attention to the early Christians if their faith had not involved adherence to a different Lord and shaped a movement apart from the cohesion of the imperial whole. The Roman authorities, permissive toward the spread of various religions, would not tolerate a movement of believers who rejected the dominant Roman definition of reality. Their motives were political, not religious. They saw the spread of the Christian message and movement as a threat to the desired monolithic unity of the Empire. That perception was accurate.

In Christendom, however, after the Constantinian shift, a central assumption was that the church in its oneness undergirded the unity of the state and society: To be held together, a society had to have just one church organizationally and confessionally. Before, during, and after the Reformation, groups dissenting from the state religion were seen as breaking away from the societal unity that had to be maintained and were persecuted as threat to the established order. Concern for right belief and theological rectitude was seldom the determining motive for persecution as actually carried out.

In the American experiment and elsewhere, it was discovered that a variety of religious groupings could be tolerated and drawn together into supporting and sanctifying nation and culture as well as a single state church ever did. Without the establishment of religion, there could be religion largely aligned with the establishment. For most citizens the nation could be the *church*, the most determinative corporate entity for personal affiliation and commitment.[16] What governments had sought to maintain, even through persecution, could be had without it. The Roman authorities noticed with alarm the contradiction between the officially prescribed definition of reality and the faith of those in the Christian movement. Lapdog churches do not present imperial authorities with any such contradiction. As Jean Lasserre brings out:

> But because the State does not persecute the Church, can one really conclude that the State is faithful and has not been "demonised"? Is it not equally possible that the State is well and truly demonised, but does not persecute the Church which grants it all it wants, and is in haste to satisfy all its whims, like a mistress afraid to lose the favours of her rich, protective lover?[17]

Throughout the Cold War, those who stood against wars and prevailing foreign policy assumptions were often accused of being subversives — basically the content of the charge against the early Christians. They were seen as undermining the national unity indispensable for the nation's role in the world. The U.S.-Iraq War brought a resurgence of this attitude. Protesters in various countries were widely regarded as intolerable threat. As one passerby told me and others vigiling in front of a city post office, "You are the enemy." Reporters who dared to diverge from the official line were berated by generals and became the objects of public fury.

But when church people stand with the imperial dominion, they unwittingly commit again the worst scandal of Christendom, supposedly put aside centuries ago: the church as advocate of persecution. Jesus warned that "brother will deliver up brother to death" (Mt. 10:21). Continuing large-scale fulfilment of that comes as professing Christians, through their political attitudes and alignments, participate in giving over millions of Christians and others of God's children into persecution by repressive governments. If the managers of U.S. society decide to undertake vigorous repression of those within the country who refuse to burn the pinch of incense to the Empire, many church folk will likely cheer the endeavor.

"The Road to Damascus: Kairos and Conversion," a statement issued by Christians from El Salvador, Guatemala, Korea, Namibia, Nicaragua, the Philippines, and South Africa, declares:

> Right-wing Christianity under whatever name is a way of believing that rejects or ignores parts of God's revelation and selects or distorts other parts in order to support the ideology of the national security state.... Right-wing Christianity is being promoted with vigorous and expensive campaigns in all our countries and in almost all Christian traditions....
>
> We have wished to make it quite clear that those Christians who side with the imperialists, the oppressors and the exploiters of people are siding with the idolaters who worship money, power, privilege and pleasure. To misuse Christianity to defend oppression is heretical. And to persecute Christians who are oppressed or who side with the oppressed is apostasy — the abandonment of the gospel of Jesus Christ.[18]

To round out the grotesqueness of this state of affairs, those who control and implement the imperial exercise of U.S. power and those who support this are for the most part church members. Pontificating television preachers bestow their blessing on repressive rulers. Worst of all, some right-wing religious groups have given direct financial and material assistance for covert military operations, such as those of the Nicaraguan Contras.[19]

In the Hebrew Bible the chief abuse of power is mistreatment of the poor. In the apostolic scriptures it is persecution. For many countries, the two have become merged. Third World elites and behind them the Western elites "oppress the poor...crush the needy" (Amos 4:1). They want to "devour the poor in secret" (Hab. 3:14), out of public view. What economic policies perpetrate, repression seeks to maintain. Of course many who resist and work for justice do not see themselves as Christians. But in countries with a larger Christian population, Christians usually constitute a central range of resistance and leadership. Not all of the Hebrew poor were looking to Yahweh, but the many who did were taken as representing the entire group. In the same way, "the poor in spirit" and those yearning for justice (Mt. 5:3, 6) who know themselves to be in Jesus' family are to be seen as standing with and representing those of parallel yearning who do not yet understand this.

Jesus crucified and risen is with "the least." What is done to them — including the terrible things — is done to him: "As you did it to one of the least of these ... you did it to me" (Mt. 25:40). Jesus, undeserving, took our deserved suffering and stood and stands with each and all in all undeserved suffering. Jesus continues to suffer and die with those who are the victims of the powers of destruction. In this Jesus God is most amazingly God[20] and comes ever again to stand with those who are his in the midst of torture chambers, prisons, concentration camps for ethnic minorities, death squad assassinations, blown-up airliners, and slaughters in Yugoslavia, Afghanistan, Lebanon, Iraq, Haiti, Guatemala, Ethiopia, Somalia, Angola, Mozambique, Liberia, and many other countries.

Answer to the horrors perpetrated in the world as in Ivan Karamazov's stories is to be found provisionally in that which his brother Alyosha took into his reply:

> You said just now, is there a being in the whole world who would have the right to forgive and could forgive? But there is a Being and He can forgive everything, all and for all, because He gave His innocent blood for all and everything. You have forgotten Him, and on Him is built the edifice, and it is to Him they cry aloud, "Thou art just, O Lord, for Thy ways are revealed!"[21]

This Jesus continuously crucified is at the right hand of the Father. His is the sovereignty that will soon win out. If disciples look to Jesus Christ in the breadth of who he was and is, they see in him God's No to the rebel powers, God's suffering with all victims, and God's Rule that is displacing misrule. Jesus on the cross was already entering into his triumph, and so it is too with those who are drawn pre-eminently into that death.

Christians not under persecution are to be "partners" (koinonoi, Heb. 10:33), sharing in spirit the suffering of those who are. When Christians reside in an imperial power very involved in persecutions, that partnership with the persecuted must find expression in resistance to such involvements.

The Cry of the People

Jews in Palestine during the earthly ministry of Jesus were a subject people under the Roman overlordship. They had virtually no access to the central power structure of the Empire. The rule under which they lived came upon them from above. They did not have a participatory voice for choosing that rule or the rulers. Jewish collaborators took part as an elite that imposed Roman authority, as well as their own, on the masses. That political situation seems quite remote from present-day democracy in the West.

Yet the most significant decision made by Roman authorities during the centuries of the Empire was that of crucifying Jesus of Nazareth, and, ironically, the local population did have a participatory voice in that decision. It was a sort of direct democracy between the crowd and Pilate. Much Roman decision-making was oriented toward killing on behalf of the Empire, and the execution of Jesus was in line with that, even though Pilate, who alone had the requisite authority, drew back. But "the people," incited by their leaders (Mt. 27:20), had their say, and Pilate went along with *vox populi*.

Contemporary political decision-making can be looked at in the light of Jesus' trial. The central decision — always partly analogous to the chief issue at that trial — is whether or not to kill on behalf of the ruling power structure (or on behalf of what is seeking to replace it). That decision has such somber significance and so many ramifications, especially in going to war or preparing to, that it usually needs to come or appear to come as the mandate of the people. Here is the most elemental "democracy," emerging under any form of government. World War II evoked this sort of mass solidarity even in the most totalitarian countries — thus under Stalin the Soviet struggle against the Nazi invasion. A formal democracy such as the United States becomes fearfully totalitarian when what seems near to being a massed totality affirms the leader's resort to massive violence, as in the bombing of Hiroshima and Nagasaki, the invasion of Grenada and then of Panama, the war with Iraq, and, by threat, in the Cuba Missile Crisis. In war, dominating rule from above is greatly enhanced by, and very dependent on, the orchestrated support of the people.

When I gaze at photographs of Jews, especially children, being rounded up for Auschwitz, I try to comprehend for those few something of the tragedy of it all. Anne Frank's legacy is that of taking us past the incomprehensible numbers into the humanity of who she, a single victim, was. In Jerusalem the Yad Vashem memorial to the Holocaust victims has a building dedicated to the children.[22] At the entrance are a few photographs of haunting faces. And then inside, into the eerie darkness of mirrors and myriad dots of light is read in endless succession name after name, each intimating the unique, unfulfilled human person from among the 1.5 million Jewish children who perished. But for the slain Iraqi children and the hundreds of thousands who continue to die in the aftermath of the war and for the forty thousand children around the world who are given over needlessly to death each day we have no Anne Frank, no Yad Vashem, and hardly any pictures. Those children and any who for us would visually represent them have been most carefully kept from our view. There were the other Germans, among them Dietrich Bonhöffer, who said, "Only he who cries out for the Jews may sing Gregorian chants."[23] If we are not to have our own humanity effaced by the alluring powers of destruction and by the tidal inhumanity of official thought control, we must see those we are not meant to see and cry out for them.

Some in Jerusalem did not join in the cry "Crucify him!" Luke pictures massive dissent before and after that execution: "And there followed him a great multitude of the people, and of women who bewailed and lamented him.... And all the multitudes who assembled to see the sight, when they saw what had taken place, returned home beating their breasts" (Lk. 23:27, 48). Offering continuation of that dissent, some in our time do not merge into the collective readiness to kill. They do not become functionaries for contemporary crucifixion. They withhold consent and live out their resistance to the purpose and deed of taking human life. What is most crucial is the stance: to see all public killing, from capital punishment to nuclear holocaust, as having its historic center in the execution of Jesus and to live life from him in struggle against all death-mongering.

Chapter 6

MASADA AND GOLGOTHA

Judas...wills to take even the judgment of God into his own hands, and himself executes it upon himself. It is in this light of a usurped self-judgment crowning all previous offences that Matthew evidently sees the corresponding downfall of Jerusalem and the whole national and religious life of the Jews. With the killing of its Messiah, Israel has entered a road on which not only is God's judgment upon its whole existence inevitable, but in sheer self-consistency it must end by committing suicide. That is what Israel finally did in the revolt against the Romans and particularly in the defense of Jerusalem against Titus in A.D. 70. Unable to live any longer, it gave itself up willingly and wittingly — we have only to think of the account of the end of the last high-priests — to the death which in itself could not be an expiation for its sins, but only their consummation....

To be sure, the Church waits for the conversion of Israel. But it cannot wait for the conversion of Israel to confess the unity of the mercy that embraces Israel as well as itself, the unity of the community of God.

—Karl Barth[1]

As Hendrikus Berkhof points out, "However and wherever Israel appears it tends to be a stumbling block and the object of excitement for the nations."[2] God set Jerusalem "in the center of the nations, with countries round about her" (Ez. 5:5). Israel/Palestine continues to draw more attention from the world of nations than any other small area. That attention is a blurred intimation of Isaiah 2:1–4 in which all the nations look toward and go up to Zion to learn the ways of peace. But ironically, the larger contours of the current situation there are in stark contrast to Isaiah's vision of Jerusalem and all the earth at peace: the most intensely militarized society on earth, the fifth most powerful air force in the world, a readied arsenal of more than two hundred nuclear weapons,[3] and repressive rule over the Palestinians in the occupied territories.

Many countries have pursued arms buildups to ward off threatening adversaries. Some other governments have carried out far more ruthless repression of ethnic groups within the country or in conquered territory. In these matters the State of Israel is not exceptional. What Israel has been doing can be seen as necessary for its continued existence and the survival of the Israeli people. The objection could, therefore, be raised: Why should special attention be given to Israel?

For a biblical-theological understanding of the contemporary world, the State of Israel is exceptional, unique. Israel is there because of an impetus through the generations stemming from the Hebrew scriptures. Whether or not it is seen as the genuine fulfilment of that impetus, Israel has a relation to scripture different from that of any other nation state.

Prophecy specialists have convinced tens of millions of people that the emergence of the State of Israel is a fulfilment of biblical prophecies and is the clearest indicator that the Second Coming of Christ must be regarded as calendrically very near. Israel's wars have also been explicated by deciphering Hebrew prophecies. Israel is seen as the site of the impending battle of Armageddon. In this outlook, it is a biblical imperative that the United States (and the West) fully support Israel militarily and otherwise. Religious justifications of U.S. policies and those of Israel become intertwined.[4] Thus, questions about Israel are closely related to the issue of what one sees as a sound approach (and what one sees as misguided approach) in seeking a biblical understanding of the present world of nations.

The primary aim in this chapter is to develop a biblically Christian perspective on the State of Israel in contrast to certain views widely held in the churches. If Jesus is Lord, those who understand this should view all nations, including Israel, in terms of that Lordship. Large sectors in the churches lack such an outlook. "The word of the cross" is a "folly" and stumbling-block, a cause of agitation and resistance (1 Cor. 1:18, 23), especially with regard to nationhood and national exercise of power. But any who confess Jesus as Lord should see the nation they live in as under that word. If they consider the State of Israel, they should see it too in the light of the message about Christ crucified.

Criticism of policies and actions of the Israeli government is often branded as anti-Semitic. But if strong criticism of the direction being taken by a Jewish government constitutes anti-Semitism, the Hebrew prophets and Jesus of Nazareth would need to be seen as the archetypal anti-Semites. The writings of the prophets are filled with such criticism. Jesus, like some of the prophets, saw a beloved populace headed toward catastrophe. Questioning the present direction of the State of Israel can be grounded in that very attitude.

But Christians who express such questioning should keep in mind that warring and repression by those bearing the name "Christian" have been vastly more extensive and deadly than Israeli warring and repression. Through the centuries of Christendom into the present, the scandal of the churches' unfaithfulness to Jesus Christ has been far greater than what may be seen as contemporary Jewish unfaithfulness to the Torah and the prophets, inside and outside Israel. Moreover, just as there are many Christians striving to be faithful in post-Christendom countries that are far from being Christian, so in Israel there is a large minority committed to the humane values of the Jewish heritage. This "other Israel," represented in fifty peace groups, does seek shalom/salaam with the Palestinians and with Arab countries.

Christians also need to ponder what Ronald J. Sider surveys confessionally:

> We must acknowledge that this Christian oppression of Jews has played a key role in current Israeli oppression of Palestinians. It is largely we Christians who have made the Jews feel they are outcasts, with no one they can trust in the world. In the Israeli soldiers' attacks on innocent Palestinians, we must see our centuries of pogroms against the Jews. In the soldiers' destruction of Palestinian homes, we must see the centuries of church-sanctioned desecration and destruction of Jewish homes and places of worship. In the Jewish failure to speak out against the injustices committed by their government, we must see the centuries of Christian failure to speak up in defense of the Jews. Israel is reacting with extreme force against the Palestinians because of its extreme fear that it will be destroyed and no one will come to its rescue. We must acknowledge our major role as Christians in planting that fear in them.[5]

Christians must remember the Holocaust and the massive involvement or complicity of professing Christians in it.

The Torah, the Prophets, and the State of Israel

God's promise in choosing Abraham was "In you all the families of the earth will be blessed" (Gen. 12:3).[6] In this is stated the intent, beginning, and goal of God's dealings with the people of biblical Israel. Psalmists and prophets offered visionary pictures of the realization of that promise. The early Christians saw the coming of Jesus and the spreading of the Gospel as the central fulfilment of God's promise to Abraham (Acts 3:25–26; Rom. 4; Gal. 3:6–29).[7] But Christians in the modern times can also recognize an additional, continuing

fulfilment in Judaism's witness to God and in the multiplicity of
Jewish contributions to the life and culture of the world, apart from
Christianity. However, there is much reason to question whether the
State of Israel as such, in its emergence and in its exercise of political
and military power, is a central realization of that promise to Abraham and of Jewish enrichment of human life. The State of Israel has
been a blessing to large numbers of immigrant Jews. But so far it has
been more a curse for the minority within and the peoples round
about, often evoking the worst in those populations. It is "a byword
of cursing" in many nations (Zech. 8:13).

In World War I Palestinians constituted nine-tenths of the population of Palestine. In 1947 under the British, Jews, mostly in cities, were
one-third of the population and owned 6 percent of the land.[8] The
1947 Partition Plan, which the United States with much arm-twisting
pushed through the United Nations, gave the Jewish State 52 percent
of the land — as compensation, strangely enough, for what Europeans had inflicted on Jews. During 1947–49, combat, massacres,
and expulsions impelled eight hundred thousand Palestinians, four-
fifths of that population, to flee from what was becoming Israeli
territory.

A number of passages in the Torah dealt with right treatment
of sojourners, non-Hebrew people living within Israel. "You shall
not oppress a stranger; you know the heart of a stranger, for you
were strangers in the land of Egypt" (Ex. 23:9). "Love the sojourner
therefore; for you were sojourners in the land of Egypt" (Deut. 10:19).
Hebrews were to be God's agents of blessing toward all other peoples
of the earth, beginning with the resident ethnic minorities.

Jews in modern times returned to Palestine first as sojourners;
they had been that everywhere else. In 1948 the remaining Palestinian population of Israel became an underclass in what (under
foreign rule) had been their own land for many generations.[9] After
the Six Day War in 1967, Palestinians in the territories occupied by Israel found themselves in a land much less theirs than before.[10] Israel
became a new Egypt, treating aliens as a cheap labor pool — even to
the point of intense concern about the birth rate of those aliens. In
parts of Palestine, Israel with its mini-empire finds itself as anomalous successor to Rome, holding down an indigenous population
determined to be free.

The precursors and founders of the State of Israel, though secular
Jews, had an idealistic hope that this new country would be a model
nation for Jews everywhere and for the world — "a light to the nations" (Is. 42:6; 49:6). That hope in its secular and religious forms

evoked a huge outpouring of energy and sacrifice in the return to Palestine and the emergence of the nation. Israel's Declaration of Independence affirms: "The State of Israel ... will be based on freedom, justice and peace as envisaged by the prophets of Israel; it will ensure complete equality of social and political rights to all its inhabitants, irrespective of religion, race or sex." Tragically, this vision has been widely contradicted in practice.

Most orthodox Israeli Jews see the rebirth of Israel as messianic, as the beginnings of redemption. (About 15 percent of Israeli Jews consider themselves "religious"; the large majority of these are orthodox.) Rabbi I. Amital has stated about Israel:

> Its internal objective is not the normalization of the Jewish Nation to be a nation like all nations, but to be a holy people, the nation of a Living God, whose center will be Jerusalem, sanctified by the presence of God's Temple. What we observe currently is the beginning of the prophetic vision of the redemption of Zion. These are the Messianic steps.[11]

(At the time of the Roman emperor Constantine, Eusebius took a comparable position and led the church in seeing a changed political structure as eschatological event.) There are now gardens in the desert, and Western-style cities where there was sand. But what has been inflicted on the Palestinians since the beginnings of the State of Israel and what this has done and is doing to Israeli society, cling like a pall. One can have high respect for the yearning, the devotion, and the sacrifice that have gone into the building of the State of Israel and still discern the hand of the God who confounds all messianisms. Here too, as for other presumptively messianic settings, one can ask, Is this what the start of redemption looks like?[12]

The "realist" argument is, of course, that only Israeli military strength has kept Israel from being driven into the sea by hostile Arab countries. But throughout the Hebrew scriptures God calls his people to rely on him and not on military might. It could be said that parts of the Hebrew scriptures support resort of violence and war. But these passages too give no basis for arms buildup and trust in military power. "Not by might, nor by power, but by my Spirit, says the Lord of hosts" (Zech. 4:6). "Some trust in chariots, and some in horses: but we will remember the name of the Lord our God" (Ps. 20:7 AV). The State of Israel (like other nations) completely rejects that call to rely solely on God. The very orthodox Neturei Karta is one small group in Israel that discerns this rejection of the core of Judaism. These believers do not accept the State of Israel:

What is the significance of the Zionist State which has emerged in our time? It signifies a denial of the basis of our faith. It asserts that the destiny and existence of God's people does not depend on the observance of the Torah and commandments, maintaining rather, that the Jewish nation will live by virtue of mortal strength and weaponry.[13]

Hebrew prophets warned repeatedly against military alliances — such as seeking "shelter in the shadow of Egypt" (Is. 30:2). But Israel is extremely dependent militarily and economically on its alliance with the United States. American church folk who promote this alliance also defy that word. All that Israel as client state has been doing, including the illegal establishment of settlements in the occupied territories, is underwritten by massive aid from the United States, which amounts to more than $1,100 per Israeli each year.[14]

If present policies continue, all of its military power will not bring Israel through in the longer term. Turning again to seek justice and peace as called for in the Torah and the prophets could bring greatly increased security. Given the present situation — and God meets Israelis or any people where they are — the security of Israel would be greatly increased if Israel withdrew from the occupied territories and allowed the Palestinians to have their own country, free from Israeli domination. The new Palestinian state, one-third the size of Israel, could remain demilitarized, with a United Nations presence; and the obsessive militarism corroding Israeli society could subside. In the summary formulation of a group of human rights activists from various of countries:

'Israeli Jews have a deep and understandable fear for their security. But the attempt to achieve security through the subjugation of another people is not only morally wrong, it is doomed to fail. Security — for both Israel and the Palestinians — can only be achieved through mutual recognition, acknowledgement of each other's right to self-determination, and peace.[15]

Jesus of Nazareth and the State of Israel

The alternatives for Israel (and all humanity) are represented by two heights, Masada and Golgotha. On the one nearly impregnable height, Jewish rebels, after the fall of Jerusalem, held out against the Roman Tenth Legion until A.D. 73. Then in the night before the Romans were about to enter through the breached wall, 960 men, women, and children died in a mass suicide (though many were probably slaughtered without their consent), with the last person setting fire to the palace.[16] The State of Israel has made Masada the prime symbol of heroic determination to fight, if necessary, to the death. Many Israeli military units are inducted in the ruins of that fortress. Inductees swear their allegiance to Israel and make the vow "Masada shall not fall again." It remains unrecognized that the Masada story, taken as a mystique, becomes a foreshadowing of the Israeli future.

On the other elevation, now not even identifiable with any certainty, Roman soldiers executed a Jew who had refused to lead his people in taking up arms against them. He gave himself into the power of his enemies — exactly what those rebels in Masada were determined not to do — and let them do their worst to him. He prayed that his enemies and all those implicated in the deed be forgiven. Soldiers were stationed to hold secure the result of the execution on Golgotha. (The legionaries who later maintained Roman control of Masada had a far easier assignment.) Suddenly, through power immeasurably greater than that of all who had set themselves against him, the One whom they had killed was no longer dead. Soldiers were total passivists at the time of the utterly decisive defeat and negation of their power. Touched by the triumphant power and choosing the way of the cross, Christians through generations lived unconquered by Rome.

Jesus, before his death, wept over Jerusalem. He saw the majority of his people rejecting him and turning to a course that would bring upon them destruction by the Romans (Lk. 19:41–44; 21:20–24). Jesus chose not to become the military deliverer to whom they would have swarmed. Though quite a number turned to him, the dominant elite carried the majority with them and succeeded in having him crucified. With Jesus' rising and the upsurge of the Messianic community, Israel was given a further opportunity, like the fig tree in his parable (Lk. 13:6–9). When that second chance brought only limited results, the Romans carried out a terrible cutting down. No longer would what had grown there "use up the ground."

The State of Israel is a remarkable revival of the militant nationalist course that led to the rejection of Jesus and of what he was calling that people to be. This Israel may seem to be the fulfilment of messianic expectations that Jesus did not fulfil. The victories that did not come in the First and the Second Revolt (A.D. 66–70 and 132–35) were achieved in 1948, 1967, and 1973. Messianism in the manner of Bar Kokhba, who led the second, even more disastrous uprising (an estimated five hundred thousand perished), seems to have succeeded. Through nearly two millennia Jews had lived in exilic vulnerability on the margins of societies controlled by others. That past with its climax in the Nazi Holocaust led to the establishment of the State of Israel. Suffering in weakness — suffering experienced most of all by the Jew who was the focal person of history — was replaced by the model of heroic fighting Jews who could vanquish all enemies and come through as the valiant guarantors of their own destiny.

This militarist nationalism can be justified pragmatically. Israel in its national sovereignty can be "like all the nations" (1 Sam. 8:20) and outdo most of them. But those who seek a Christian perspective on any nation must recognize that the mentality and course of action that constituted rejection of Jesus then still (anywhere in the world) constitute that today. If Jesus is indeed the Messiah, what he called his own people to then he still calls that people to now.

Strenuous objection may be made that, after what Christians have done to Jews, it is perversely presumptuous of them to view Israel in terms of the life, teaching, death, and rising of Jesus. But such scrutiny of the Israel of the time was a main motif in the apostolic scriptures. If Jesus is Lord, every human being and every grouping is to be seen in the light of who he was and is. It should be clear that if he is Lord, no amount of wickedness perpetrated by those who profess to be his people can suspend that Lordship.

The Holocaust is pointed to continually as the primary justification for Israel and whatever it undertakes for its own survival. Violence is given its rationale in those millions who were violated. Christians can ponder the horror of what was inflicted on Jews in the Third Reich and hold nonetheless to a fully contrary justification in a suffering Jew. They can refuse to believe that (instead of vulnerability) there must be the military capability to fend off all threats. They can declare, rather, that because Jesus still loved as he became totally vulnerable, the way to restored relationship with God and with other humans was opened for all. Instead of dominance in the frozenness of broken relationships, with God's sanction for that, comes the God-given healing of alienation — alienation first of all from God. The suffering and death of those millions of victims is then taken, not as exonerating justification for one nation state, but as complement to the sufferings of the One through whom all human beings from every nation are offered forgiveness and acceptance by God.

Since the Constantinian shift, professing Christians in many countries have been at the centers of power — where the Jewish elite had been in the Gospel story. Through the centuries Jews were often where Jesus said his disciples would typically be: on the margins of society, in persecution and distress. In the ghettos, in the pogroms, and into the Auschwitz gas chambers, the unseen Messiah moved in the midst of a people who knew him only as expectation yearned for. In their suffering and in their expectancy they have been his people.

I was walking along the Via Dolorosa in the Old City of Jerusalem, looking for the traditional stations of the cross. At a corner just beyond the Ecce Homo Arch, a group of Israeli soldiers had stopped a bearded young Palestinian and were checking his ID card. One soldier slapped him on the cheek — a big insult already in biblical times. I thought of the teaching of Jesus and of his being slapped like that. The Palestinian seemed unintimidated and rather matter-of-fact about the situation. I stood by watching as the soldiers drew out the procedure. A tourist couple came along. A small boy was on his father's shoulders. Just as they passed next to me, the boy caught sight of the Palestinian and asked, "Is that Jesus?" The Jewish Lord stands with "the least" in Palestine and around the world.

The Question of Promised Land

The basic religious argument for a divine sanction undergirding the State of Israel is this: God gave the land of Palestine to Abraham and his descendants; modern Israel has come into existence and continues as God's contemporary fulfilment of that promise after a lapse of almost nineteen hundred years. This view is held by most religiously observant Jews and by large numbers of "conservative" church people, especially in the United States.

If Jesus of Nazareth came as the fulfilment of the Torah and the prophets, a key question in relation to the State of Israel is whether or not the territoriality of the Hebrew story (the base in that particular land) received transformation in him.

In the Hebrew scriptures those who are humble before God do not seize land. God deals with the proud who are wrongly in control of land and people and gives it to those who wait for his saving acts. Jesus promised that those who live in humble subordination to God "shall inherit the earth" (Mt. 5:5, quoting from Ps. 37:11), the future earth on which God's will is fully done, not just the small land of Canaan as in the promise to Abraham. Jesus is meek, "humble and trustful toward God"[17] (Mt. 11:29; 21:5), and in this respect "stands radically opposed to the Zealots...and to all the champions of a political Messianism." To all "who on the basis of their oppressed situation acknowledge not their own will but the great and gracious will of God...Jesus promises the inheritance...of the coming aeon, which includes (cf. Mt. 19:29) secure dwelling in their own land."[18] This outlook correlates with the covenantal condition- ality of God's giving the land to the people of Israel. When that people turns away from the required trust in Yahweh, the gift can be withdrawn. Jesus points to trust that looks ahead to God's renewed gift of land.

Impelled by God's word, "My house shall be called a house of prayer for all nations," Jesus cleansed the Temple (Mk. 11:15–17). But he foresaw that the Temple would soon be destroyed. Jesus in his resurrected body would become what the Temple in its lapsed state was not and could not be (Jn. 2:19). Jesus told the Samaritan woman: "The hour is coming when neither on this mountain nor in Jerusalem will you worship the Father.... The true worshipers will worship the Father in spirit and truth" (Jn. 4:21, 23). Soon each revered place would be desolate; the Father seeks spiritual worship not bound to a particular place.

What Jesus had called all Israel to be, the apostolic church became. The reach of the witness commissioned by Jesus was to take in all nations and all the earth. The risen Lord laid claim to the *oikumene*, all the inhabited world. The faith lost its linkage to a particular place; it was deterritorialized or, rather, now took in all territory. Jerusalem and Palestine were the starting point for that missionary outreach, but there is no indication that they were seen by the early Jewish Christians as still having a unique status and importance for the people of God. The early church had no holy sites and nothing com- parable to what Jerusalem, Rome, or Mecca became as pilgrimage centers.

As Paul saw it, the promise given to Abraham and his (spir- itual) descendants had now expanded to become as wide as the Messianic community's missionary outreach, moving toward the consummation: They are to "inherit the world" (Rom. 4:13). Through the coming of Jesus, God's promise to Abraham about the land, like the other promises, had received a far more than literal fulfilment. Colin Chapman writes of Paul:

> He seems to show no interest in the land in the purposes of God.... The reason for this silence must be that Paul believed that Jesus was the fulfilment of *all* the divine promises.... It is difficult to see how he could say that *all* believers are the seed of Abraham and therefore inheritors of the promise, but at the same time believe that one aspect of the promise does *not* apply to all believers.[19]

Acts 1:6-8 records that just before Jesus' ascension his apostles asked him, "Lord, will you at this time restore the kingdom to Israel?"

He turned away from their question toward all the world into which he was sending them as witnesses. He did not tell them they were simply wrong with regard to their continuing hope that he would be the One who would restore the Kingdom to Israel. Evidently they were not. Jesus left them with the implication that he would do this upon his return "in the same way as [they] saw him go into heaven" (Acts 1:11) — that is, beyond the course of history as humans have experienced it.

Jesus had told the apostles: "Truly, I say to you, in the new world, when the Son of man shall sit on his glorious throne, you who have followed me will also sit on twelve thrones, judging the twelve tribes of Israel" (Mt. 19:28). "In the new world" the pre-eminence of the initially chosen people and of the first chosen witnesses will be manifest — as this is manifest in all of scripture. It will be actualized in terms of place and promised land, but these as God's gracious gift rather than by human arrogation. When "the Lion of the tribe of Judah, the Root of David" (Rev. 5:5), enters into gracious dominion over all, the Kingdom will have been restored to Israel. Within this view of history, however, the State of Israel can hardly be viewed as part of what moves toward that culmination. Yet just as ascendant false prophets are a sign of the approach of the End, so too is the State of Israel as predominantly structured by false prophecy.

Yahweh declares in Psalm 2:6, "I have set my king on Zion, my holy hill." For the apostolic church the true Jerusalem was the domain of God's acting in Jesus. The Hebrew prophecies of the coming incomparable glories of Zion were understood in terms of that domain.

In Hebrews 11:8–16 it is said that Abraham, sojourning in the land of promise, "looked forward to the city which has foundations, whose builder and maker is God." The people of God are "strangers and exiles on the earth," never geographically at home but "seeking a homeland...a better country, that is, a heavenly one." Thus those who are in faith descendants of Abraham do just the opposite of cleaving to a particular geographical area. (This scriptural teaching goes against all primary attachment to place and country.) What is determinative for them is not "the present Jerusalem...but the Jerusalem above" (Gal. 4:25, 26), not earthly Jerusalem and its territory, but "the city of the living God, the heavenly Jerusalem" (Heb. 12:22).

One tie to geographical Jerusalem is appropriate for all who look to the God of biblical story: "Pray for the peace of Jerusalem!" (Ps.

122:6). Pray that the city of no shalom, the city of strife and violence, will yet learn "the things that make for peace." And weep with the One who weeps over the intransigent city.

Many Hebrew prophecies picture the glorious fulfilment of God's purposes set in the land of Israel and centered in Jerusalem. John on Patmos, recasting such prophecies, leaves earthly geography behind. The New Jerusalem as the resplendent realization of God's purposes is the place of perfect breadth and length and height, which receives into itself all whom God draws into that consummate harmony (Rev. 21–22). If that Jerusalem is not as wide as the New Earth, all other place is not really other but its environs. Geographical Jerusalem's central place in salvation history is, in transfiguration, taken over by the New Jerusalem. And when in the End all the nations come up to the New Jerusalem, the Jews as a people returning will be among them. They too will bring their glory and honor — in part their suffering — into it (Rev. 21:26).

The State of Israel and the End of the World

Jeremiah, Second Isaiah, and Ezekiel declared that there would be a return from exile into Palestine. Those prophecies need not be taken as predicting and awaiting a twentieth-century fulfilment. They were fulfilled when bands of Jews returned from Babylon. They did have an eschatological overreach: They were picturing far more than what came with the Jewish return from Babylon and its sequel. Thus in Ezekiel 37:14, 25–26, 27: "And I will put my Spirit within you, and you shall live.... David my servant shall be their prince for ever. I will make a covenant of peace with them; it shall be an everlasting covenant with them.... My dwelling place shall be with them; and I will be their God, and they shall be my people." In the view of the apostolic church, prophecies such as this one had been fulfilled in Jesus Christ and the emergence of the Messianic community, and that still hidden fulfilment was moving toward its consummation. In terms of this view the movement toward the glorious redemption envisioned by the prophets proceeds in a different direction than through the current re-established sovereignty in Palestine.

Jesus, foreseeing the destruction of Jerusalem by the Romans, said: "this people... will fall by the edge of the sword, and be led captive among all nations; and Jerusalem will be trodden down by the Gentiles, until the times of the Gentiles are fulfilled" (Lk. 21:24).

The establishment of the State of Israel in 1948 and the "liberation" of the Old City of Jerusalem in 1967 have been widely seen as fulfilment of the latter part of that prophecy. But the age of nations in clamorous revolt against God and in collision with one another has not come to an end. The kingdoms of this world have not yet become "the kingdom of our Lord and of his Christ" (Rev. 11:15). Jerusalem and Israel are still trodden down by the Gentiles. They have been molded by reaction to what the Nazis and so many others did. They have been driven by what Arab states and groups (especially the Palestine Liberation Organization) have done or might do. They conform to worldwide modes of thought about wielding power and having security. The age of dominance by those who refuse to live as God's people has not come to a close, even in Israel.

Under the Nazis one-third of the Jews on earth met annihilation. The specter of another annihilation, roused through decades by much Arab rhetoric and violence, impels the frenzy of Israeli militarism and repression. But that dark possibility becomes more probable because of the course Israel has been taking to prevent it. Israel, with its small area, could be more easily devastated or obliterated than any other major military power. As the Middle East arms race continues, Arab missiles, even without nuclear warheads or later with them, could end the existence of Israel as state and people. Immense military strength can deter attack, but the jeopardy of Israel (as ironic relapse into that Jewish weakness through the millennia) increases with each passing year. Richard Falk writes of what looms ahead for the State of Israel if it continues its present course: "To contemplate such a destiny of Israel is to remind oneself of the Jewish heritage of tragedy. What lies in wait if Israeli hardness prevails is a destiny of blood and destruction that might in the end have to be compared to the Holocaust itself for its magnitude."[20] An awesomely direct fulfilment of Jesus' warning, "all who take the sword will perish by the sword" (Mt. 26:52), came with the destruction of Jerusalem by the Romans in A.D. 70. That warning remains as ominous for present-day Israel as it was originally for Israel in the first century.

Jesus, weeping over Jerusalem headed for destruction, said: "Behold, your house is forsaken and desolate. For I tell you, you will not see me again, until you say, 'Blessed be he who comes in the name of the Lord'" (Mt. 23:38–39). This Lord, rejected, was departing from Temple and city, leaving them empty and unshielded from impending doom. But later the Day would come when this people and city would join in the cry of acclamation to the Messiah.[21] Paul's teaching about Israel in Romans 9–11 with its climax in the assurance "and so all Israel will be saved" (11:26) is to be understood in the light of this prophecy of Jesus. When he appears in unveiled glory as Messiah, this people as a whole will recognize him at last, at the End, and be saved. The ruined height of Masada will sink away into the valley of marveling contrition.

Chapter 7

"FALLEN IS BABYLON!"

This repeated collapse of every earthly imperialism is the most impressive demonstration of the fact that no divinization of any earthly power can stand, that every absolutizing of any earthly absolute always carries within itself the seeds of death. God sets up His throne on the wreckage of human earthly thrones, and the history of the world is strewn with the wreckage of demolished imperialisms and smashed altars, whose debris reveals impressively the sole Lordship of God.

—Karl Heim[1]

Some Christians gather on the north bank of the Potomac between the White House and the Pentagon. One after another they read from Isaiah 13, 21, 47–48, Habakkuk 1–2, and then from Revelation 18, echoing Hebrew prophecies: "Fallen, fallen is Babylon the great!" (v. 2). Last they read from Jeremiah 50–51, concluding with Jeremiah's instruction to Seraiah: "When you come to Babylon, see that you read all these words.... When you finish reading this book, bind a stone to it, and cast it into the midst of the Euphrates, and say, 'Thus shall Babylon sink, to rise no more, because of the evil that I am bringing upon her.' " Two of the readers take the Bible that has just been passed around, bind it to a damp stone, and cast that projectile into the river. No laws are broken; no arrests are made. Those who hold power in the city perceive no threat and do not take notice.

Those witnesses on the Potomac do not make the simple identification of the United States with Babylon. But they know that God's word against all that is Babylon endures. Babylon in the Bible is far more than the Babylon of Nebuchadnezzar and more than imperial Rome. Babylon is what collectively exalts itself against God. Like the primeval tower, Babylon is the central embodiment of human defiance of God. "She has proudly defied the Lord" (Jer. 50:29). Babylon seeks to gather to itself all nations, all peoples, in a devouring greed insatiable as death (Hab. 2:5). Babylon is the world system in its centeredness and its multiformity. Babylon is *Bab-ilim,* "gate

101

of the gods." "For it is a land of images, / and they are mad over idols" (Jer. 50:38). Those who presume to be lords over the world pay homage to what their own hands have fabricated, seen as securing that dominion.

In the proclamation of the Hebrew prophets the three great sins of Babylon are arrogance, violence, which is the chief derivative of that, and affluence, which is the living out of that arrogance over against the poor of the earth. In Revelation 18:5 it is said of Babylon, "her sins are heaped high as heaven." That height is the achieved tower of Babel. In scripture the primeval tower becomes a mountainous immensity, a "destroying mountain" (Jer. 51:25), as it displaces all in its advancing spread, "mercilessly slaying nations for ever" (Hab. 1:17). Babylon can destroy all that is cherished on the earth. For in Babylon is found the blood of God's witnesses "and of all who have been slain on earth" (Rev. 18:24). All slaying has its origin in Babylon — murders, pollution as manslaughter, drunk driving, executions, covert wars, interventions and invasions, nuclear arsenals, weapons production and sales as most notable economic activity.

The center of the mystery of iniquity is this: What vaunts itself as the highest good — all its actions being therefore justified — becomes abysmal wickedness: *Pax Romana*, established religion in the crucifixion of Jesus, "the true church" in the Inquisition and other persecutions, communism in the Stalinist purges and slave labor camps, Nazism in the subjugation of Europe, "freedom" under U.S. auspices in many Third World countries. Overarching the horrors perpetrated is the implicit claim to absoluteness, to divinity.

Babylon is also convivial temptress, "holding in her hand a golden cup full of abominations and the impurities of her fornication" (Rev. 17:4) and extending it to all the nations (Rev. 14:8). The dynamic of her lust after everything evokes a responsive lust among the nations; in it they are joined carnally with her. By economic enticement more than by conquest Babylon draws the nations into configuration around her. In imperial subversion Babylon dispenses her culture through the media.

Yet by complementary dynamic, "the merchants of the earth have grown rich with the wealth of her wantonness" (Rev. 18:3). The picture given applies so well to the multinational corporations of our time. Babylon and all that is conjoined with her serve the worldwide mercantile elite. Her "merchants were the great men of the earth" (Rev. 18:23). Through what Babylon is and does they become richer and richer. As a president emerges as front man for the elites controlling power behind the scenes, so even mighty Babylon is in many ways a front for and creature of the global corporate elite. When Babylon falls, the merchants "weep and mourn for her, since no one buys their cargo any more" (Rev. 18:11).

A mightier hand grasps that Babylonian hand and cup; for "Babylon was a golden cup in the Lord's hand, / making all the earth drunken; / the nations drank of her wine, / therefore the nations went mad" (Jer. 51:7). Under God defiance veers into folly and madness. Invigorating sips are never enough. The whole intoxicating draught is gulped down. Babylon leads that descent into madness.

Yet the drained cup is brimming over with "a double draught" (Rev. 18:6) of wrath and judgment. One nation after another drinks that cup, and "after them the king of Babylon shall drink" (Jer. 25:26). Babylon can be agent of God's judgment. Yet because of what Babylon perpetrates, it brings God's judgment upon itself. Cataclysmic judgment reaches the crowning height of human presumption — sequentially through history and at the End. The "cup from the Lord's hand" given to Jeremiah to pass on was for "all the kingdoms of the world which are on the face of the earth" (Jer. 25:26), all in his time and in subsequent eras. That cup and God's call to turn back are for all time. Either human beings partake of the cup of Babylon's doom pressing upon all, or they partake of the cup of Jesus' blood poured out for all.

The Shattering of the Imperial Image

In Daniel 2, Nebuchadnezzar, king of Babylon, archetypal representative for the rulers of the earth, saw in a night vision an "image, mighty and of exceeding brightness...and its appearance was frightening:" head of gold, breast and arms of silver, belly and thighs of bronze, legs of iron, feet of iron mixed with clay (vv. 31–33). The great image was, first of all, Nebuchadnezzar's Babylon but then the successive empires in the likeness of Babylon. This idol is imperial man rising up against God, man not in creaturely delimitation but as magnified construct.

A stone cut out by no human hand smote the image on its feet of iron and clay and broke it to pieces so that its debris became no more than chaff on the summer threshing floor swept away by the wind. "But the stone that struck the image became a great mountain and filled the whole earth" (v. 35). The demolition of the image comes successively throughout history and climactically at the End. Empire in its successive lineaments does not endure. God's Word pulverizes it. The reality of God's Rule smites repeatedly and becomes at last a mountainous height extensive as the earth and reaching to the heavens. Like Daniel, present-day disciples are to declare the meaning of the vision to rulers.

Jesus Christ is the huge stone, God's Kingdom in its coming, as it hurtles toward final collision with the imperial image. One can so easily be taken in by the seeming solidity of that construct. Like the Temple for the first disciples (Mt. 24:1), the Capitol, the White House, the Pentagon, and the New York skyline seem so imposing and permanent. What transforms the vision of disciples is to see God's Rule embodied in Jesus breaking in (Mk. 1:15). Seeing this, they discern how ephemeral the image is. "The world passes away, and the lust of it" (1 Jn. 2:17); but disciples yearn for God's Kingdom.

The stone and mountain come into public view only at the End. Before that the smiting stone remains out of sight behind the visible agents of demolition. God's declaration to Jeremiah is carried out again and again: "Behold, I will stir up the spirit of a destroyer / against Babylon" (51:1). In Isaiah 13 a tumult of nations attacks Babylon, an eschatological, more than historical, Babylon. In Rev. 17:16 ten kings and the beast destroy Babylon. One mad configuration of hubris shatters another, as in the World Wars. The kingdom of the beast is shaken by civil war. Jacques Ellul comments: "There is an auto-destruction of political forces at the interior of history. That which makes them live, that which gives them authority, that upon which they are based, is the very spirit that finally repudiates them, because it is the annihilator."[2]

Even when Babylon in biblical prophecy refers primarily to the historical Babylon (as in Jeremiah 50–51), it looms as more than that. The prophecies of this Babylon's destruction had an overreach; much less came to pass than had been prophesied. At the time of its political overthrow, Babylon was not destroyed in the manner pictured in Jeremiah 50–51 and Isaiah 47. It opened its gates to the Persian emperor Cyrus in 539 B.C. and later to Alexander. After its fall Babylon ceased to be Babylon — chief rebel nation against which the prophecies had been spoken. It lost its commercial importance to the rival city Seleucia and gradually declined into an uninhabited ruin. Precisely because the Hebrew prophecies against the original Babylon were in part not fulfilled, they became God's warning to all that is Babylon. What is brought into view in Revelation 18 is the eschatological Babylon and all that converges toward its culmination. "In a single day" terminal woes are to come upon Babylon, "and she shall be burned with fire" (18:8). (In this passage those who weep for Babylon weep, not for human beings overwhelmed by catastrophe, but because of the ruination of their economic self-interest. The rejoicing in heaven is over the collapse of Babylon as infernal power structure.) The sudden destruction that the original Babylon avoided has come upon many later Babylons and impends for all that is Babylon now. This current and future Babylon could be engulfed by a cataclysm climaxing the destruction visited upon all earlier Babylons. "Hallelujah! The smoke from her goes up for ever and ever" (Rev. 19:3): Indication of Babylon's utter defeat by the Lord God the Almighty will continue throughout eternity.

In Ezekiel 32 the ruling elite and army of country after country go down into the Pit, into Sheol, and are given somber greeting by the slain hosts already there. The decisive guilt of each national group is that they had "spread terror in the land of the living." Terror then as now was chiefly the work of dominant elites and their agents, not of desperate individuals or gangs. The transience of nations and empires is pictured as a sequential entry into collective death. That sequence continues as surely as does the global spreading of terror. Now as then, the imperial elites and their underlings are blind to this pattern in history until they themselves also go down into the chasm of all that has become fully past. What is different in our time is the prospect that the nations may all together go down into the Pit.

The Beast

In Daniel 7 four beasts in succession dominate the earth. (*Four* in biblical imagery expresses completeness, totality.) The seer's field of vision, which has been filled by the beasts, is suddenly redirected to a glimpse of God enthroned in majesty and of "one like a son of man," who appears before him and receives "dominion and glory and kingdom" (v. 14). As marginal event to what is happening in heaven, the climactic beast is slain on earth and its body burned with fire. That triumph corresponds to the demolition of the imperial image in Daniel 2.

This redirection of attention is of the utmost importance for disciples. Far more than recognizing the beast, imposing as it is, they are to catch sight of God's sovereign Rule and overruling. What has real decisiveness is not "the great words" of the beast (v. 11) but the sovereignty of the Ancient of Days and the breaking in of his Rule. Reading Daniel 7 and 2 in the light of the apostolic scriptures, Christians see Jesus Christ as the Son of man, whose dominion replaces all other kingdoms and lasts for ever. "The saints of the Most High shall receive the kingdom" (7:18) through their being part of the dominion of the Son of man.

The beast in Revelation represents Rome, every power structure in the likeness of Rome, and the culminating manifestation of such power at the close of history. One of the heads of the beast "seemed to have a mortal wound, but its mortal wound was healed, and the whole earth followed the beast with wonder" (Rev. 13:3). The beast itself is mortally wounded, yet revives into continued exercise of dominion (Rev. 13:12, 14). A Nero, a Napoleon, a Hitler, with governing entourage, is struck down, but other heads emerge out of the violent overthrow. Again and again comes infernal resurrection of evil and of wicked leadership. What appears on the world stage is not a repetition, say, of Hitler and the configuration around him but rather another persona for the beast, doing its will.

For those who appropriate biblical prophecy to forecast the future, much hinges upon identifying the beast, which supposedly appears just before the end of the world. This identification — usually with the nationally designated enemy — confirms the outlook that the end is very close in ordinary reckoning of time because the emergence of the beast is understood as a primary sign of the end. But Daniel 2 and 7 picture imperial hegemony and revolt against God as a main continuity moving through history. Revolt just before the End is the culmination of that continuity. Demolition at the End is the consummation of all earlier shattering of such political power. Therefore any identification of what is beastly, even if accurate, cannot be rightly taken as basis for forecasts about the calendrical nearness of the End.

Emigration from Babylon

Disciples should remain aware of those who are in Babylon but not of Babylon, those not involved in spreading terror but about to be overwhelmed by judgment upon it. In Babylon, like Nineveh, there are many "innocent children...as well as many animals" (Jon. 4:11 TEV). Unlike the mercantile profiteers, disciples, already before Babylon's fall, are to weep for all its citizens. They are to seek the welfare of this Babylon of human beings and "pray to the Lord on its behalf" (Jer. 29:7).

God's people, though, are to leave Babylon: "Come out of her, my people, / lest you take part in her sins, / lest you share in her plagues"

(Rev. 18:4). Originally Jewish exiles were to depart literally from the geographical Babylon (Jer. 50:8, 28; 51:6, 45; Is. 48:20; 52:11). God was bringing to an end their Babylonian captivity. But their leaving became the paradigm for the departure in mind and spirit (if not by geographical movement) from all that is Babylon throughout history.

Only when disciples recognize where and what Babylon is can they depart from it. In any century disciples are to struggle for discernment of what constitutes Babylon, the beast, and the imperial image, lest they be drawn into that insurgency against God. The original Babylon became for the Jewish people an occupying power. Those under occupation view such a power from outside it, not as a part of it. Babylon should always be seen as occupying power. Yet through the centuries of Christendom/post-Christendom, the churches have mostly identified themselves with whatever imperial or national insurgency was close by. Churches are largely characterized, not by any identification of how their country is Babylon, but by identification with this Babylon — with imperial arrogance, violence, and profligate consumption. The film *The Godfather (I)* reaches its crescendo in a double scene: The celebrative baptism of an infant son takes place at exactly the same time as the killing of every one of the family's rivals. That is a dual image for much of Western history. On countless days, presumptively Christian countries have had baptisms, communions, and worship services while simultaneously slaughtering those seen as rivals. A Mafia-like blindness to any incongruity has pervaded all this.

Jesus spoke of trying to gain "the whole world" (Mt. 16:26). The stymied individual drive to be the center of the universe and draw everything to oneself feeds into the massed imperial attempt. The Assyrian emperor (Is. 10:12, 14 NRSV) in "arrogant boasting" and "haughty pride" was a prototype:

> My hand has found, like a nest,
>   the wealth of the peoples;
> and as one gathers eggs that have been forsaken
>   so I have gathered all the earth;
> and there was none that moved a wing,
>   or opened its mouth, or chirped.

The goal is to assert unchallenged dominion. Even a chirp, as from Nicaragua or Iraq, must be silenced.

An intention of God for the New Jerusalem is that "the kings of the earth shall bring...into it the glory and honor of the nations" (Rev. 21:24, 26), and "nations shall bring you their wealth" (Is. 60:11

NRSV). But imperial powers seek that for themselves. What ancient empires were able to do in this regard was paltry compared to the drain of wealth from poor countries and groups by multinational corporations under the auspices of the rich countries. What Babylon consumes most of all is other peoples, external (along with internal) proletariats — "slaves, that is, human souls" (Rev. 18:13).

In talking with friends in Russia before the breakup of the Soviet Union, I found that nearly all of them saw communism as a dismal failure. In the West and especially in the United States the wide collapse of communism was taken as vindication of Western economic and political systems. There is much in U.S. and Western societal arrangements that serves human well-being, and Christians should remain aware and supportive of whatever does that. But the dynamisms that are taking the world toward catastrophe dominate. If the imperial powers continue with massive military forces and the reckless poisoning of the biosphere, sooner or later all the brighter aspects of those societies will not count for much. Like those dismayed Russians, Christians in the West should recognize the abysmal failure of the economic and political system around them, which (to mention only one indicator) leaves forty thousand of the world's children to die unnecessarily each day. God's judgment upon communism in the East should be taken as warning that comparable or worse judgment impends for the West. Recognizing such things, God's people depart from Babylon.

Helping others come to faith in Jesus Christ is the most important task on earth. Witnessing for peace and justice is not to be seen as a diversion from that task. This Lord does not will human destruction of the earth but stands against it. Disciples are called to stand with him. They are to plead with others to give their allegiance to Jesus Christ. Ahead for those who worship the beast lies the second death (Rev. 20:4–6). The beast can be identified most of all as the fearful, money-mad, militarist Empire, enthralling the masses and imperiling humanity. God's call away from adherence to the beast and into discipleship to Jesus must be given to those in the churches and to those beyond.

"The form of this world is passing away" (1 Cor. 7:31). Babylon is tottering and is about to collapse. The scriptural call to come out of Babylon is filled with tremendous urgency. Salvation hinges on it. Doom comes upon that vaunting, deluded arrogance. Escape the closing trap. Flee as from a conflagration. Remove yourself from that disintegrating rebellion, turn from those sins, and enter into the sphere of God's Rule.

PART III

THE MESSIAH'S TRIUMPH

Chapter 8

"THE JUDGMENT OF THIS WORLD"

Human history seems always to be without God. Yet God's will and working run through everything. Ultimately His will is done.
—Christoph Blumhardt[1]

In the Hebrew scriptures those who perpetrate evil are pictured as not reckoning with God who sees and acts. They say in their hearts, "There is no God" (Ps. 10:4), or of whatever deity might exist, "He will never see it.... Thou wilt not call to account" (vv. 11, 13). "Those who hide deep from the Lord their counsel, whose deeds are in the dark," say, "Who sees us? Who knows us?" (Is. 29:15). Babylon says, "No one sees me" (Is. 47:10). God is regarded as short-sighted, unobservant. "To the wicked God says,... 'you thought I was one like yourself... you who forget God'" (Ps. 50:16, 21, 22). They suppose the Ultimate to be conveniently conformed to their reasons and actions. In such passages the innermost determinant behind what is perpetrated is not greed, arrogance, or hatred but brazen denial of God, who sees such things and moves against them.

Most worldviews and many theologies feed into that denial. "All who do evil hate the light, and do not come to the light, so that their deeds may not be exposed" (Jn. 3:20 NRSV). In the apostolic scriptures darkness is the delusive domain hidden supposedly from all scrutiny, especially God's. It is characterized most of all, not by the evil done there, but by the desire, in doing the evil, to be autonomous, unobstructed, and unaccountable.

Yet even the passion for secrecy, in power structures and in individuals privately, points by implication to the scrutiny it would evade. Terms again and again in the news signify the global spread of what governments do in secret: espionage, covert (cloak-and-dagger, undercover) operations, low-intensity conflict, secret police, CIA, KGB, deniability, disinformation. Secrecy is fundamental to the

111

military and to much of foreign policy as nations carry it out. The control of governments by vested interests is concealed. Hardly ever does the threat of human exposure disappear, and that intimates the far more ominous scrutiny and prospect of exposure.

When "God" is seen as compliant with power structures that have much to hide, witness must be given to the God of Israel and of Jesus Christ. God sees, with a seeing that is entry into acting. "The eyes of the Lord are in every place, / keeping watch on the evil and on the good" (Prov. 15:3). Jesus taught that God does not overlook a single sparrow (Lk. 12:6). The motif of God's seeing is most vividly stated in Hebrews 4:13: "And before him no creature is hidden, but all are open and laid bare to the eyes of him with whom we have to do."

The nations, though supposing themselves beyond that scrutiny, are totally under it. His "eyes keep watch on the nations — / let not the rebellious exalt themselves" (Ps. 66:7). Psalm 33:13–14 (NRSV) gives the picture:

> The Lord looks down from heaven;
>   he sees all humankind.
> From where he sits enthroned he watches
>   all the inhabitants of the earth.

What so notably follows from God's seeing is expressed just before and after (vv. 10, 16):

> The Lord brings the counsel of the nations to nothing;
>   he frustrates the plans of the peoples....
> A king is not saved by his great army;
>   a warrior is not delivered by his great strength.

The power-seeking of the nations centers in military might, but sooner or later God overturns all that. Governments project worst-case scenarios in relation to their adversaries, but they do not consider the most ominous worst-case scenario: that God is moving to cast down their might. And that threat behind all others can be coped with only through repentance.

To stress that God sees may appear too elementary. But in the contemporary welter of religious movements, the divine is usually not One who sees and knows all. Many theologies do not point to the transcendent living God, the Creator, who sees, wills, and acts. Even when such a God is looked to, the focus ordinarily remains private and individualistic. God's wider dealing with his called-out people and with the nations is nearly out of sight. God is not understood as seeing in the manner in which the God of the biblical story saw. To discern God's scrutiny of the nations, especially one's own nation, is of the utmost importance.

God as Judge

To think in terms of the judgment of God is to go against the dominant relativism of our age. If truth claims and moral judgments by human beings are inveighed against as quite unacceptable, how much more intolerable is judgment by One who comes as ruling Lord. The managers of nations and of the human present and future cannot be bothered by any such thing. For anyone to be "judgmental" is seen as obviously intolerable; and when humans set the standards for ultimate reality, God must not be "judgmental," must not be Judge.

The understanding that God is Ruler-Judge (*shophet*) over all of life and over current history has been much weakened in the churches. What commonly remains is a vague sense that individuals may be in need, after death, of God's approval for going to heaven. God is viewed as "gentle Philanthropist."[2] Beyond that, God is recruited as a principal ally of one's own nation but is hardly reckoned with as present Judge of that nation and of all the nations. Or "God" is understood essentially in terms of immanence, thus excluding the biblical view of God as Judge. In segments of the churches where social concerns (presently summarized as justice, peace, and the integrity of creation[3]) have come to the fore, God is typically seen as the ground and source for these concerns but relatively little as the One who in Jesus Christ has acted and constantly acts, against all opposition, to bring about what he requires.

A main reason for sloughing off the biblical view of God as Judge is the desire not to have God burdened by the darker aspects of judgment. A "God" apart from judgment and wrath, a "God" with no attributes that disconcert or threaten, may seem worthier of human reverence. But the secret and more decisive motivation has to do with the comfortableness of not being accountable to "a judge who is God of all" (Heb. 12:23). One's wrongdoing is enough of a problem in terms of one's own and others' response to it. One would like to be relieved of the unfathomably more acute problem of the divine reaction to it. When the radical malignancy of sin before God is not acknowledged, humans seem to have it much easier. They conceive for themselves a "God" thoroughly congenial and fully to their liking. This inclination is strong, whatever one's theological commitments or lack of them.

The Hebrew prophets cried out their anguished sense of the horror of collective sinning before God and the consequent utter jeopardy. The prophets felt the extremity of the problem brought on by any sinning as rebellion against the God of the covenant. Surrounded by, and implicated in, immensely more extensive wrongdoing, one is either drawn somewhat into the prophets' perception or remains largely without it. One either discerns, or does not, that God's judgment most surely comes upon such wrongdoing.

In the evangelical tradition within the churches, individuals are to see the magnitude of their sin and recognize their extreme need for repentance and forgiveness. But wide ranges of those identified as evangelicals currently have little sense of the *collective* sinning in and by the society and of the urgency of a turn-around. They are Augustinian for private transgression and Pelagian in insistence on the basic goodness of the nation they so profoundly identify with. Their nation is seen as the best and most righteous in the world. They deplore the enormities of private or underworld sinning within the society — breakdown of the family, sexual promiscuity, pornography, traffic in abortions, drug abuse, crime. They may see these as evoking the threat of catastrophic judgment upon the nation. Most of them, however, do not understand that threat as being brought on as much or more by what is done by their nation as nation and by its vested interests: neglect of the least privileged in the country and beyond it, economic exploitation, support of oppressive client regimes, interventions, covert wars, endless military buildup, mindless corporate destruction of the environment. People in peace and justice movements, on the other hand, often see only the latter types of wrongdoing but hardly the more private types. Biblically, both sin and judgment are individual and collective. For the Hebrew prophets, such was the sense of cohering corporate identity that they hardly thought in terms of such a differentiation.

A standard objection to understanding God partly in terms of judgment is that this outlook is an inferior part of the Bible, found in the Hebrew scriptures, and cannot be taken as truth about God. These scriptures have often been dismissed or largely ignored with the claim: "The Old Testament has a God of wrath; in the New Testament, God is a God of love." Jesus supposedly revealed a God of love quite beyond those demeaning traits pictured in the story of Israel.

This Marcionite contrast, however, is untenable. The Hebrew Bible is filled with passages about the love and mercy of God. The apostolic scriptures have much to say about the judgment and wrath of God. The most somber pronouncements in this regard are by Jesus himself. If Jesus had seen a need to correct the understanding of God given in the Hebrew scriptures and discard mistaken elements in it, one would expect that intention and effort to have found expression in his recorded teachings. This is not the case. Jesus at times set his ethical teachings against popular interpretations of the Torah, the primary covenant documents, (as in Mt. 5:43–45) or against some statement in the Torah (Mk. 10:2–9=Mt. 19:3–9 in contrast to Deut. 24:1–4). But there is no indication that he saw his teachings about who God is as contradicting those found in the scriptures he grew up with. The God of Jesus was the God made known in the Hebrew Bible. Yet in Jesus this God revealed himself far more fully. Through Jesus God's self-disclosure to Israel was clarified and fulfilled. "The God of the New Testament is the same as that of the Old Testament, not in the sense of absolute identity of conception, but in the sense of a continuity of salvation history."[4]

Confirmation of this continuity with the God of Israel is to be found also in who Jesus was as evidenced in the Gospels. P. T. Forsyth wrote:

> If we take but two features alone in Christ we find ourselves before elements which it is impossible to combine in any conception except that of personality with its alogical and inconsistent unity; and in this case it is a personality great and contradictory beyond the mould of any other.... In Christ there are two features which are to be unified in no fair picture but only in one mighty person. The severity of judgment in Christ and the tenderness of the pity form a contradiction which seems as final in its own region as the antinomy of the divine sovereignty and human freedom is in another plane.[5]

In the Gospels that severity of Jesus flares up again and again like an inner fire. This One, superlatively compassionate, rebukes his disciples, becomes angry, cries out against unbelief and hardness of heart, warns of judgment, confutes his adversaries.[6] That is, the seeming opposites that run throughout the Hebrew portrayal of God also run through the accounts about Jesus in the Gospels. Having come from God, he bore within him and expressed the intense holiness of the God of Hebrew faith. Christians cannot with honesty ignore in Jesus what they may be inclined to dismiss from the Hebrew witness to God. In him were and are "the kindness and severity of God" (Rom. 11:22). And in the witness of the apostolic scriptures Jesus Christ is the coming Judge of all humanity.

A prism refracts light into the rainbow colors that comprise it. We may experience from another human being empathy, courage, vulnerability, questioning, hopefulness, rigor, gentleness; but behind that refraction is the one person. So it is far more with the mercy, the wrath, the tenderness, the judgment from God, who is One.

About God Jean Danielou has written:

> Essentially, anger is not the same as *Ressentiment*, the typical reaction of wounded self-love; but rather a refusal to have any dealings with what is beyond the pale.... Wrath, so understood, is purged of every connotation of pettiness, meaning simply that intensity of existence which nothing whatever can withstand.... So far from representing God in the image and likeness of man, it brings us to an apprehension of just that in which he most of all excels us, namely the supreme and perfect intensity of his being, which is out of all proportion and analogy with our own.[7]

God's holiness is an aspect of that intensity in relation especially to who humans are in having sinned. That intensity comes as love but also as wrath, which the Hebrews understood as "the driving force by which God asserts himself despite all human resistance."[8] Critically important for disciples is a deepening perception of the intensity of existence with which God meets them. They must never suppose that they have moved beyond the imperiling threat of God's holy rejection of their sin.

Humans have, when it is not atrophied, a derivative intimation of the wrath of God. If it is essential to one's humanity that one cry out and act when terrible things are done to others, is not the corresponding source of that to be seen in God himself? The basic rightness of such reaction in humans derives from its total rightness in God. Human caring, though, even at its best, usually remains marginal to how dominant power is exercised in the world. What brings utter seriousness to wrongs inflicted on others is God's caring, caring that issues into judgment.

Counterpoised to the riddle of the vastness of evil in the world is the actuality, always partial but continually emerging, that defeat and disintegration come upon any dominion of evil. Hubris in the world is so ascendant and encompassing. Yet again and again it is cast down, if only by a more successful embodiment of hubris. Such dominion is always contested, collapsing, or about to collapse. In God's ordering of human disorder, rebel brazenness does not continue indefinitely, unmet and unchecked. The One whose eyes keep watch over the rebel nations "makes destruction flash forth against the strong" (Amos 5:9). Mary of Nazareth gave echo to a psalm of Hannah, mother of Samuel: "he has scattered the proud in the imagination of their hearts, / he has put down the mighty from their thrones" (Lk. 1:51–52; cf. 1 Sam. 2:6–7). Throughout the Bible God is portrayed as moving against evildoers with the incomparable intensity of his being.

Collective defiance of God takes on a face, a spirit, a configurative cohesion of those involved in it. God does not put the No, the defiance, the rebellion, into human hearts but diverts the course of that No toward fulfilling his purposes for overcoming it. In his movement against evil, God commandeers the evil that humans do. "Behold, I am bringing evil upon this people, / the fruit of their devices" (Jer. 6:19). Under God's Rule, evil comes consequentially upon evil, sin upon sin, hubris upon hubris, as judgment — and this in the world brought before us by the evening news and the daily paper. Also under that Rule, good overcomes evil in hidden or manifest ways.

In sin the will is contrary to God. God moves against that willfulness. When I am in conflict with someone else, the other person's attitude of conflict affects me and our relationship. I come to recognize that this is far more the case for my conflict with God. If I go against God, he is not benignly passive or undifferentiatingly loving. God graciously moves to thwart my disregard and resistance. The "good" sought apart from God becomes my punishment. Under judgment I encounter God, not God who zaps me with a punishment, but God who meets me as Judge in the coming of the consequence or in his rescuing me from it. I must face, behind the consequence, the One who is dealing with me.

As consequences come upon human willfulness, God's movement against that willfulness impinges into these. God relates to it with all the intensity of his being, even though the defiance typically may include no intention to take God into account. Judgment is not simply immanent cause-and-effect in an autonomy removed from God. Evil brings on its own demise; God does not impose that as something from without. It comes by the impulsion of evil, yet as determined by God's word. Walther Zimmerli writes of the Hebrew view: "His judgment takes the form of a direct sentencing; it must never be reduced to the neutral process of an action involving its own consequences."[9] Nor is judgment to be regarded as one way the process of history works, with the whole viewed somehow as "God." Judgment is one aspect of how history proceeds as ruled and overruled by the God of biblical faith.

In biblical perspective, when a cataclysm comes, such as that experienced by the Germans in the latter part of World War II, the people who bring it on are not in a deist world running by itself, somewhat removed from God. They are not in the midst of something bracketed away from God or something in which God moves only as co-sufferer. They are being met by God, the sovereign Judge, whether they recognize this or not. Germans, having done what they did, were being dealt with not simply by their human adversaries but by God.

Again and again in the Hebrew scriptures, the violence of one nation against another was viewed (though not always) as God's judgment and as God's acting. God was pictured as bringing the end of the Northern and of the Southern Kingdoms, and even as himself doing the worst that came. But Samaria was destroyed by the Assyrians, and Jerusalem by the Babylonians, not by God smiting supernaturally from heaven. When the prophets wrote that God would destroy or had destroyed, they were quite clear as to the human agency involved. They were stating that the populace, confronted by prospective or actual destruction, were (behind that human agency) being met and dealt with by God. "'Yet you did not return to me,' / says the Lord. / 'Therefore thus will I do to you... / prepare to meet your God, O Israel'" (Amos 4:11–12). The prophets felt so intensely this encounter with God as the utterly decisive matter that the destruction was attributed without qualification to God — a dramatic oversimplification that may seem jarring. The conclusion of history on the cataclysmic side is often pictured in the Bible simply as God's acting. But in this prophetic perspective, it will come through human agency, yet as God's judgment. Then beyond all human agency except that of Jesus Christ, God will overwhelm and with finality overcome the worst that humans could do.

When a person commits suicide, that act is not what God wills. God was striving with the person against that conclusion. Yet to some degree, that ending ordinarily comes as judgment for refusal to live what God wills. Correspondingly, God does not will nuclear holocaust. It would come as something utterly against what he wants for the human family and yet as judgment upon all that defies what he wants.

The prophets frequently pointed to judgment coming upon nations that had been the agents of judgment, precisely because of terrible things they had done. Judah reaps the destruction it deserves, but the destroyers sow toward their own destruction. God does not exonerate those who do what must not be done, even though he channels that against other unrighteousness. The nations that were the conquering agents of judgment in World War II have, through what they did then, come under judgment that is far from completed. What the Allies inflicted on their enemies, most of all the obliteration bombing of cities, was not what God wanted. They did not have

God on their side. What they sowed is still springing up for them into ghastly harvest. The victory of the Allied powers was no more confirmation of their righteousness than victories by the Assyrians and Babylonians were that for them.

Government as such is to be seen essentially, not as an order of creation, but as judgment upon a people. This is indicated by the way the monarchy was given to rebel Israel (1 Sam. 8). Government may be quite evidently a dominating, occupying power, or it may be that only covertly: if not an Assyrian or Babylonian emperor, then a Solomon or a Jeroboam and the elites alongside them. The degree of judgment in government itself may be mild or severe. On the other hand, much of the evil that a government does should not be seen as judgment on its victims.

If I do something nasty to someone and that person retaliates with nastiness that hurts me, I reap what I have sowed. It is effect from cause, but, more than that, it is a mode of God's dealing with me in my wrongdoing. God does not will the retaliation, yet commandeers it, seeking my good. The person coming back at me also goes against God's way in Christ and elicits judgment. If the person had absorbed the injury from me and responded to me with surprising love, God would in that have judged and dealt with me in his preferred mode. God would have acted into that acting.

The same holds for nations. If in other countries there had been the corporate will and creativity to face the Nazis nonviolently, that would have been God's preferred mode. But God is not shut out by human refusal on both sides of such a conflict to seek his way. He can commandeer for his purposes massive inhumanity pitted against massive inhumanity. Also when persons and nations go totally against the way of Jesus, God draws those contrary moves into the overriding chess-like strategy of his purposes.

Jesus as God's Judgment

The Hebrew scriptures repeatedly picture God as coming to judge the world.

> for he comes,
> for he comes to judge the earth.
> He will judge the world with righteousness,
> and the peoples with his truth.
>
> (Ps. 96:13)

In Jesus he did so come. The world has been judged by Jesus' life, death, and rising, by who he was and is. All God's judgments before and after are subsumed in that judgment.

In Jesus' dying God bore the brunt of all contrary will and was still holy — in contradiction to that will. God said through Jeremiah, "I will pour out their wickedness upon them" (14:16). In Jesus God who is behind such inundation stepped under it. Jesus lived all God's contradiction to human willfulness and then in the place of all others came under it. This God of judgment and of the severity of Jesus is the God who in Jesus so loved the world and each human being.

"In all their affliction he [Yahweh] was afflicted" (Is. 63:9).[10] What prophets through their anguish intimated about God, Jesus lived and died to the fullest. All evil is assault against the Rule of God. Jesus came as God's focal counterassault. Throughout his ministry he acted with utter decisiveness to break the sway of evil and shatter all infernal will captivating human wills. "If it is by the finger of God that I cast out demons, then the kingdom of God has come upon you" (Lk. 11:20). But then in Jesus God let come upon himself the totality of evil's assault. At the cross evil was not recoiling on itself or veering over to bring down other evil. The retribution did not fall upon those who deserved it but upon the One without sin. Jesus took upon himself the status of those under judgment for sin and bore the intensity of God's movement against evil. God's commandeering of evil into collision with evil for its collapse as discerned throughout the story of Israel shifted amazingly into evil's doing away with the Son of God and, by that, coming to its own undoing. At the least likely point, evil, through its being borne by Jesus, was made to subserve the purposes of God.

Also in the Hebrew scriptures the God of judgment against sin is the God of tender mercy and compassion. In Jesus' death these seemingly opposite poles in God are shown to be a unity. Jesus' death, rather than giving assurance of a God of love apart from judgment and wrath, reveals God in holy, unfathomable love bearing to the full that judgment. This means that the prophets' warnings of disaster and doom, no matter how dark they are, should be understood christologically: God in Christ has suffered in whatever horrors of punishment have come. When Jesus told of the imminent destruction of Jerusalem and wept over the city, he brought clarification to even the most dreadful of those pronouncements: The God who warns weeps. That Jesus bore the punishment of all gives intimation of God's presence in him with all who come under punishment by God.

In the Bible God judges as the One who overcomes wrong, sets things right, restores relationships. Judgment in its more negative biblical range of meaning is God's giving over to dire consequence. But that sort of judgment is intended to serve the grander theme. It is meant to turn people back to God, to restore that and other relationships. Throughout the story of Israel God smites his people as a step toward healing them. "Because of the iniquity of his covetousness I was angry, / I smote him.... / But I will heal him" (Is. 57:17, 18). A prophecy, pointing to the conversion of the nations beyond Israel, states: "And the Lord will smite Egypt, smiting and healing, and they will return to the Lord, and he will heed their supplications and heal them" (Is. 19:22). Just as pain in the body can evoke steps to remedy its causes, so can judgment.

Success and contentment in evildoing is doom confirmed.

> For when thy judgments are in the earth,
> the inhabitants of the world learn righteousness.
> If favor is shown to the wicked,
> he does not learn righteousness.
>
> (Is. 26:9–10)

But "there is no peace, says my God, for the wicked" (Is. 57:21). God's retribution with "no peace" is meant to break an opening for his gift of peace. When evil is brought to collapse, its delusive grip is broken. A way is cleared for the incursion of truth. God "has scattered the proud" (Lk. 1:51) and out of that crumbling phalanx draws persons into his regrouping. God's primary intent in such judgment is the same as that in the coming and death of Jesus: to rescue his human creatures from what ensnares them and bring them home to himself.

Shortly before Jesus was nailed to a cross, he said, "Now is the judgment of this world, now shall the ruler of this world be cast out" (Jn. 12:31). The world in its fallenness is not simply or primarily an aggregate of individuals in their wrongdoing. The world in its autonomy is organized against God. The Creator orders his creation, but the world sets against this its (dis)order. Biblically, the world *is* that (dis)order. Behind that is the organizer, "the ruler of this world." What moved against Jesus was the religious, political, social, economic, and military power structures of that time and place. Individuals coming against him did so as actors in (or reactors to) those power structures. Jesus' death on the cross was judgment upon that world so organized and upon that world throughout history. As all the Bible discloses, humans defy God, not mainly as private individuals, but as collective groupings. The Adversary is not simply the tempter of individuals but the infernal one who presses his counter-reign and misleads individuals most of all through the collective dimensions of that counter-reign. Human revolt against God reaches its gigantic breadth and power through mass adherence to that contrary ruler.

Most of all in going to the cross Jesus revealed who God is, and he did that in collision with the onslaught of rebel structures. This God is overwhelmingly different from such structures and from any "God" taken as auxiliary by them. God is not the hallowing sponsor of those structures, but in Jesus has taken upon himself the worst they can do. They are exposed in their dark opposition to the One who has come as God's light. They are exposed in their weakness, for from the cross he exercises unequalled power for good, drawing all human beings to him (Jn. 12:32). He is the Reality upon which all the competing realisms are shattered. All that is like the structures Jesus collided with comes into that same collision with him.

Nations hardly figure into the view of "last things" that looks only to the accumulating individual transitions from this life to the beyond. But for biblical faith God at the End judges the nations. The age of the pagan nations (Lk. 21:24) is not vacant as regards the severity of the End but is infused with it. All that is to pass away at the End is already in process of passing away. The more one sees Jesus and in him what God asks of humankind, the more one discerns the overwhelming magnitude of impending judgment.

Jesus came "that through death he might destroy him who has the power of death, that is, the devil" (Heb. 2:14). This is the most encompassing characterization of the evil one. Behind the state's power to kill, in all its aspects, is that infernal power. But Jesus met the focal concentration of that power and vanquished it. Its supposed ultimacy collapsed, for those with eyes to see.

Wherever those who belong to Christ suffer and die under the judgment of those who wield power, there too is the judgment of this world. They may seem to go down in impotence and defeat. But even in their suffering the world is exposed in the grotesqueness of its rebellion against God. And the ones who seem so dominant are no more in real control than were Caiaphas and Pilate and the elites around them. Any who see Jesus' suffering and death as God's judgment of this world may themselves need to join many others in whom reiteration of that judgment is made manifest.

In John 12 the counterpoint to judgment of this world is stated: "Father, glorify thy name" (v. 28). What could be greater glory to

God and more against human self-glorification than this death on the cross? What could be more unlike the subservience of auxiliary gods than this sovereign self-giving?

Criteria for Testing the "Just War" Tradition

Dominant traditions in church history have viewed politics and war-making as an autonomous sphere where the revelation in Jesus Christ is not looked to as determinative or even as relevant. In rhetoric at least, the "just war" tradition has been taken as a basis for political thinking and action. Because of practical considerations and necessities, God's command in Jesus has to be suspended, put to the side; one has to go by other norms. God's revelation centered in Jesus has seemed too remote from what is politically practicable.

In the light of Ephesians 6:10–20 and related passages, the "just war" tradition can and should be seen as a principality, a power, a rebel dynamism. In the interpretations given by Hendrikus Berkhof[11] and John Howard Yoder,[12] religious and ethical systems and governmental and economic structures are to be seen as manifesting what Paul pointed to; they are meant to serve the right ordering of human life, but they characteristically veer into rebellion against God. The "just war" tradition has had a major role in history. To some quite limited degree it may have been a restraining, ordering factor. (If its guidelines had been strictly observed, the countries of Christendom would have fought few, if any, wars.) But through the centuries any serious application of the guidelines has been far outweighed by a "just war" mentality bent on seeing one's own side and all its military violence as justified. This principality has been a prime impetus for insurrection against God.

It can be said that the popular "just war" mentality needs to be challenged by careful application of the traditional guidelines, for example, with regard to nuclear war. There is a place for that.[13] But according to Ephesians 6 Christians are to take the whole armor of God and with it the word of God in order to stand against any principality. The "just war" tradition has its roots in Roman thought, not in Jesus and not in the Hebrew scriptures. Especially "evangelicals" and "Bible church" people should be helped to recognize that reliance on this tradition as an autonomous norm constitutes a desertion of the Gospel. Disciples live out of the reality that Jesus in going to the cross has disarmed (taken the captivating power away from) this principality and the others (Col. 2:15). This rebel power that has shaped much of human history has been decisively defeated by Jesus' victory on the cross and at the tomb.

Response to these issues gives an answer to that most basic question: Does one really believe that the world has been redeemed in Jesus Christ and that one is to live out this redemption toward its consummation? Apart from Jesus the "just war" tradition may seem to make good sense. But the reality of Jesus' life, death, and rising expose it as a lie, delusion, and defiance of this Lord. If people are to have attitudes transformed and turn back from doom, it is surely more promising to look to the word of God for that than to "just war" analyses. Followers and leaders must be won away from perverted use of unbiblical concepts to the incomparably Good News of the peaceable Lordship of Jesus in the midst of and over the nations.

The decisive ethical question is this: What does God require? According to Jesus himself and all the apostolic witness, what God requires has been put before humanity in Jesus. Autonomous ethical norms can have no tenable grounding for those who believe that God's continuing judgment of history, moving toward the Last Judgment, issues from the judgment carried out in the life, death, and resurrection of Jesus Christ. When governments and peoples are given license to disregard the way of Jesus, the actuality and basis of God's judgment coming upon that disregard is not recognized. To name this Jesus as Lord and yet advocate ethical norms apart from and contrary to him is not only to delimit his Lordship but also to assume that judgment, however conceived, is, and will be, based only in part on Jesus and what he has revealed. But those who believe that Jesus Christ is *the* norm for God's judgment now and at the End must strive to hold to this norm even in their political discernment and action.

The 1983 Vancouver Assembly of the World Council of Churches approved a most significant declaration:

Nuclear deterrence, as the strategic doctrine which has justified nuclear weapons in the name of security and war prevention, must now be categorically rejected as contrary to our faith in Jesus Christ who is our life and peace. Nuclear deterrence is morally unacceptable because it relies on the credibility of the *intention to use* nuclear weapons: we believe that any intention to use weapons of mass destruction is an utterly inhuman violation of the mind and spirit of Christ which should be in us.[14]

What is so starkly clear with regard to nuclear bombs should be clear enough for other means of warmaking. The burden of proof lies with those of contrary persuasion: to show that *any* readiness for war and *any* fighting of a war is other than "an utterly inhuman violation of the mind and spirit of Christ."

The Sermon on the Mount has as its close the parable about the two houses, the one built on rock and the other on sand (Mt. 7:24–27). Some hear and do the words of Jesus and thus build on rock. Others hear those words and do not do them and thus build on sand. And the storm comes. Jesus was pointing most of all to eternal life and to definitive ruin. The storm that tests the two houses is, in its final intensity, the closing collapse and the Last Judgment. But storms foreshadowing the last one burst upon individuals and nations. The parable should not be seen simply in terms of the eternal destiny of individuals in their private decisions for or against the way of Jesus. Whatever may sweep over parts of this planet or the whole of it, the revelation in Jesus is the one sure and solid reality that will endure. Those whose lives rest in that reality are brought through whatever comes. Jesus was explaining how one goes about being realistic.

The Torah and the prophets stressed the two contrary directions for human beings under God — "life and good, death and evil" (Deut. 30:15). The destinations of those directions were seen as being reached again and again within history. One catastrophe after another was reckoned as God's judgment because of disregard of his will revealed in the Torah. As prophet greater than Moses, Jesus proclaimed from a mountain what God asks of his people. To go against Jesus' teaching in this Sermon is to be given over to the catastrophic collapse of what has been built up. Much of the meaning of the parable is social and corporate in direct continuity with the primary emphasis of the Hebrew scriptures.

In the word of God through Jeremiah, "the way of life and the way of death" (21:8) corresponded, at that juncture, to the acceptance or rejection of God's command to surrender to the Babylonians besieging the city. Because the people of Jerusalem a few hundred years later were unwilling to learn from Jesus "the things that make for peace," their enemies were soon to dash them to the ground and "not leave one stone upon another" (Lk. 19:42–44). Jesus called both individuals and the Jewish people as a whole to love their Roman enemies and not to enter into violent resistance against them.[15] All Israel could have begun building on the rock. Rejection of his call brought on the storm of A.D. 70. "Unless you repent you will all likewise perish" (Lk. 13:3, 5). That Jesus was intensely concerned not only about the Last Judgment but also about the impending judgment on Jerusalem indicates that the alternatives presented at the end of the Sermon are to be understood in relation to national and international affairs.

The blindness of the majority around Jesus to his being Israel's Messiah was in considerable measure political and had enormous political consequences — climactically in the destruction of Jerusalem and the Jewish state. But now too, when the political realm is viewed apart from Jesus the Christ and not in his light, there is a comparable blindness. The most portentous factor in the politics of any country is the giving over of the populace more and more into blindness — blindness to the poor near and far, blindness to covert wars and death squads, to the accelerating destruction of the environment, to ruinous economic policies, to "the march of folly" in militarism and nuclear weapons, blindness to the God of biblical faith. This blinding pervades wide segments of the churches, as the One called Lord is left out of account politically. The claim to sight compounds the blindness and the guilt (Jn. 9:41). Television and other media have brought an unending barrage of sights so that people "see and see, but do not perceive" (Is. 6:9). But some, even for the political side of life, do seek to see with Christ and in his light. And partly through them the light shines in the darkness.

When "all the nations" are gathered before the Son of man, the dividing judgment comes upon individuals (Mt. 25:31–46). But individuals do or fail to do what the King requires, not only in private and locally, but also in their formative relation to wider groupings, chiefly the nation. In the contemporary world more than in the past, each person has some weight, however slight, toward moving governmental policies in the direction of the Matthew 25 norms or away from them. For judgment within history and at the End, who each has been is constituted in considerable measure by how each has lived as constituent part of the nation.

A common objection is this: One's hope for the day of judgment should be in God's mercy through Christ and not in one's fulfilment of what God requires; God's mercy can cover what people have to do politically, proceeding by sub-Christian norms because Jesus' commands are quite impracticable for that side of life. But the latter stance amounts to sinning intentionally with the expectation that grace will abound — a posture that Paul rejects as outrageous (Rom. 6:1–2). Only those who see Jesus as the fullness of what God requires recognize the extremity of their need for God's mercy and rightly hope for his transfiguring pardon at the End. No reassuring lesser standards intervene to hold in abeyance God's command. The

One who came as incarnation of God's imperative to humanity will be that in unobscured majesty on the Last Day.

The ethical issue concerning resort to violence needs to be considered also in terms of human *being* as shaped by God. The Christian ethic comes not only as God's word spoken to human beings; it has to do with the intention of the Creator implanted in every human being. God created man and woman for oneness in marriage. Any who veer into promiscuity or infidelity go against God's command; but as the underside of that, they go against their true humanity, God's intention molded into them, to which the command corresponds. Conscience, however faltering, is the inner voice arising from that God-given mold.

Jesus stated imperatives; but, antecedent to that, Jesus came into the human midst as the all-righteous, all-loving being. He lived life as God meant it to be lived. "Love one another as I have loved you" (Jn. 15:12). What was set before humanity in Jesus has also been molded as orientation into each person. No matter how much one may go against that orientation, it still inheres as intended basis of who one is.

It is relatively easy to suppose that certain aspects of human life, notably the political and military aspects, need to be bracketed away from the imperatives given by Jesus. For that side of life it is rather easy to claim a suspension of those imperatives, ultimately by God himself. There can, however, hardly be a suspension of what God has impressed into human *being*. Much of the time and in diverse ways, humans go against God's intention stamped into the mold of who they are. Yet what is being considered here is a stance in which a warrant, a charter, a definitive justification is given for proceeding apart from Christ's way and thus from what has been molded into each human being. War is given justification in terms of what "has to be done," seen as the imperative. But killing in combat and alignment with that always diminish the humanity of those who act in this way. However strong the claim to God's permission, those entering into war lose something of their own soul. Those who kill or give their assent to killing go not only against Jesus' commands but also (and most tellingly) against God's will for humanity inscribed in their being. Leaders and led, doing what "has to be done," effect the erosion of their own humanity. Any such erosion is judgment.

Discerning God's Judgments in Contemporary History

In human affairs judgment may be slow, covert, and generally disregarded; or it may be sudden, manifest, and convulsive. Even when the latter is not recognized as judgment, its devastating content cannot be ignored. Slow judgment comes more and more over many societies: in the emptiness of affluence, in economic decline, in the blighting influence of so much of mass culture, in child abuse by the media, in social disintegration, in deterioration of the infrastructure, in the effects of polluting the environment, in drugs and crime. Like a mass of snow and ice before an avalanche, all this gradually accumulates into an onslaught of cataclysmic judgment.

Dramatic judgments of God can be discerned in our time. The Thousand-Year (millennial) Reich lasted twelve years, four months, and eight days. The greatest military power on earth was defeated in the Vietnam War and stymied in the Iran hostage crisis. The Soviet Union was caught in the Afghanistan snare. The Pentagon papers were published, the Watergate burglary was investigated, the Iran-Contra scandal came to light. The Three Mile Island disaster, so near to becoming unspeakably worse, imperiled much of the eastern United States. The Chernobyl catastrophe shamed Soviet technology and spread radioactivity, fear, and the shadow of death over much of Europe. After vociferous Cold War exploitation of the Soviet downing of a South Korean jetliner, the United States found itself guilty of shooting down an Iranian jetliner. The space shuttle *Challenger* exploded, and with it much of the U.S. advance in the militarization of outer space. The world's greatest creditor nation became the world's greatest debtor nation. Communist governments across Eastern Europe were overthrown by nonviolent uprisings as inundations of grace. For communism the economy is the alpha and the omega, and yet economic failure more than anything else brought on that collapse. Cathedrals in the Soviet Union were taken over for the casting of monumental statues of Stalin and Lenin. Then those statues were toppled, and the cathedrals became "working churches" again. One Third World despot after another has been overthrown. In the United States the frenzied elation evoked for the U.S.-Iraq War gave way to deepening economic and social malaise. The economic decline of the United States in relation to Japan and Western Europe continues.

One must not, however, suppose that all misfortunes and disasters are God's judgment. Israel's slavery under Pharaoh was not seen as judgment. Job's counselors were mistakenly convinced that his affliction was punishment for sin. Jesus rejected the alternatives proposed by the disciples: "Rabbi, who sinned, this man or his parents, that he was born blind?" (Jn. 9:2). The world is filled with the suffering of the innocent (the very young) and the relatively innocent ("the wicked swallow those more righteous than they" — Hab. 1:13 NRSV). A hurricane with a ferocity brought on perhaps by First World pollution cuts a swath of devastation across the Caribbean. Governments in the arrogance of power do terrible things within and beyond their borders. When collective wrongdoing leads into disaster, many suffer who led lives more against, than for, that dynamic. From Sodoms generally the righteous are not led out.

But when the spirit of the age draws away from any thought of judgment under God, what is so largely ignored must be given special attention and emphasis. The Hebrew prophets were not making inferences like Job's friends or like Jesus' disciples with regard to the blind man. They discerned mad rebellion against God and what it was leading to. Christians seek to discern what around (and in) them is that and what is not. Only the consummation of judgment will make fully clear what has been judgment and what not.

Jonathan Schell in *The Fate of the Earth* presents Christians with an oblique, unintended, but most significant question: Does Christian faith tend to diminish a sense of urgency for resisting the drift toward nuclear annihilation? For Schell, if the human species is extinguished, all is lost; the most urgent imperative is to work against that. But Christians believe that God in sovereign mercy will not allow all to be lost, that beyond death humans are to be raised to eternal life, and that the plea "Thy will be done on earth as it is in heaven" is to be fulfilled. Is the task of working against human extinction and for peace therefore less urgent?

There is awesomeness in becoming and being a mother or a father, in having that central responsibility for creating and shaping an emergent human life. But the awesomeness of that responsibility is far greater if that child is indeed faced with the future of resurrection into new life and the utterly opposite nonfuture of descent into doom. If these, rather than human survival or extinction, are the ultimate contrary prospects, the urgency of siding with Life against all that threatens life is still greater. Attitudes and actions are then seen as helping to determine, not only whether there will be a continuing earthly future, but also who and what will become part of the everlasting future God gives.

Cataclysmic judgments have their macrocosmic exterior and their multitudinous interior of persons before God in judgment or deliverance. Nuclear war cannot cut off the future promised by God. But alignment with the forces of destruction can cut persons off from that future. Those forces impel toward what Schell calls the second death, human extinction, but beyond that to what in the closing chapters of Revelation is termed the second death, final doom seen as fire. Of this Otto Weber has written: "The person who utters and acts out a No to God's grace, including the grace he encounters in the commandment, is moving toward God's No. Judgment is only the final binding of man to what he already is in contrast to the gracious self-disclosure of God."[16]

God's judgments continue in the lives of persons and in collective human events. The world is full of the types of things that in the Bible are seen as judgment under God (and as signs of the approaching End): wars, civil turmoil, overthrow of governments, epidemic diseases, famines, travail in nature. The people of God are not placed beyond the reach of such happenings. But they are being drawn apart from that which God gives over to destruction. When they too are caught within cataclysmic judgments (as Jeremiah was in the fall of Jerusalem), their acquittal in Jesus Christ redefines what they undergo. At the End they are to be rescued from evil's demise, and prefigurations of that rescue shape their lives even in the midst of disaster. In the Risen One, God, who has broken the sway of evil, moves with the might of his love to rescue his human creatures from that collapsing domain.

Chapter 9

FATE AND FAITH

Infatuation, a form of political madness whose inevitable end was self-destruction, meant much more to the whole of the ancient east as to the Greeks than it does to us, and they found it impossible to regard the causes of something so atrocious, such a plunge into madness and ruin at one's own hands, as lying simply on the human and immanent level: in the last analysis they could only be the inscrutable working of the deity."

—Gerhard von Rad[1]

Gabriel Marcel has written: "What is the essence of the act of despair? It seems as though it were always capitulation before a certain *fatum* laid down by our judgment."[2] In our time, this capitulation has taken a variety of forms. It is argued that, though the present world economy imperils the environment, radical shifts to a viable ordering would be very difficult to carry out and hardly practicable. The extreme poverty of many hundreds of millions of people on this planet is deplorable, but the problem is so huge that relatively little can be done about it. Having and at times using vast military might is regrettable but necessary, the world being the way it is. Many who openly or secretly reckon with the possibility of nuclear annihilation see it as what may be the ultimate *fatum:* We hope the bombs will bring us through; but if they don't, we did what we had to do.

To capitulate to what is viewed as a *fatum*, inexorable necessity, puts a person or a people under its control. Capitulations of various types determine the political, economic, and military contours of our world. But the despair that is their inner essence is kept down and obscured by orchestrations of optimism: We are coming through; we have plenty to consume; our country is still at the top in the world; we have won another war.

"Just war" thinking as actually practiced is basically capitulation to what is seen as inexorable necessity. The Allies entered World War II by such a capitulation: The adversaries being who they were, this war against them had to be fought. The ever-repeated questions about fighting Hitler and Nazism have to do essentially, not with "just war" by the classic criteria, but with what is still regarded as inexorable necessity. In the Cuba Missile Crisis, that time of greater peril for humanity than any other that has come till now, the U.S. administration and populace were committed to forcing the Soviets to back down, even if that meant nuclear holocaust: This stand *had* to be taken. During the buildup for the war with Iraq, the Bush administration gave the appearance of seeking some "peaceful" solution; but by ultimatums and refusal to make the slightest concessions for face-saving on the other side, it was proceeding in a way that would bring on the war it was determined to have. Through the subservient media it made the war seem the inexorable result of the actions and attitudes of Saddam Hussein and the Iraqis.[3] In that war and most others, justice and justifiableness were taken up as the reassuring rationale; but the quintessential experience, evoked or actual, was that of being forced by the grip of dark necessity into war. Of course, that which "has to be done" because of what a nation is up against in its enemies would seem to be justified even if some "just war" criteria are not met, as in modern wars (and arguably in all wars) they never are.

Fate, as Langdon Gilkey defines it, is what comes upon us "as overwhelming and oppressive, as destructive of our powers and so of our freedom." He writes:

> It is, moreover, evident that the central aim of politics and of most historical activity is to achieve freedom from fate, to restore our "lot" as destiny.... To understand the ultimate concern and so the fanaticism latent in patriotism we must understand the deep sense of being and of autonomy latent in national strength and the deep fear of fate implicit in national weakness.... To be fated is to be stripped of one's humanity, and so anxiety about being fated is a fundamental anxiety — and central to all politics.[4]

One could speak simply of the individual and collective fear of being weak, defenseless, impotent.

The regnant irony is that the collective drive to avoid what Gilkey identifies as fate proceeds as capitulation to such supposedly inexorable necessities as the ones just considered. Thus, the struggle to escape coming under the domination of those long perceived as inhuman adversaries has taken the form of surrender to the *fatum* of preparedness to destroy the world and of being unimaginably impotent under the bombs, should they begin to fall.

In the peace movement as well the military buildup and the readiness to resort to war are widely seen as an immense dynamism that has become almost irresistible. Most peace activists waver between frail hope that a turn-around in the direction being taken by their country can still be brought about and some distraught equivalent of the cry in Revelation 13:4 about the beast, "Who can fight against it?"

Capitulation to a *fatum* and justification of that leave sin and God out of view. Response and action are determined by circumstantial necessity. A sense of necessity, of doing what "has to be done," brings seeming release from the burden of sin and guilt. With no acknowledgment that God's commands given by Jesus have been flouted, sin is not seen as exceedingly sinful (Rom. 7:13).

Throughout history most politics has proceeded by such capitulation. But what should be decisive for Christians is that Jesus stood in dramatic opposition to such politics. He did not see a Jewish war for independence as inevitably necessary to counter impotence. He did not lead in trying to throw off the Roman yoke. He lived in freedom under its shadow, even, at the last, the freedom of giving himself over to the death imposed upon him. Because he refused to copy the attitudes and means of those who moved to do away with him, he did not let them dominate or efface him in what is always the most extreme way — the eliciting of retaliatory attitude and action. By giving himself over to the preponderance of oppressive and lethal power (not as a fate but in obedience to God), Jesus overcame it.

The Enslaving Power of Sin

Jesus warned, "Every one who commits sin is a slave to sin" (Jn. 8:34). What is decisive is not the impingement of inexorable necessity from without. Rather, sin as intensifying momentum controls. Temptation lures, and the wrong choosing doubles back to lay deepening hold on those who have chosen. "You once yielded your members to impurity and to greater and greater iniquity" (Rom. 6:19). Again and again, in lust, in greed, in hate, this doubling-back comes upon us. It moves in the vortex of political and economic processes and in the capitulations under discussion.

In contrast to what is otherwise seen as deterministic necessity or fate, the Bible points to God's hardening of hearts — certainly one of the more difficult biblical teachings. In the Exodus story it is said that God again and again hardened Pharaoh's heart. In John 12:40 somber words from Isaiah 6:10 are rephrased to explain the general rejection of Jesus: "He has blinded their eyes and hardened their heart." Paul, treating that same rejection, wrote: "So then he has mercy upon whomever he wills, and he hardens the heart of whomever he wills" (Rom. 9:18). But it is also stated that Pharaoh himself hardened his heart (Ex. 8:15; 9:34; 1 Sam. 6:6). King Zedekiah, in rebelling against Nebuchadnezzar, "stiffened his neck and hardened his heart against turning to the Lord" (2 Chron. 36:13). Zechariah 7:11–12 gives the picture: "But they refused to hearken, and turned a stubborn shoulder, and stopped their ears that they might not hear. They made their hearts like adamant lest they should hear the law and the words which the Lord of hosts had sent by his Spirit through the former prophets." In Hebrews the warning given in Psalm 95:7–8, "Today, when you hear his voice, / do not harden your hearts as in the rebellion," is taken up like a refrain (3:7–8, 15; 4:7). The human responsibility is clear in Mark 3:5, when Jesus gazed at his antagonists "with anger, grieved at their hardness of heart," and in Mark 10:5, when Jesus said to his questioners, "For your hardness of heart [Moses] wrote you this commandment" on divorce.

Evil willing by the individual is not willed by God. Nor is evil willing rampant in history willed by God. In scripture, hardening as what God does is seen in correlation with the reprehensible human choice of hardening one's heart. It is never viewed as transferring to God, and away from human beings, guilty responsibility for that state of mind. In Romans 1:24, 26, 28 Paul wrote that, because of the rebellious human rejection of God, he "gave them up" to "impurity, to the dishonoring of their bodies among themselves... to dishonorable passions... to a base mind and to improper conduct." That rejection of God is not simply a No; it is an utterly foolish Yes to "images... a lie... [worshiping] the creature" (vv. 23, 25). Enslavement to sin resulting from the idolatrous turn away from God is not simply a psychological process. God gives humans over to the rebel attitude in its expansive doubling-back. The momentum of hardening comes, not as God's initiative, but as God's giving over to the rebel human initiative. Humans choose to be in control, but God moves against that presumption to expose it as illusion, precisely by allowing it.

The militarization of nation states, the nuclear arms race, the acute disparity between the haves and the have-nots, and the devastation of the environment are not inexorable necessities but the global actuality of God's giving human beings up to what comes with the choice against God. "The Lord will smite you with madness and blindness and confusion of mind" (Deut. 28:28). To choose the militarized nation state, its providence, and provisions rather than God is to come under that contrary lordship. The grip of that lordship is, most basically, the expansive doubling-back of what has been chosen. Leaders represent the many in the choosing, and the doubling-back comes most of all through the leaders and their misleading.

In this connection the Hitler analogy can be examined further. One of the most frequently used arguments for justifying hard-line military approaches to world problems is that there must be no appeasement of an evil adversary. It is held that the British and French governments appeased Adolf Hitler, and this led directly to World War II. As the United States and a subservient UN Security Council kept issuing unconditional ultimatums to Saddam Hussein about withdrawing from Kuwait, the rationale stated repeatedly was that even the appearance of appeasing him would open the way for this new Hitler to do still more terrible things in the future.

Appeasement is commonly understood as giving in to a ruthless leader of another country, who then becomes stronger and bolder. Actually, appeasement so defined has been going on all the time around the world. For many years the United States and other countries appeased Saddam Hussein. They ignored his human rights abuses, his slaughter of Kurds, and his war with Iran, and gave him much of what he wanted. The guiding assumptions of imperial foreign policy have led to appeasement of many tyrants. Appeasement has come especially in the form of military aid and weapons sales. Monstrous behavior abruptly becomes the basis for punitive measures or going to war only when a leader does not remain adequately co-operative with supposed U.S. and Western interests or when a leader is no longer seen as the one most fitted to serve those interests. Otherwise appeasement continues in many countries and does feed into further repression.

The importance of attempting to stop any leader and nation that are about to become at all like Hitler and Nazi Germany seems obvious. Hitler led collective evil on a rampage. Such evil has broken loose again and again in history, most massively in the twentieth century; and the threat of that, along with the immense covert actuality of what could break loose, overshadows our lives. The drive to stop a demonized leader focuses on the designated enemy of the moment. Quite understandably, the vantage point is related to that of the British, French, and Americans in the years before and during World War II. But the more critically relevant parallel is with the Germans themselves during those years, though this is hardly ever recognized. The danger of an expanding dominion of evil and of its breaking loose must first of all be identified and resisted in one's own nation, especially if one lives in the world's lone superpower. How can such a national momentum be slowed and stopped by people of that nation?

The rhetoric about appeasement has to do with not giving in to a wicked leader, not yielding to the march of evil. But the deeper issue must be recognized: that of giving in to evil, going along with it as chosen means. When a leader and country, seen as the enemy, are resisted by cold war or hot war, this may seem the opposite of giving in to the evil posed by the adversary. But it actually constitutes going along with the march of evil. One gives in to evil as the supposed means for standing against it. Usually both sides before a war are very intent on saving face. Yet what is lost in war still more than before is the human face and heart. Retaliation is "unconditional surrender to evil."[5] The United States has come to demand unconditional surrender from each wartime adversary; but strangely, in prosecuting the war, it had already made such a surrender to the supremely inimical power.

Those who defeated Hitler did so by outdoing him in massive violence. The attitudes that found such destructive incarnation in Adolf Hitler and the Nazis were not really stopped by the Allied victory in World War II but continued as central to the Cold War, the nuclear arms race (especially the readiness to immolate millions of human beings), the East-West wars in Third World countries, and the exploitation of impoverished populations by the industrialized nations. In going to war against what is seen as ultimate evil, one succumbs to it.

The Hitler analogy served well those who brought us the U.S.-Iraq War. But who can hold in check the victors in that war? What can restrain the military hubris and the supposedly vindicated readiness to resort to war for solving problems? What is to stop the master race (technologically more than biologically) from lording it over lesser breeds? Much in the relations of other countries to the United States constitutes appeasement with regard to world domination.

Reinhold Niebuhr wrote:

> The development of atomic weapons to the point of the hydrogen bomb for the sake of exercising our responsibilities toward the free world is the measure of our growing political and moral maturity. We now know that we cannot be responsible without guilt. For all responsibility is exercised in a field where partial and fragmentary values are supported against contending forces, and the ultimate exercise of responsibility may involve the guilt of the destruction of life. We must be realistic enough to guard our liberties against any use of force by the foe. [emphasis added]

Niebuhr proceeded to warn that we must not "rely too much on military strength in general and neglect all the other political, economic, and moral factors which give unity, health, and strength to the nations of the free world."[6] That Cold War "realism" so persuasively articulated by Niebuhr did include some recognition of the terrible evil inherent in building and relying on nuclear bombs. But reliance on those weapons was seen as utterly crucial for the preservation of "the free world." And it was supposed that nuclear weapons would, very probably, never have to be fired to annihilate "the foe."

Jesus in the last petition of the Lord's Prayer was far more realistic about evil than was Reinhold Niebuhr: "And do not bring us to the time of trial, / but rescue us from the evil one" (Mt. 6:13 NRSV). In the petition is a strong sense of how ominously threatening the power of evil is and of how weak even disciples are for the task of withstanding it. "Temptation" or "the time of trial" (*peirasmos*) is, most of all, the dire testing and moral peril at the close of the age. But since all alluring deceptions and times of testing foreshadow and move toward that culmination, disciples ask that God not give them over to what could so easily bring them to ruin. They look to God who acts to deliver from ensnarement by sin. But if God's rescue is rejected, the will stands aligned with the infernal will of "the evil one" against God, who moves to bring out the full seriousness of that by giving over into the constriction of that alignment. Humans live out God's grace prefiguring the final liberation, or they live out that giving over as prefiguration of eternal ruin.

A prevailing conception, in the churches as elsewhere, has been that of doing the lesser evil when no other option is available. But if this "necessity" is so basic in human affairs as is claimed, how strange that the revelation in Jesus Christ gives no attention to it. Jesus' life and teaching provide not the least indication that he knew of any necessity to do wrong, which is therefore justified, or that he saw himself or anyone else as ever under such a constraint.[7] In biblical perspective, when people see themselves caught in a choice only between a greater and a lesser evil, it is because they are not enough in touch with God to discover what the content of faithfulness in the situation would be. Apart from Christ one can be in the grip of dark necessities from without and within. But through Christ the trap is sprung.

With regard to weapons of mass annihilation, most church people in the United States have said in effect, "We have to have them because of the extreme danger our enemies pose for us." Military buildup and most specifically nuclear deterrence have been a sort of unacknowledged prayer to the weapons, "Deliver us from evil that the enemy would like to inflict upon us." The greater jeopardy before God is not recognized. Many people of moderation and good will align themselves with armaments, with the present economic order, and with wars of intervention. They fail to recognize the enslaving momentum of alignment with evil and the urgency of the plea to be preserved from its sinister power. Commitment to imperial military might is sin, captivation in sin, "a covenant with death" (Is. 28:15). The hold of the infernal dynamisms behind the means employed tightens. This is just what has been happening more and more in the escalating militarization of the world, the nuclear arms race, exploitation of impoverished countries, and the consumptive poisoning of the biosphere.

The God of biblical faith makes evil subserve his purposes against evil. It has been widely held that human beings can and must do the same. The prevailing assumption, even in the churches, has been that "the free world" could rely on dark instrumentalities and remain essentially above them. Paul denounces a formulation of this outlook: "That would be the same as saying: Do evil as a means to good. Some slanderers have accused us of teaching this, but they are justly condemned" (Rom. 3:8 JB). This outlook is completely lacking in the biblical realism about evil. One cannot consort with evil and maintain a desired mastery over it. Those who seek to use evil as an instrument for good are drawn into being instruments of evil. They may think they can imitate God in commandeering evil, but they fail. That attempt, rather than being under God's sponsorship, is actually a usurpation of God's prerogative. Humans are not God, who from beyond the plane of human affairs makes even the worst actions subserve his purposes. The evil they resort to is commandeered against them. Jesus warned of this in his saying, "All who take the sword will perish by the sword" (Mt. 26:52). Retribution comes upon the wrongness of human attempts to set things right. Doing evil as a means to good has its own inevitably destructive momentum into the web of human interaction. Of itself, it moves against God's intention for human life. Only in the mystery of his sovereign action against it is it brought to ricochet toward his goal for his creation.

Even before August 6 and 9, 1945, the construction of the first three atomic bombs unleashed forces that enthralled and drove those who supposed they were the Promethean masters of that power. According to the strategy of nuclear deterrence, what a nation or alliance has to have is nuclear weapons sufficient for inflicting "unacceptable damage" on the adversary even after a first strike by the adversary. At some point in the 1950s or later the United States government could have declared: "We have that. We don't need more nuclear weapons." Such a halt at a "survivable minimal deterrent" would have been consistent with that strategy and would have made some pragmatic sense. Instead, the nuclear arms race was pursued to what George F. Kennan characterized as "levels of redundancy of such grotesque dimensions as to defy rational understanding."[8] Then the Soviet Union broke up; the chief adversary of the West disappeared. But the dynamic of militarization has continued in the United States and among its allies (and of course in other countries too) essentially the same as before. Even cuts in military spending and some dismantling of obsolete types of weapons converge with "modernization" of what remains the dominant institution in the society. The leaders of the major powers work at arms *control;* but they have not the least intention of disarming, even multilaterally, for that could end their domination of the world. Why all this has been happening can be analyzed politically and militarily. But the deeper explanation is in the teaching of Jesus: To proceed with sinning is to become still more dominated by that sin; to go in a direction opposite the plea "Rescue us from the evil one" is to succumb to the prodigious power of evil.

God's Plan, Human Choice, and the End of History

Again and again in the Exodus narrative what constituted Pharaoh's hardening of his heart was this: "and he would not listen to them [Moses and Aaron]; as the Lord had said" (7:13, 22; 8:15, 19). His refusal to allow the Hebrews to leave Egypt stemmed from his rejection of God's declared message. God's word to Moses was that Pharaoh would persist in this refusal to the end. A similar situation emerged repeatedly in the prophets. The people refused to heed God's call to turn back from imminent catastrophe toward God. At times a prophet would declare that because no change of heart would come, the impending judgment was virtually certain. The rejection of God's warning was to continue "until the cities lie waste / without inhabitant... / and the land is utterly desolate" (Is. 6:11). "So you shall speak all these words to them, but they will not listen to you.... Therefore... the land shall become a waste" (Jer. 7:27, 32, 34). Jesus foresaw that the Jerusalem populace would persist in rejecting God's call, with awesome judgment as the result: "Would that even today you knew the things that make for peace! But now they are hid from your eyes.... Your enemies ... will dash you to the ground, you and your children within you, and they will not leave one stone upon another in you; because you did not know the time of your visitation" (Lk. 19:42, 43, 44). "How often would I have gathered your children together as a hen gathers her brood under her wings, and you would not!" (Mt. 23:37). That "and you would not" remains archetypal for all collective rejection of Jesus that leads to doom.

It may be that the current world situation is similar and that God, who sees the hearts of all, knows that in the period ahead humanity will not turn back from folly and world cataclysm. But if God knows that, humans have no way of knowing it. No contemporary prophet is given a sure word from God on that.

The years pass. Global catastrophe in nuclear or other form does not yet sweep over the world. God holds it back still longer and gives additional time, "not wishing that any should perish, but that all should reach repentance" (2 Pet. 3:9). In the light of the Hebrew scriptures, such time is given for turn-around not only in terms of individual conversion but also in terms of collective avoidance of cataclysmic judgment within history.

In sending his Son, God knew that Jesus would be killed, humanity being what it is. He gave himself over into what he saw coming. Scripture teaches that God has comparable knowledge that humanity will plunge history into ruin and death just before the End. Into that too God will give himself over. But since Christians dare not presume to know the timing of the End, the possibility that in the period ahead a determining portion of humanity will turn back from catastrophe to God must be kept very much in view. In any case, the urgency of the turn-around presses upon all human beings.

In this connection an influential view held by great numbers of people in "Bible-believing" churches can be considered. According to this view, nuclear cataclysm is a central part of God's plan for the near future of the earth, and believers can be sure of this through the study of biblical prophecy. Thus, U.S. nuclear weapons find their necessity and justification as an element in God's plan, and fighting a nuclear war is seen as carrying out God's purpose. Such believers, when in the armed forces, can suppose themselves to be prospective agents in executing God's plan. The conclusion is that Christians can do nothing, and are meant to do nothing, against the coming of nuclear war. They must not be drawn into a futile struggle against nuclear annihilation or other catastrophes (or for social justice) and diverted from the all-important task of winning persons to "a saving faith in the Lord Jesus Christ." Such a perspective meshes dynamically with the political mindset dominant in many countries.

Persons who reject this view usually dismiss it as obviously perverse and appalling, especially in its understanding of God as a sort of super Pentagon commandant, who, after his great patience has run out, blasts his enemies, even if that means destroying the earth. Richard J. Barnet offers this summary: "God is planning to destroy the world. So when we blow it up, we are doing God's will."[9] But people who hold such a view see it as part of the biblical revelation, to which they want to remain staunchly loyal. What must be made clear is that a deplorable misunderstanding of this revelation is involved.

In the biblical story, impending judgment could be averted if the people turned to God. The God of Israel gave this gracious warning: "If at any time I declare concerning a nation or a kingdom, that I will pluck up and break down and destroy it, and if that nation, concerning which I have spoken, turns from its evil, I will repent of the evil that I intended to do to it" (Jer. 18:7–8). That is, any such judgment is not seen as a predetermination by God that nothing can change. (Passages that might seem to speak of some such predetermination are to be understood in terms of God's knowing that the people will not turn back.) Prior to any onslaught of judgment, God gives time for the turn-around: "As I live, says the Lord God, I have no pleasure in the death of the wicked, but that the wicked turn from his way and live; turn back, turn back from your evil ways; for why will you die, O house of Israel?" (Ez. 33:11).

The alternatives in Deuteronomy 30 summarize God's message proclaimed by all the prophets: "I have set before you this day life and good, death and evil. . . . Therefore choose life, that you and your descendants may live, loving the Lord your God, obeying his voice, and cleaving to him" (vv. 15, 19–20). Throughout the story of Israel and through all the later centuries, these have always been the awesome contrary possibilities: Trust in God, cleave to God, and be greatly blessed; or defy God, rebel, and move into catastrophe. Again and again as that people called by God headed into disaster, the prophets cried out, "Turn back, turn back to God, and live." In contrast to Greek and contemporary views of fate, even the forewarnings that were stated most unconditionally bore at least the implication from their wider context that there could be the turn back from destruction if those in such jeopardy would do that. In somber words Jesus warned, "Unless you repent you will all likewise perish" (Lk. 14:3, 5). He was saying: You need not perish; you can turn back from that ruin. This remains God's word to humanity with regard to nuclear catastrophe and all other impending doom.

The continued imminence of nuclear annihilation as the chief among many threats to the human future is to be seen in terms of these biblical motifs. God has no pleasure in the death of multitudes in a nuclear holocaust. That is not what God wants or insists on. Holocaust does not impend as part of a plan that God holds to but as the prospective termination of vast arrangements and efforts that governments and peoples (among them a great many "Bible-believing" persons) hold to. It would come as judgment from God (as delineated in the previous chapter), and certain Hebrew prophecies about destruction of all the earth could be taken as descriptive of it.

Church folk contradict Deuteronomy 30 and the whole message of the Bible when they suppose that nuclear war is inevitable and that efforts to prevent it are a waste of time. This outlook assumes that God is not giving humanity the choice between life and doom. Biblically seen, however, God does offer this choice. If there is no turning back, nuclear or other global catastrophe will come. For collective sinful pursuits in history as a whole, it must be said, "The end of those things is death" (Rom. 6:21). Yet God still gives time and strives with humankind for the turn back from cataclysm. Christians are to be part of that striving. God wills peace for the human family on earth. Because of this, extraordinary positive changes in human affairs can come if God is looked to as the One to bring about such changes. Because the Messiah is at work creating wholeness of relationships within the world, disciples can rightly work for local, national, and global breakthroughs giving expression to something of that wholeness.

A friend may be very ill. In the usual human perspective, this person is going to die sometime. But one would be wrong to jump to the conclusion that this particular illness will cause death and nothing should be done toward preventing that. Even for what is diagnosed as a terminal illness in oneself or in someone else, one should hope and strive against death and for life. The Bible does picture a death (or death-throes) of history before its resurrection. But as Jesus emphasized, none can know the timing of that termination. The impending death that at present so threatens the earth may be postponed for a long time.

God can deliver from any seeming *fatum*. When some of those encompassed by collective choice of death choose life, then for all the world the realm of life is a little enlarged and the realm of death a little diminished. Even if most do not turn back and global disaster comes, any human being can turn back and not *perish* in it.

So far in this chapter the concept of inexorable necessity has been considered with regard to those who capitulate in carrying it out. But there is the other side, that of the victims. What seems to be fate presses upon them in more crushing ways. In Auschwitz, Dresden, Hiroshima, Soweto, Afghanistan, El Salvador, Ethiopia, Baghdad, and innumerable less known places, multitudes of victims have not escaped what the perpetrators carried out. But if such acting is gross inhumanity and defiance of God, victims should see it as that rather than as fate or God's will. The only "necessity" is the perpetrators' enslavement to sin; and as nonviolent resistance seeks to make clear, liberation even from that enslavement can come. Victims can learn from the Hebrews in Egypt, from the early Christians in the book of Acts, and most of all from Jesus. They can live out that same freedom under God. They can let God shape and inspire the life they find together in community. They can live that life resiliently out toward structures of death. With this Lord, they can bear whatever victimization they cannot practically or rightly escape. When not directly victimized, disciples are to stand with victims, and that may be entry into becoming victims.

Total Reorientation

God's word through the prophets often centered in the verb *shuv, turn* — *turn* from disobedience and rebellion and *return* to Yahweh. A turning of one's whole existence toward God is conversion, actualized in obedience to his will, and involves unconditional trust in him and renunciation of all competing sources of help. Jesus took up this imperative as central to his proclamation, "The time is fulfilled, and the kingdom of God is at hand; repent [turn, be converted], and believe in the gospel" (Mk. 1:15). God's Rule has come into the human midst in the person of Jesus. In the Greek text of the apostolic scriptures, *metanoia*, usually translated *repentance*, comes as the entering into a new relationship with God so that the whole life of the person is claimed by the divine Lordship in Jesus. It includes the unconditional turning from all that is against God and brings the transformation of who one is.[10]

That total reorientation, individual and corporate, is not a human possibility; it is not something simply within human power to decide and effect. But what is humanly impossible is "possible with God"

(Mk. 10:27). Faith is "not your own doing, it is the gift of God" (Eph. 2:8). Conversion is brought about by the Spirit of God moving in a person. Only the Spirit can liberate from increasing hardness of heart and from all contrary capitulations.

Zacchaeus stood up at the table and said to Jesus: "Behold, Lord, the half of my goods I give to the poor; and if I have defrauded any one of anything, I restore it fourfold" (Lk. 19:8). That was radical conversion. What Zacchaeus committed himself to do could not be accomplished that same day. As a process it was going to take some time. But in the presence of Jesus, the turn-around and transformation had come upon him.

What is imperative in relation to military power is that individuals and societies turn from it to full trust in God. Global disarmament correlated with the building of alternative security systems can only be carried out as a step-by-step process over a longer period of time. A breakthrough into that process could possibly come if people of faith everywhere make the turn-around with regard to wealth, weapons, and the resort to war that Zacchaeus made regarding his riches. The rejection of all reliance on military power can proceed only when joined with the rejection of overconsumption and the desolating injustice of prevailing economic structures. These changes would involve huge problems (for example, economic conversion from military production) and would take time to carry out, but the fully redirected collective will in a society would set the new direction. For any country in which such a turn-around does come, undismantled weapons would be analogous to ill-gotten wealth of Zacchaeus that had not yet been returned fourfold.

The gravest weakness in the American Roman Catholic bishops' *Pastoral Letter on War and Peace* is its "strictly conditioned moral acceptance of nuclear deterrence." The most determinative criterion for this acceptance is that "nuclear deterrence should be used as a step on the way toward progressive disarmament."[11] This is somewhat like a young man's saying to himself: "I really must shift from these random sexual encounters into a good marriage. I will from now on engage in such encounters only as a necessary element in the transition to the marriage I hope for." In the biblical ethic and in common experience of life, sexual promiscuity cannot provide a helpful transition toward covenantal marriage. Within the context of a Christian conversion or on his own, the woman chaser must commit himself in a resolute No to promiscuity; and the change that issues from that No can shape a prelude to the desired marriage. As a Christian he would be praying, "Deliver me from this evil."

Since 1945 (and since the bishops' *Pastoral Letter* in 1983), reliance on the nuclear arsenals, however conditional in the wishes of ethical theorists, has been the opposite of transitional means toward progressive disarmament. Even after the close of the Cold War, there is no tenable basis for supposing that such reliance can serve in that desired way. The continuing momentum of militarism around the world is too strong. The one hope politically in this connection is that enough people will come to something like Zacchaeus's decision and the woman chaser's committed No — a giving up on military power, recognition that it is intolerable threat rather than source of security, and determination to do away with something so utterly inhuman. Disciples are to live out and proclaim that dimension of *metanoia*. But that dimension takes form in all sorts of people who do not yet or no longer know the Christ.

The global sense of fatedness, of being driven by forces beyond human power to reverse, gives support to the biblical understanding that humanity cannot save itself and that, without the turn to God, catastrophe does come. God alone can rescue human beings, individually and collectively, "from the evil one." The turn back from doom can come only if multitudes cry out: "Deliver us from being corporate partners in dominating, exploiting, and persecuting the poor. Turn us back from mindlessly degrading the environment. Deliver us from the war system and nuclear evil, from alignment with it, from complicity in it, from perpetrating the ultimate horror. Don't give us over into fearful testing on a devastated planet." Such cries are the embattled transposition of the plea "Thy Rule come!"

Hebrew prophets typically saw themselves as nearly alone in heeding the call of God. No current successor to the prophets needs to see things in that way. God, who gives over into the momentum of nuclear and other follies, has a scattered people, who have been turned around and who, however falteringly, do listen to his present call. This remnant is identifiable, vocal, and growing. The story in Jonah 3 of the repentance of the Ninevites and their rescue from destruction can be set against the intimations that global catastrophe is sure to come. In our present Nineveh as well the incredible could come to pass.

Chapter 10

"ARISE, O LORD!"

I was envious of the arrogant,
when I saw the prosperity of the wicked....

Therefore pride is their necklace;
   violence covers them as a garment.
Their eyes swell out with fatness,
   their hearts overflow with follies.
They scoff and speak with malice;
   loftily they threaten oppression.
They set their mouths against the heavens,
   and their tongue struts through the earth.

Therefore they draw large crowds
   and their words are sipped like water.

—Psalm 73:3, 6–10[1]

The Hebrew question about the wicked flourishing had to do generally, not with criminal elements on the margins of well-ordered society (as in a present-day "law and order" outlook), but with the criminality, the lawlessness, of those who held prevailing power in the society, defied God's will for the harmonious ordering of relationships, and wreaked havoc near and far. In one fashion or another, as Hebrews or as oppressing pagans, the wicked were on top, and they were rich.

The first half of Psalm 73 depicts the correlation between violence and the words of those who perpetrate it. Terrible things are being done, but still more confounding are the arrogant claims, the smooth talk, the cynical justifications of the perpetrators. Most of all with words they continue to win the popular support they need for their vicious exercise of power. "Their tongue struts through the earth." What stands out most in world affairs currently is not the menacing destructive potential lodged in the nuclear arsenals nor the crushing oppression and victimization of a large segment of the human race

146

but rather this strutting of the tongue by which rulers "bestride the narrow world."[2] As in Psalm 73, those with power hold, savor, and exercise it through words. And now too those with this power are "still getting richer" (v. 12 JB).

That articulated domination can extend beyond a populace that laps up the words and beyond those who are its more direct victims. The poet of Psalm 73 surveys the wickedness of the powerful but is dismayed by their continuing success. The triumphant advance of everything he deplores becomes an onslaught upon his faith. All his struggle to be faithful to God remains without any outward confirmation in events. "As for me, my feet had almost stumbled, / my steps had well nigh slipped" (v. 2). The arrogant show by their deeds that they do not reckon with a sovereign God who sees and acts. "And they say, 'How can God know?' " (v. 11). But the psalmist from his contrary perspective has come close to that same conclusion: Those with the upper hand determine and define the way things are. The psalmist, confounded by what is, has yielded grievingly to that actuality and paid the powerholders the compliment of his envy.

Much of the time the dominant mood in the peace and justice movement in various countries is comparable to the despairing protest of the psalmist. Leaders whose policies are based on violence and oppression move from one success to the next. Deception and manipulation seem regularly to win out. Those who resist the Empire are a marginal minority. They have little access to the establishment media. The means at their disposal — especially truth-telling — seem so weak in relation to what they are up against. For the resistance, even little successes so often fade into defeats. And if certain managers of a society lose their hold on power, others continue that exercise of power. Frustration, despondency, and a sense of impotence in the resistance, including the Christian resistance, have as background the secret surrender to the definition of reality projected by those in power. They do, it seems, have the determining say. The poet in Psalm 73 begins with, but then questions, the affirmation, "Truly God is good to the upright, / to those who are pure in heart" (v. 1). Contemporary protesters often find their belief in God overshadowed by the ways political, economic, and military power is wielded in the world. Their field of vision can be largely filled by the ruling structures and personages.

But the psalmist proceeds to describe the extraordinary inner breakthrough that comes for him:

But when I thought how to understand this,
    it seemed to me a wearisome task,
until I went into the sanctuary of God;
    then I perceived their end.
Truly thou dost set them in slippery places;
    thou dost make them fall to ruin.
How they are destroyed in a moment,
    swept away utterly by terrors!
They are like a dream when one awakes,
    on awaking you despise their phantoms.

When my soul was embittered,
    when I was pricked in heart,
I was stupid and ignorant,
    I was like a beast toward thee.
Nevertheless I am continually with thee;
    thou dost hold my right hand.
Thou dost guide me with thy counsel,
    and afterward thou wilt receive me to glory.
Whom have I in heaven but thee?
    And there is nothing upon earth
    that I desire besides thee.
My flesh and my heart may fail,
    but God is the strength of my heart
    and my portion for ever.
                                        (vv. 16–26)

The psalmist is about to give up. But then he thinks of God's people and his place among them (v. 15). He goes into the sanctuary, probably the Temple in Jerusalem, and is overwhelmed there by the reality and nearness of the God of Israel. As Artur Weiser brings out:

It is a Copernican turn which the poet accomplishes in revaluing the former values; he no longer squeezes God and the interpretation of everything that happens into the narrow compass of his own egocentric trains of thought, but conversely seeks to understand and evaluate the realities of human life in the light of the reality of God which takes hold of him and surrounds him in the experience of God's presence (v. 23). It signifies a radical change in man's attitude of mind when he abandons the ground of visible data as the starting-point of his thinking and relies on the invisible reality of God to such a degree that it becomes by faith the unshakable foundation of his seeing and thinking.[3]

God is now seen as in control of human affairs. The ascendancy of those who violate others is only a giddy tottering before their fall. God deals with them and already, so contrary to appearances, has set them on slippery terrain sloping to the precipice. The plunge into ruin that God will surely bring about is seen as already occurring. Those who have so dominated the field of vision are like phantoms from a dream. Their power and their imposed conception of the world are illusion. The word translated "phantoms" in v. 20 ordinarily refers to images of deities. What had seemed most concrete and awesome are mere semblances, apparitions.

The alternatives that Weiser analyzes press upon human beings. People tend to take what impinges on them from the world round about as the starting-point for their outlook on human affairs. Most people simply conform to the impingement of the embracing technological context of living, the images and information presented by the media, the actuality of economic, political, and military power structures. Others resist from the margins of that dominating status quo.

But the contrary possibility is to start with "the reality of God which takes hold of" a person and to understand and evaluate the onslaught of the data of this world in the light of that reality. One then relies "on the invisible reality of God to such a degree that it becomes by faith the unshakable foundation of . . . seeing and thinking." One catches sight of God's ruling and overruling, and all that had seemed so imposing shrinks toward its demise. This God becomes the defining Reality.

"Nevertheless I am continually with thee." To be in the presence of God is what truly has significance and promise. God, who had seemed a do-nothing in relation to the wicked, is now clasping the up-stretched hand of the worshiper to lead and guide. For the psalmist God has become so completely the good he yearns for that even the good things of earthly life are, by comparison, insignificant. The psalmist's communion with God will be brought to glorious fulfilment beyond death. God is his portion, the gift allotted to him, forever (v. 26).

Some may object that the poet turns his back on the grievous injustices around him and retreats into contemplation of his personal relationship with God. The private quest for spiritual exaltation that lifts hands toward heaven but not a finger to help those struck down by violence and oppression is all too common in the world. The poet, however, does not cast off his intense concern about the monstrous wrongs around him. Because God has now become for him the central, determining reality, the psalmist is able to view the wrongs and the perpetrators in a very different way. He does not retreat into a spiritual realm isolated from the world; the realm that is sought moves to right what is wrong in the world. This is no flight into quietistic spirituality but the most radical resistance possible to the claims and dominion of the violent, resistance that centers in recognizing and proclaiming God's works (v. 28).

What is most decisive for Christians in relation to the confusions of the world is that they have eyes spiritually open to see the gracious might of the One who is Lord of history. They are not to seek first justice and peace as imperative autonomous goals but rather the God of biblical faith who in his present and coming Rule establishes justice and peace.

When professing Christians take up revolutionary arms against oppressors, they adopt the means and the definition of power held over them by those oppressors. Or hope may be directed toward "the democratic process" as the way to unseat those who wield power in desolating ways. Yet precisely within that process, the managers of the society are on their chosen ground of control of the media to manipulate the public. But when the foundation of Christian understanding is the reality of God's Rule in history and human lives, disciples see the structures of oppressive power undercut, negated, and about to be demolished by God through what he has done in Jesus Christ. That power no longer impresses. Disciples need to reckon with it as they stand with or are among its victims. Yet they see that power as discredited and destabilized by the incomparably greater power of a righteous, loving God. Prefiguratively they act upon and intimate the overthrow that God is about to accomplish. All barrages of lying words subside, "but the word of our God will stand for ever" (Is. 40:8). Over against that plethora of deceptions stands the *pleroma*, the fullness of God in Jesus (Col. 1:19).

The crowning satisfaction for a tyrant or demagogue is to assess the relative impotence of the opposition. But if an opposition has a very different calculus of power and proceeds in an assurance that its seeming impotence is drawn into the might of God in the struggle, the strutting leader may need to recognize the threatening political significance of this counterposed understanding of reality. Such confidence among the early Christians living under Roman persecution, confidence expressed superlatively in the book of Revelation, baffled and unnerved the imperial authorities. When Christians in our time live out a comparable confidence, imperial authorities are unnerved.

Coming to Power

In peace and justice movements generally, the overriding question is this: How can we muster power sufficient to change abhorrent policies and conditions? Strategies abound. With upswings of activist hopefulness large numbers of people take part in such efforts. But when political breakthroughs do not come, the ranks thin out. Most people who are concerned about such issues remain immobilized, mainly by the feeling that they cannot do anything about the direction of national and world affairs. Those who keep trying contend typically with a keen sense of political powerlessness.

Such powerlessness can seem like an astonishing and anomalous development to persons conditioned by Western thinking about democracy. But in the biblical world and biblical thought, that was a most familiar condition of people, including the people of God. Much in the story of Israel has apparent political impotence as somber background. Paul wrote, "Not many of you ... were powerful, not many were of noble birth" (1 Cor. 1:26). The early Christians were an "internal proletariat"[4] with hardly any access to the central concentrations of political power. Christians in our time should not be surprised or dismayed by their typical lack of political power to change pernicious government policies. They are naturally saddened when all efforts fail to stop the vast poisoning of the environment, the warfare state, the nuclear madness, and sponsorship of Third World oppression. Yet sadness must not impel into resignation or despair. Disciples do not lack access to the central wielding of power. They can have the ear of the sovereign Lord.

If resisters (Christians and others) are the ones who somehow have to stop the imperial hubris, a sense of futility may be appropriate. In the Bible, however, this task belongs to God. Throughout scripture God is looked to as the One who casts down what otherwise appears irresistible. In Isaiah 13:11 God's promise is given: "I will put an end to the pride of the arrogant, / and lay low the haughtiness of the ruthless."

If an international adversary is indeed defying the good, that one and many are already on the slippery slope. People of faith must not rush onto it to do the casting down; for God, even when long delaying, deals most surely with any who place themselves on that terrain. God out of the whirlwind tells Job: "Look on every one that is proud, and bring him low; / and tread down the wicked where they stand" (Job 40:12) — that is to say, "You think you can play God and do what only God can do?" "Just war" and violent revolution try to take on that task. But so do peace and justice movements. When, however, Christians in the resistance really listen to that gracious taunt out of the whirlwind, they can shift from the question, How do we muster sufficient power? to the quite different one, How can we relate expectantly and supportively to God's accomplishing what we cannot?

Psalms 9 and 10, originally one psalm, give a part of the answer to the question how people of faith can relate with expectancy to what God is committed to doing. Here as in Psalm 73 is an outcry and protest before God against terrible injustice.

> He sits in ambush in the villages;
>> in hiding places he murders the innocent.
> His eyes stealthily watch for the hapless,
>> he lurks in secret like a lion in his covert;
> he lurks that he may seize the poor....
> His mouth is filled with cursing and deceit and oppression;
>> under his tongue are mischief and iniquity.
>>> (Ps. 10:8–9, 7)

The images call to mind the Contra incursions in Nicaragua, death squads and official terror in other countries, and those who sponsor such atrocities. Violence proceeds behind a screen of cursing, deceptions, and lies.

The psalmist utters the far more ancient, recurring Hebrew cry, "*Quma Yahweh* — Arise, O Lord!" (9:19; 10:12). God, who has been seated as King over all but in restraint and delay, is called upon to arise, act, and show his saving power.

> Rise up, O Lord; O God, lift up your hand;
>> do not forget the oppressed....
> the helpless commit themselves to you....
> Break the arm [the strength] of the wicked and evildoers.
>> (10:12, 14, 15 NRSV)

The little people of the land are defenseless against the depredations of the violent. They cannot save themselves. They look to God to shatter the might of their adversaries. God hears their entreaty: "'Because the poor are despoiled, because the needy groan, / I will now arise,' says the Lord" (Ps. 12:5). In First World churches it is little recognized that no less than eighty-seven of the psalms express the cry to God of the poor, the victimized, the oppressed.[5] Again and again they utter a plea such as: "Rescue me, O my God, from the hand of the wicked, / from the grasp of the unjust and cruel" (Ps. 71:4 NRSV).

Jesus can say, "Blessed are you poor" (Lk. 6:20), because of their characteristic attitude of dependent trust. In the Hebrew scriptures the poor are those wrongfully deprived who, precisely because they are without the resources or means to change their lot, look to Yahweh, who stands in special relation to them as defender. What they have and who they are provide them with no basis for trust and confidence. Inferior and abjectly dependent within the society, they shift that dependence toward Yahweh. They hope in God. Under oppression and in exile Israel corporately becomes the poor who in their extreme need look to God. For Jesus, it is not simply the outwardly poor who are blessed (as the Lukan wording of the beatitude might be taken to mean) but those who in such circumstances (and in keeping with the Hebrew connotations of the term) trust God to bring them through.

Disciples recognize an ascendancy of wickedness that they cannot topple. They become the poor who see that they lack the means for doing what needs to be done and who therefore in their powerlessness look to God. What they do most decisively is to rely on God's acting. That stance is what the waiting Habakkuk summarized: "The righteous live by their faith" (2:4 NRSV). In answer to their doubt, Christians experience with Israel: "See, the Lord's hand is not too short to save, / nor his ear too dull to hear" (Is. 59:1 NRSV).

With psalmists and prophets in the darkest periods of Israel's history, disciples cry out to the sovereign One who is mightier than the reign of evil: "Rise up, come to our help! / Deliver us for the sake of thy steadfast love!" (Ps. 44:26). They pray that God cast down the hubris of the nations and thwart infernal schemes of leaders: "Arise, O Lord! confront them, overthrow them!" (Ps. 17:13). "Scatter the peoples who delight in war" (Ps. 68:30). Disciples implore God, "Save all the oppressed of the earth" (Ps. 76:9). This plea "Arise, O Lord!" is not the totality of their response, as if they then have nothing more to do; rather it expresses what should be the determinative outlook for all else that they do in this regard. They act, believing that the seemingly absurd inadequacy of their acting can be taken into the adequacy of what God is doing. Disciples listen for how their acting can be drawn into God's.

Only with trembling should First World Christians utter the plea "Arise, O Lord!" They are not free of the hubris. For each of them too imperialism has been captivating. Immensities of judgment that they dimly foresee press also upon them. With Habakkuk they must plead, "In wrath remember mercy" (3:2).

Some may object that the prayer "Arise, O Lord!" is directed against persons wielding power and is therefore contrary to Christian love and to the command to pray for rulers (1 Tim. 2:2). However, the plea that God arise is not really aimed against persons but against their misuse of power. Psalm 10 has the remarkable intercession, "seek out his wickedness till thou find none" (v. 15): Confront it, expose it, overwhelm it until the evildoer is freed from it. And this is much of what characteristically happens in conversion. As the entreaty of Psalm 83:16 puts it, "Fill their faces with shame, / that they may seek thy name, O Lord."

Praying for Vindication

Jesus in Luke 18:1–8 points to just the sort of praying found in Psalm 10. In the parable the poor widow keeps coming before the godless judge with her plea "Vindicate me against my adversary" (v. 3). Finally, so as not to be bothered further, the judge acts to give the widow her just rights. How much more (Jesus wants his disciples to understand) will God act on behalf of those who bring their pleas to him: "And will not God vindicate his elect, who cry to him day and night? Will he delay long over them? I tell you, he will vindicate them speedily" (vv. 7–8). Much from the psalms is drawn into those words. In spite of delays, God's promise that he does act on behalf of those who cry out to him was fulfilled again and again in the life of the Hebrew people corporately and individually. Jesus reaffirmed God's promise. This, he said, God's people can confidently expect.

The translation given in the Authorized Version has the widow saying, "Avenge me of mine adversary." In the common understanding, this would refer to desired revenge to be carried out by a judicial authority. In an important study of the Hebrew root NQM, which lies behind the Greek verb *ekdikeo* of Luke 18:3–8, George Mendenhall demonstrates that the texts with a word from this root are generally misunderstood because of the usual connotations of the words *vengeance* and *avenge*, used in translation. He shows that in the prebiblical Amarna letters the "root NQM signifies the executive exercise of power by the highest legitimate political authority for the protection of his own subjects." The uses in the Hebrew scriptures "strongly indicate that they have to do with the use of power against the enemies of that power, *whether internal or external.*" Such opposition "may involve either action against the authority itself, or actions consisting of past attacks on those under the protection of the sovereign." Ultimately, only Yahweh has legitimate power and sovereignty. Some uses of the root are to be seen as "defensive vindication"; others, as "punitive vindication." "Uncertainties of interpretation make it difficult to say in specific cases whether the action is defensive or punitive. After all, the rescue of one party from another in a conflict almost inevitably involves the use of force against the attacker, and therefore the defensive and the punitive aspects are merely two sides of the same coin." Mendenhall writes of Isaiah 35:4:

The usual translation, "Behold, your God will come with vengeance, with the recompense of God. He will come and save you," is highly jarring and completely inaccurate. It is a description of the expected deliverance from a long-continued situation of want and misery by the "setting right an unjust situation" or by remedying or relieving suffering. There is no hint in the poem of satisfaction in the form of seeing opponents or oppressors punished or exterminated.[6]

Commenting on stories in 1 Samuel 24 and 26, Mendenhall develops a most significant point: "Such an appeal to the executive defensive vindication of Yahweh excludes self-help on the part of David. Such actions in self-help constitute a claim to an imperium on the part of the individual which is incompatible with and actually rebellious against the Imperium of Yahweh."[7] Wronged individuals or the Hebrew people must not take matters into their own hands but rather must look to Yahweh to set things right. Those who resort to violence and war try on their own to bring about vindication. By implication they give No as their answer to God's question, "Or have I no power to deliver?" (Is. 50:2).

Jesus drew upon Psalm 37:11 for the saying, "the meek...shall inherit the earth" (Mt. 5:5). Throughout that psalm "the meek" are the poor and oppressed who wait on the Lord for vindication, rather than seeking to accomplish it on their own. The psalmist had in view any such "one who is utterly humbled before the majesty of God, that is, one who has become willing to let God alone be sovereign."[8] At the End and before, God vindicates those who do not presume to vindicate themselves. Vindication by God is what Jesus promised in the Beatitudes.

Empire is set inevitably against the Imperium of God. Indeed, Mendenhall writes: "In all of these usages from Jeremiah to 2 Isaiah one receives the very strong impression that the new emphasis upon the Imperium of God led to the conclusion that all political sovereignty stood under divine condemnation as an enormity that competed with God himself."[9]

Within a society and its legal structures, the government has a measure of delegated authority to punish those who do wrong (Rom. 13:4). The widow naturally turned to the judge as an agent of the governmental authority to redress the wrongs done her. But actually he was a quite unreliable and callous functionary. Where judicial systems do indeed serve to bring vindication to those who have been unjustly treated, they have their provisional place under God. Yet governments all too often do terrible things to groups and individuals within their domain, connive with criminal gangs, and, like the unjust judge early in the parable, do not act to redress wrongs against those victimized within the society. "Sovereign" governments do not recognize a higher authority or a shared and subordinating context of law. Through its armed forces, multifaceted projection of power, and war, each government as imperium seeks to get what it can and vindicate itself. All this is rebellion against God's Imperium and God's acting to vindicate. But God, sovereign over history, causes any such avenger to cease (Ps. 8:3). This Judge hears the cries of all those unjustly dealt with by the powerholders and judiciaries of this earth. And God's people pray, "Your Imperium come!"

On Not Taking Matters into Human Hands

In some (mostly earlier) passages of the Hebrew Bible, God is understood as delegating to his people or their leaders the execution of his punitive vindicating Rule. Church people who try to make God's self-disclosure in Jesus Christ conform to the Hebrew scriptures commonly believe that the resort to war by Christians and other compatriots amounts to taking up a task delegated by God. But for one thing, no nation or leader now receives a direct command by God to wage a particular war, though a vague equivalent of that is of course typically claimed. If there is no contemporary parallel to those ancient commands as recorded in the narratives, the Hebrew scriptures too provide no basis for going to war. Apart from such authorization (if indeed it was ever given to the Hebrews), waging war is upstart human imperium set against God's Rule. Jesus, in any case, makes very clear that followers of his, like their Lord in his earthly ministry, have no such assignment from God.

In the parable of the weeds among the wheat (Mt. 13:24–30), Jesus gave an answer with regard to what is wrong in the world: "An enemy has done this" (v. 28). But the wronged master in the story instructs the servants not to pull out the wheat-like weeds lest "you root up the wheat along with them" (v. 29). An underlying question has to do with moving forcibly to eliminate what is set against the good. That initiative is forbidden because it inevitably involves destroying so much that is good — as most notably in war. Yet in the coming harvest the sovereign Lord will remove all growth of evil, as humans by presumptuous violence cannot.

Jesus instructs disciples to pray God's blessing upon people who do terrible things to them. Followers of his must bless, not curse, enemies. Paul wrote to Christians in the imperial city: "Bless those who persecute you; bless and do not curse them.... Repay no one evil for evil.... Beloved, never seek your own vindication but leave it to the wrath of God; for it is written, 'Vindicating rule is mine, I will repay, says the Lord' " (Rom. 12:14, 17, 19, altered[10]). The Hebrews had been commanded, "You shall not take vindication into your own hands or bear any grudge against your own people" (Lev. 19:18, altered). Paul in this passage points twice to "all [human beings]": "take thought for what is noble in the sight of all.... so far as it depends on you, live peaceably with all" (vv. 17, 18). By this usage he indicates that the ancient prohibition holds for relations with all humans.

Disciples are not to occupy the terrain of retribution with their own attempts to carry it out, but are to step back (literally, "give space") for God's acting across that terrain. They are drawn into the outlook of the Servant of Yahweh, Jesus: "He who vindicates me is near" (Is. 50:8). In leaving the matter to God, they dare not wish or pray that the worst come upon their enemies. A number of psalms do have pleas that crushing judgment fall upon enemies. (Even these outcries express, though quite inadequately, the hunger and thirst to see right prevail.) Christians must not direct such pleas against anyone. To pray for God's blessing upon enemies and to give place to his wrath are not opposites but go together. "If favor is shown to the wicked, / he does not learn righteousness / ... and does not see the majesty of the Lord" (Is. 26:10). What is really the worst for those enemies is their being caught up in the evil they are doing. When God in judgment defeats and brings down that worst, those who have been doing the evil are given a way out of it. God's vindicating Rule moves to rescue all victims and victimizers from their entrapments.

The context of the first line of Deuteronomy 32:35, quoted in Romans 12:19 (and Heb. 10:30), needs to be kept in view. After an indictment of Israel for its terrible unfaithfulness, God's further warning is given (vv. 35–36, altered):

Vindicating rule is mine, and recompense,
    for the time when their foot shall slip [cf. "slippery places"];
for the day of their calamity is at hand,
    and their doom comes swiftly.
For the Lord will vindicate his people
    and have compassion on his servants,
when he sees that their power is gone. . . .

Quite clearly in this passage, vindicating Rule is defensive and punitive. The word for *recompense* (*shillem*) is from the same root as *shalom*.
When the wholeness of ordering under God's Rule is broken apart,
that jagged opposite of shalom is not allowed to stand indefinitely
in its fractional autonomy; it receives its negative rounding out,
God's recompense. God draws into shalom completion or thwarts
in fulfilled defeat.

Jesus let come upon him the attempt of the establishment leaders to carry out God's verdict against sin. Their presumption and
everything in history that has moved parallel to it fell upon him.
Through the total mistakenness of that attempt, God accomplished
what they failed to do.

The death and rising of Jesus was in fact God's supreme act of
vindication. At the cross God met and overwhelmed the ultimate
human challenge to his gracious sovereignty. Condemned and executed as a criminal, Jesus was then shown to be utterly in the right.
The powers arrayed against him, against all humanity, against God,
lost out on the third day. The One who had seemed most impotent
sat down "at the right hand of Power" (Mt. 26:64). Yet that vindication and that victory over those powers remain mostly hidden,
awaiting the Day when they will be made resplendently manifest
to every human eye. He who did not turn to violence for defending
himself and his followers brought into being a new people who in
their defenselessness and ill repute live out of that vindication and
long for the Day.

God's love of enemies is the heart of the Gospel: "While we were
enemies, we were reconciled to God by the death of his Son" (Rom.
5:10). Jesus' imperative to love all enemies is at the heart of discipleship. In his call it has been the greatest *skandalon* (stumbling-block).
But that in life which is most difficult to do becomes somewhat less
so when it is seen as imitation of God's way with enemies, that is,
with every human being. To take to oneself the hate and violence of
others and still show them love as Jesus did can evoke that which
Jesus, more than any other, has called forth: the great change of heart
in enemies. "No, 'if your enemy is hungry, feed him; if he is thirsty,

give him drink; for by so doing you will heap burning coals upon his head' " (Rom. 12:20).[11] If "burning coals" means pangs of shame and remorse (as most commentators hold), then what disciples hope for when showing kindness to enemies is what God aims at in judgment.

In universal human experience, revenge does not of itself lead enemies to conversion but works against it. No human being is righteous in revenge. No revenge brings forth the right; human "anger does not achieve God's righteous purposes" (Jas. 1:20 TEV). But God's judgments are directed toward the righting of what is wrong and the rescue of those who are lost. Jesus bore the judgment against evildoers called for in some of the psalms, judgment that they (and all humans) have indeed deserved. Because God says, "Vindication is mine," and has accomplished that most of all in Jesus, those outcries in the psalms are replaced by prayer that God will bless one's enemies. The plea that God act to set things right keeps in view the hearts and minds of enemies. Such prayer implies the understanding stated by C. E. B. Cranfield: "The wrath of God which was revealed in its full awfulness in Gethsemane and on Golgotha [is] the wrath of the altogether holy and loving God. To make way for this wrath is to recognize that one deserves oneself to be wholly consumed by it, but that the Son of God Himself has borne it for one: it is therefore to have the vengeful sword dashed from one's hands."[12] Christians must not treat enemies in ways that go against prayer for them and the Gospel's coming to them.

Through the Hebrew generations the people of God prayed, "Arise, O Lord!" The central fulfilment of what they waited for so long came on the first Easter morning. "The Lord has risen indeed!" (Lk. 24:34). "He arose, / With a mighty triumph o'er his foes."[13] God has raised the poor — first of all Jesus — from the dust (Ps. 113:7).

If Christians truly await the consummation of what has been revealed in Jesus, they see its adequacy as ground for all their living. Thus in situations of conflict and dehumanizing injustice, disciples seek to be filled with what God had done and continues to do in Jesus. They know nothing of any imperative to "fill in" now for God's sovereignty by modes of action contrary to God's acting in him. To move in directions opposite to that is to go against not only the ethic but the total *work* of Jesus and its adequacy for individuals and for history. When church people go to war, supposedly to defend those under attack and to stop evil, this is within a situational atheism that sees no God who is doing or about to do what is so desperately needed. Disciples understand that in Jesus God has done that which was and is most of all needed — even when for jeopardy or victimization no rescuing action seems evident. The God whom they look to is still the "author of saving acts throughout the earth" (Ps. 74:12 JB). As disciples contemplate what God has done in the central saving act, they discern derivative acts in this time. God saves through the compassion, the sharing, the solidarity, the risk-taking, the resistance, and the martyr witness of those who are his.

In the parable of the unjust judge, Jesus recognizes the element of God's delay: The elect cry to him day and night. The recurrent Hebrew query "How long, O Lord?" continues. Christians may find themselves echoing that cry. They may have difficulty seeing fulfilment of Jesus' promise, "I tell you, he will vindicate them speedily." Jesus lived and died God's acting to set things right in the world. His disciples have become agents of *his* vindication. In Jesus God does come soon, quickly, suddenly to vindicate all who cry out to him. This coming continues hour by hour around the planet and moves toward the instant when the "How long?" of God's people will receive its full answer.

Chapter 11

ARMAGEDDON MIRAGE

The sixth angel poured his bowl on the great river Euphrates, and its water was dried up, to prepare the way for the kings from the east. And I saw, issuing from the mouth of the dragon and from the mouth of the beast and from the mouth of the false prophet, three foul spirits like frogs; for they are demonic spirits, performing signs, who go abroad to the kings of the whole world, to assemble them for battle on the great day of God the Almighty.... And they assembled them at the place which is called in Hebrew Armageddon.

—Revelation 16:12–14, 16

In the Hebrew prophets there is a motif of a culminating assault by the nations on Jerusalem and their total defeat by Yahweh (Is. 17:12–14; 29:5–8; Ez. 38–39; Joel 3:1–3, 9–16; Mic. 4:11–13; Zech. 12:1–9; 14:1–5, 12–15). The motif draws upon a still older tradition vividly expressed in Psalms 46, 48, and 76. This assault is depicted in Revelation 16:12–16; 19:11–21; 20:7–10. Revelation 16:16 has the single biblical occurrence of the word *Armageddon*.

Shortly before the Bull Moose convention of 1912, Theodore Roosevelt shouted some words that could be taken as a keynote cry in the twentieth century: "We stand at Armageddon and we battle for the Lord." Though the immediate reference was to Republican politics, Roosevelt had the same fiery attitude in his fight to draw the United States into World War I. In early April 1917 this attitude swept through the country. A sense of being in climactic struggle against monstrous evil, identified in enemy nations, has merged with a secularization of the antichrist motif to become a main factor shaping societies during the twentieth century.

Especially in U.S. churches there is a widespread Armageddon ideology, which presses this scriptural motif into the service of militarist nationalism.[1] Prophecy specialists have long predicted that Russia will be the leader of a coalition of nations that will invade Palestine from the north and deploy its forces on the plain next to Mount Megiddo (a geographical decoding of Armageddon); those armies are then to be annihilated. In fanciful speculation without basis in reputable biblical scholarship, "Meshech" (the Mushki of Asia Minor) in Ezekiel 38:2 is said to be Moscow; and *rosh*, Hebrew for *head, chief*, in the same verse, is taken to be Russia.[2] All the dark pictures of the Soviet Union that were standard fare in the Western media, such as its supposed aggressive expansionism, have been thought to receive biblical confirmation in these prophecies. The Soviet Union/Russia has been seen as the chief adversary, not simply of the United States and Western Europe, but of God the Almighty in the final military confrontation of history. The nuclear weapons of the United States (and of its allies) have been widely regarded as the means God will use to annihilate the coalition forces. The ideology has a continuing momentum, even when Russia is no longer officially viewed as the beastly adversary.[3] Though it has less influence at present, international developments that could make it seem more relevant again may bring its resurgence.

This Armageddon ideology has been very much in the minds of some U.S. leaders who have had the power to bring on a nuclear end of the world. Ronald Reagan, who frequently referred to Armageddon, said: "This could be the generation that sees Armageddon. This very well could be that generation." According to Jerry Falwell, Reagan told him, "Jerry, I sometimes believe we're heading very fast for Armageddon right now." In 1983 President Reagan invited Falwell to briefings of the National Security Council to discuss plans for thermonuclear war with the Soviet Union. Reagan also approved of having Hal Lindsey, author of *The Late Great Planet Earth*, give a lecture on nuclear war with the Soviet Union to Pentagon strategists.[4] It is still likely that some of the men who have the power to unleash the nuclear fury view that action through the lens of this Armageddon ideology, which makes it "an implementation of the return of Christ to earth."[5] Even if such warriors are less certain about the adversary, the headiness of the ideology remains. The U.S. nuclear arsenals and those who control them are thus given a messianic role not just of securing a continuing provisional salvation for the world but also of helping to usher in the return of Christ. Through the centuries of Christendom/post-Christendom the military forces of one's own country have been commonly seen as allied with God's Kingdom and purposes on earth. But never before (except for a few ephemeral messianisms) have they been given quite this lofty a part in God's regimen for the world. In the extreme tension of some military confrontation, those in high places and at the control panels who suppose they know so much about God's plan for the End of history could decide that they were apprehending God's will with regard to the timing of their part.

Criticisms of this Armageddon ideology have nearly always been developed in terms of the danger it poses; and it is summarily dismissed as fundamentalist obscurantism contrary to the main tenets of the Judaeo-Christian heritage. Needed, however, is a more basic critique that gives serious consideration, first of all, to the biblical passages that the Armageddon speculators appeal to.

In these passages the nations generally — "the kings of the whole world" (Rev. 16:14) — join in the offensive. To identify one superpower and a quite limited coalition of nations as veering into final collision with God has all along been a crude mistake. "All the nations" (Joel 3:12; Zech. 12:3; 14:2) are viewed as engaging in that assault. Revelation 20:8 pictures Satan as coming "out to deceive the nations which are at the four corners of the earth, that is, Gog and Magog, to gather them for battle." In this recasting of the prophecy given in Ezekiel 38–39, the totality of rebel nations is seen as Gog and Magog. Gog therefore must not be identified as a single nation (Russia) or its leader. Prophecy specialists of the religious right claim that the United States and its allies at the time will be on God's side for the battle. But in the Armageddon imagery God does not have nations on his side.

The biblical images of the uprising of the nations need not and should not be understood with the geographic literalness that ordinarily characterizes pop apocalyptism.

Certain oracles in Isaiah, most notably 17:12–14, have a breadth of vision encompassing far more than the contemporary Assyrian threat:

> Ah, the thunder of many peoples,
> > they thunder like the thundering of the sea!
> Ah, the roar of nations,
> > they roar like the roaring of mighty waters!
> The nations roar like the roaring of many waters,
> > but he will rebuke them, and they will flee far away,
> chased like chaff on the mountains before the wind
> > and whirling dust before the storm.
> At evening time, behold, terror!
> > Before morning, they are no more!
> This is the portion of those who despoil us,
> > and the lot of those who plunder us.

As von Rad comments, "Oddly enough, the nations here spoken of are not historically determinable; they appear rather as a formless, surging mass completely without political configuration."[6] The same

applies to the picture of the nations in all the passages being considered (thus Psalm 46:6: "The nations rage, the kingdoms totter; / he
utters his voice, the earth melts"). All of history's dark side finds
representation in these images, as does all of God's sovereign action against that darkness. In spite of the immensity of their chaotic
thundering, the nations are as nothing before God when he speaks
his word against them. In the brief night of God's judgment those
phantoms are swept away.

In the Hebrew story Israel, Judah, and Jerusalem were attacked
one time after another. The passages about a culminating assault
would initially have been understood in a geographical way. However, as has been shown, Jerusalem as a habitation in Palestine was
for the apostolic church no longer a focus of spiritual attention. When
Paul quotes Isaiah 28:16, "Behold I am laying in Zion a stone that will
make men stumble" (Rom. 9:33), the stone, already figurative in the
prophecy, is located in a spiritual Zion. Not the present Jerusalem,
but "the Jerusalem above . . . is our mother" (Gal. 4:25, 26). In Revelation 20:9 the attacking nations surround "the camp of the saints
and the beloved city." But this most certainly does not mean that
the Christians of the world will come together in a literal military
encampment. (Revelation is a book of symbols and metaphors; it is
"an allegory of God and of his work."[7]) Yet in spiritual encampment
and as citizens of the nongeographical city of God they are together
and well defended. The rebel nations come together, not for a final
invasion of Palestine, but for concerted global attack (throughout history) on the people of God wherever they are. As Joachim Jeremias
explains, Armageddon "is thus the mountain of the world which
as the place of assembly of hostile forces is the counterpart of the
mountain of God in Hb. 12:22 ff."[8]

*Even if it were correct to hold that an impending global war will be
the battle of Armageddon, the attitudes and policies that take the world in
that direction are set against the God of biblical revelation, and Christians,
rather than going along with these, must resist them.* That nuclear horror
would come as a more extensive revolt of the nations against the
love and sovereignty of God the Creator and Redeemer than any
previous event. To go along with the forces that could bring that
culmination is already to participate in that assault against God and
God's people. It is to rally with the Armageddon hosts.

Any who align themselves with the nuclear arsenals play with the
power to end history. Church people who seek to give that power an
apocalyptic Christian basis and justification magnify the affront to
God's sovereignty. That sort of perspective goes against everything

the apostolic scriptures say about the Messianic community under the Lordship of Jesus Christ. This community knows nothing of any assignment from God to take part in bringing history to a cataclysmic end. Those who by assent or direct involvement are prepared to do what could bring on the desolation or extinction of human life on this planet are far from understanding the God of Jesus Christ.

According to a widely held conjecture about the motives of Judas Iscariot, he hoped through the betrayal to force Jesus' hand for some seizure of power. Jewish revolutionaries in the first and second revolts against Rome were convinced that they would evoke God's intervention to give them victory. They were of course not saying that they would compel God to do what they expected of him. But their way of proceeding amounted to that. Current apocalyptic militarists are quite similar in stance to those revolutionaries and that conjectural Judas. They think they know enough about the purposes and designs of God that they can prepare for and engage in the violence that will come as necessitating prelude to God's climactic intervention. Such presumption has again and again been shattered.

A related approach (already scrutinized in chapter 9) asserts that nuclear Armageddon is part of God's plan and will for the end of the world. However, as viewed in the texts about the uprising, the rebel nations do not fulfil the will of God, but move madly against it, and are vanquished in the attempt. Armageddon is not what God wants of the nations. Satan, not God's word in Jesus Christ, draws them to this (Rev. 20:7–8). Salient throughout history is an Armageddon process, the revolt of the nations against God and God's Messiah (Ps. 2; Acts 4:24–30). Yet even that revolt subserves and yields to the fulfilment of God's will. Looking to the God revealed to Israel and in Jesus, Christians can believe this even for the crazed collective will that is taking the world toward cataclysm.

In scripture the nations have their rebel plans; God has his well-deliberated plan for bringing the nations into submission. In a battle a general considers what the opposing forces are doing and are likely to do and devises his strategy accordingly. But the resistance on the other side is not of the general's doing and does not have his backing. So it is with God, whose chief means is totally unlike that of a general. In accordance with God's plan Jesus was crucified and was then raised from the dead (Acts 2:23; 4:28; Eph. 1:10–12). God's soon-to-be-completed victory over all opposition comes from that Midpoint event. "Man's evil planning has already been encircled by God's superior plan."[9]

Joel 3:10, 12 does give an ironic call by God:

Beat your plowshares into swords,
  and your pruning hooks into spears....
Let the nations bestir themselves
  and come up to the valley of Jehoshaphat [Yahweh shall
      judge];
for there I will sit to judge
  all the nations round about.

This, however, is God's taunting challenge to combat directed at
those intent on fighting against him: "Go ahead with what you are
determined to do, for in your doing that you move right into the
total defeat I bring upon you." In this fashion God does assemble
the nations (Mic. 4:12; Zeph. 3:8; Zech. 14:2). That "plowshares into
swords" is not in the least a biblical justification for military buildup,
though it is sometimes misused as that. Rather, it is entrapment in the
supreme folly of fighting against God. Ironically, those who suppose
they would be executing God's judgment in a nuclear holocaust are
correct. But they would not be acting from God's side. Rather, in
the horror of strike and counterstrike, they would be in that other
divided, self-destroying side that brings such judgment upon itself.

"At evening time, behold, terror! / Before morning, they [the
nations] are no more!" (Is. 17:14). Such is our nuclearized world
that what seems a hyperbolic image for the transitoriness of power
could be actualized as vast smouldering wasteland, and quite literally within that time frame. Within the hours of one night the terror
wielded could become the terror experienced. The threat of that,
whether reduced or increasing, will remain as long as those weapons
are held in readiness. The continuing possibility of that global collapse intimates the magnitude and scope of God's judgment hanging
over the nations.

*In these passages the attacking hosts are not defeated by an opposing al-
liance or Jewish military prowess but by the action of God. This is especially
clear in Ezekiel 38:18–39:6; Revelation 19:11–21; 20:7–10. No righteous
human warriors vanquish the enemy or are even in view.*[10] "The nations
...marched up over the broad earth and surrounded the camp of
the saints and the beloved city; but fire came down from heaven and
consumed them" (Rev. 20:8, 9).[11] "The name by which he is called
is The Word of God.... From his mouth issues a sharp sword with
which to smite the nations" (Rev. 19:13, 15). Such passages describe
the revolt of the nations throughout history, seen in terms of its ter-
minus and of God's consummate victory over them. This victory is
intimated by the recurrent collapse of nations and is grounded in the
triumph of Jesus over the powers that crucified him.

That sword is Jesus' spoken and written word that smites the insurgent nations and vanquishes all that vaunts itself against him. According to John 12:47–48 (NRSV), Jesus says about judgment: "I do not judge anyone who hears my words and does not keep them, for I came not to judge the world, but to save the world. The one who rejects me and does not receive my word has a judge; on the last day the word that I have spoken will serve as judge." Jesus came as God's Word set in starkest contrast to the ways of the nations. When Jesus warned, "all who take the sword will perish by the sword," that word became a part of the edge of the sword that issues from his mouth. When individuals and groups defy the word of Jesus, they are smitten by it. That smiting of all opposition remains mostly hidden, but at the End it will demolish the final assault of the nations.

This motif of God's vanquishing the nations has within it this imperative: Turn from all reliance on military measures and power strategies; trust in God alone to bring deliverance and the new era of peace. Thus, the intent central in the motif is the opposite of the dynamic in the militaristic Armageddon ideology of the religious right and in the justifications of warmaking that have dominated the churches since Constantine.

Isaiah proclaimed that imperative to a populace faced with the grim threat of vastly superior Assyrian military power. In one period he saw the Assyrians as the instrument of God's wrath upon Judah, denounced the maneuvers for seeking independence from Assyria, counseled surrender, and prophesied disaster for rejection of God's command (1:4–9; 5:26–30; 28:14–22; 30:1–17; 31:1–3). But later, with Sennacherib and the Assyrian army advancing toward Jerusalem, Isaiah proclaimed, as God's promise, that the city would not be taken or even besieged and that Yahweh would overwhelm the invaders. The people were to desist from all military and political efforts and await God's deliverance (2 Kings 19 [Is. 37]; Is. 14:24–27; 31:4–9). In the biblical account the Assyrians were routed without a Jewish sword being drawn, and Sennacherib returned to Nineveh and death by assassination (2 Kings 19:35–37=Is. 37:36–38). God, who quite alone had delivered the Hebrews from the Egyptians and made of them a nation, had again shown himself able to rescue. With this deliverance from Sennacherib and the Assyrian host as a paradigm, faithful Jews looked ahead still more expectantly to a comparable eschatological quelling of all the nations. In that as well, Jewish military capability could have no role at all and needed to give way to waiting in faith and hope for God to act.

However, Isaiah's proclamation of God's promise in a specific situation, the older tradition behind it, and the miraculous deliverance that did come were later taken as basis for the dogma of the inviolability of Jerusalem: The city could not be captured; God would intervene to prevent that. Jeremiah, urging surrender to the Babylonians, had to combat this view, held by leaders who took it as a warrant to pursue their own political and military efforts as energetically as possible. This conviction about the inviolability of Jerusalem also undergirded the Jewish revolt against the Romans in A.D. 68–70. In both periods Jewish leaders took that earlier promise of inviolability as God's immutable commitment to deliver the city; they separated it from the complete trust in God upon which, according to Isaiah, God's deliverance is contingent. Similarly in the characteristic outlook of the religious right, a seeming reliance on God's anticipated intervention becomes an adjunct to gigantic political and military enterprises. To preach Armageddon and promote military buildup is the opposite of trusting in God alone to bring the great deliverance.

Taken together, the passages speak of an inviolability of Jerusalem that is spiritual and eschatological rather than geographic and military. Jesus recast the promise: "The powers of the underworld shall not overcome" the church (Mt. 16:18), not even in their culminating assault.[12] This church of Jesus Christ, assailed, under siege, so near defeat, stands nonetheless, by the encompassing might of its Lord, invincible.

In this motif the nations are seen as transient, deluded, and about to be swept away "like chaff on the mountains before the wind" (Is. 17:13). Christians who hold this view cannot take the preservation of the nation they happen to reside in as their most overriding concern. One's personal security cannot be sought in "national security" if one's nation is seen as about to disintegrate under the impending judgment of God. In this biblical understanding, the nation does not count for that much, does not loom that large except in its doomed rebellion, and is not the locus of one's concern for inviolability. A Christian identifies not with the nation but with the people of God wherever they are as they prefigure the coming unity of humankind.

The nations, though, are to be liberated from their own rebel entrapments into the global symphony of praising God. "Chaff" and "they are no more" do not give the full ending of their part of the story. All that is against God vanishes in the swirl of judgment, but all that can be redeemed is drawn into the New City. The assault by the nations on the city of God gives way to pilgrimage there: "Come, let us go up to the mountain of the Lord" (Is. 2:3). "Then every one that survives of all the nations that have come against Jerusalem shall go up year after year to worship the King, the Lord of hosts" (Zech. 14:16). The previously insurgent "kings of the earth shall bring their glory into" the city (Rev. 21:24). The goal of Jesus' Great Commission that all nations be drawn into discipleship to him (Mt. 28:19) is reached.

Psalm 110, which has some elements of the Armageddon motif, is the passage in the Hebrew Bible most often quoted in the apostolic scriptures. Jesus Christ was seen as recipient of Yahweh's promise: "Sit at my right hand, / till I make your enemies your footstool" (v. 1, quoted in Acts 2:34; 1 Cor. 15:25; Heb. 1:13; 10:12–13). All rebellion is to be vanquished — because of who Jesus was and is. And *footstool* is a hopeful image: Groupings that had kept their defiant distance are to be brought near into the kingly use of God's Anointed One.

Chapter 12

THE POLITICS
OF THE HILLTOP CITY

The question of whether theology, my private theology, just as much as the public theology of the church, serves the radical and total character of the attack of the gospel on the reality of the *status quo* or instead blunts it, domesticates it, and renders it harmless — that is the criterion of all Christian theology.

—Helmut Gollwitzer[1]

In the original Jewish context the choice for or against Jesus was in part a choice between opposing directions for the society. Through the centuries and in every society this has continued to be the case for all who have been confronted by his message. Jesus was calling all Israel to turn to him and his way.[2] If the chicks had been willing to be gathered under his wings (Mt. 23:37), a new spiritual-political entity would have emerged, a Kingdom unlike all others yet in their midst. But a short time later such an entity, without the King visible, did come into being.

The Jews who became disciples before and soon after Jesus' death were, representatively for Israel, choosing Jesus' way. They remained a rather small minority. Their choice could not set the direction for Israel in its entirety. As a community within the wider unconverted society, they were seeking to live out the way into which God through Jesus had called all the people. In every time and place this should be the stance of those who are Christ's. Their decision for Jesus Christ includes the understanding that the wider society, indeed the whole world, must turn around to go Christ's way. They do not have it within their power to bring about this turn-around, but in their lives and community they strive to embody and attest God's will for the world as a whole.

Jesus was calling his fellow Jews to a transforming way of living their lives together. He was saying that this way could be entered into then and there in Palestine. But there was not the wider corporate readiness to turn to Jesus and his way. The absence of that has shaped all later periods in all parts of the world. Still, his perspective for the society around him gives indication that societies now could enter into this way, if there would be the will for it. Complete living out of this way is not an earthly possibility for larger groupings or even for individuals; but entering into it and striving to live it through the empowerment of his Spirit most certainly are. This striving decisively characterizes those who go with Jesus as his people.

The Messianic City as Counter-reality

Each nation inculcates traditions and a history about its origins, founding, times of deliverance, and role in the world. School children are taught all this for their particular country. The societal shaping of minds and of the common mind continues throughout each citizen's life. Most citizens have learned well the lesson that fighting (*killing* is not mentioned) and sacrificial dying is what has given them their "freedom."

Disciples of Jesus need not stand fully outside the nationally cherished history. But it is not for them the determinative history. It is far from primary for their understanding of who they are in the world. They claim another history, a very different founding and winning of freedom — in the coming and ministry of Jesus, the upper room, his passion and crucifixion, his rising from the dead, the mission and proclamation of the apostolic church, and the strands of faith and obedience through the centuries.

Generation after generation, believing Jews have cherished the personal understanding: I was delivered out of Egypt; I was in the corporateness of what was then led out. Similar to a faithful Jew, a Christian can say: What was done in the Gospel beginning was done for me and toward me; through God's intention for me I was already a participant then. The Messianic community is "a chosen race, a royal priesthood, a holy nation, God's own people" (1 Pet. 2:9) with this contrary history. The story of Israel as source and preparation for what fulfilled it is also theirs. Disciples do not ignore the exalted history of the nation in which they reside; but in the light of the history that is constitutive for them, they discern for that relatively alien history what they can view positively and what negatively. In contrast to the nation's current making of history, derivative from its earlier, largely misguided history, they seek to live out a transformation of human life derivative from the history that comes to them in the revelation of Jesus Christ and in his risen presence.

With modifications and refinements (as in Reinhold Niebuhr), the Constantinian stance with regard to the alliance of government and church is still dominant in most countries of what had been Christendom. This stance can be pictured as that of seeking political leverage: taking the levers of political power or exerting leverage on powerholders. In such a social ethic, relatively good people take on the management of the society, basically on the terms it sets, and seek to do better at this than bad powerholders would have done. Among the oppressed and in much liberation theology, revolutionary violence is turned to as the necessary means for getting to the levers of power.

The apostolic scriptures give no hint of any such conception about Christians relating to the wider world. Jesus refused to assume power on the world's terms. He called his Messianic people to be "the salt of the earth... the light of the world... a city set on a hill" (Mt. 5:13–14). Joachim Jeremias writes that these verses, along with the Beatitudes, "concern the whole Sermon [on the Mount], just as in a mathematical formula a number before a bracket concerns every entity within the bracket."[3] Insofar as the community of disciples lives out the way of Jesus described in the Sermon, it illustrates for the unredeemed world what that world is meant to be. If the community truly provides that arresting contrast, many from beyond it turn, give glory to the heavenly Father, and enter the city. God gave his Servant Jesus as "light to the nations" (Is. 42:6; 49:6). Disciples, living in reflective relation to him, become "a light for the nations" (Acts 13:47 JB) — for nations in their collective breadth and not simply as aggregates of individuals.

In the saying about "a city set on a hill," Jesus recast the imagery of Isaiah 2:2–3 — "the mountain of the house of the Lord" to which "all the nations shall flow."[4] Jesus does not picture the nations of the world as coming to the holy place of God in Jerusalem to learn to walk in his ways. Instead, the Messianic people, walking in those ways, are to constitute that place wherever they go; and they are to "go into all the world and preach the gospel to the whole creation" (Mk. 16:15). As polis set on the terrain of the wider polis, they are to stand out by striving to actualize God's alternatives for humanity. Through much of history cities were built on hills for defense. Jesus' city is on its God-given elevation so that it may be seen. It becomes the place where God answers the still fitful yearning of the nations that "he may teach us his ways" (Is. 2:3). It is "a colony of heaven"

(Phil. 3:20 Moffatt) and prefigures the New Jerusalem that is coming to earth from beyond.

Biblically seen, there is the old aeon and the new. God's Rule in Jesus is breaking in. The structures of the old aeon, such as nation states, are tottering toward collapse and are to be displaced by the new aeon. Disciples seek to embody and proclaim the incursion of God's Rule and therefore resist, rather than stand with, structures set against that.

If nations are seen as the primary bearers of meaning in history and as the main vehicles for what counts, the politics of leverage and of doing what "has to be done" makes sense. (The U.S. founding fathers liked to view the new nation as fulfilment of the vision of "a city set on a hill.") Disciples, however, know that the central meaning of history lies, not with the imposing might, wealth, and spectacle of nations, but in "Jesus Christ the faithful witness, the firstborn of the dead, and the ruler of kings on earth" (Rev. 1:5). His community embodies and proclaims that meaning. For it the politics of the hilltop city displaces the politics of leverage, which no longer has a tenable basis. This community cannot collaborate in what the nation state is impelled to be when that goes against what its Lord calls it to be for the nations. To collaborate in such a way is to desert God's reshaping of history for renegade adherence to its chief rival.

The Messianic community orients its politics toward the imperatives given by this Lord, not toward any seemingly imperative necessities for the nation state. Disciples do not join in the idolatrous assumption that the nation state in which they happen to reside has to survive. For them the nation state does not have that paramount importance. They understand that under God it will not for all that long endure. In it they recognize structures that do on balance serve human well-being but also structures that should not be defended or preserved. Far from ignoring it, they scrutinize, commend, warn, resist. God wills that any populace live rather than perish. But a people must come to a total reorientation of its life if it is not to perish. It must, among other things, break with reliance on the means deemed sufficient for assuring national survival. Disciples echo Jesus' warning that those who seek to save (the collective) life will lose it. They present his converse offer of life through willingness to lose it.

The standard objection to the stance being delineated can be stated like this: So inestimably much is at stake in politics and government; if Christians do not get involved, they consign themselves to relative insignificance and irrelevance with regard to this overridingly important part of human life. It may seem obvious that Christians must throw themselves into something so comprehensively determinative for the human condition.

But the discipleship stance being set forth does not at all amount to withdrawal and noninvolvement. In the contemporary world, political and social issues loom larger for human beings generally than ever before in history. Questions of political loyalty and compliance are pressed upon us — almost as in the Roman coercion to burn the pinch of incense to Caesar. Unless persons are quite out of touch with the wider society and the world of nations, they cannot be politically uninvolved or neutral. To claim political uninvolvement as an individual or a church is to support the status quo. Each so-called democratic society is pluralistic, with many different social and political groupings. Government proceeds by coalition of dominant elites and electoral constituencies. Church people ordinarily figure in, not as communities of disciples, but as persons blended into various other groupings, constituencies, or elites. They let themselves be absorbed into things as they are.

In contrast, what is being described here is the hilltop city as countersign. Together in faithfulness to their Lord, disciples strive to live out God's incursive New in the midst of the collapsing old. They are actors on the political stage just as their Lord was — speaking God's word, challenging, resisting, comforting, standing with "the least." They share Gandhi's outlook: "Politics begins with the person next to you." They serve as emissaries of a Sovereign, whose life, teachings, and call to his people are utterly counter to societal structures reverberating violence. When those structures abet the rich "by grinding the face of the poor" (Is. 3:15), disciples stand with the poor (if they do not happen to be by prior circumstance among the poor). They share with them and cry out to oppressors. When those structures proceed in reckless exploitation and poisoning of the environment, disciples embrace that creation, care for it, and plead for it as still more vulnerable and voiceless than the poor among God's human creatures.

Little more than a century after the apostolic period, Tertullian, addressing Roman authorities, wrote of Christians: "Why! without taking up arms, without rebellion, simply by standing aside, by mere ill-natured separation, we could have fought you! For if so vast a mass of people as we had broken away from you and removed to some recess of the world apart, the mere loss of so many citizens of whatever sort would have brought a blush to your rule."[5] If, instead of such an imagined geographical emigration, tens of millions from among the much larger number of church people in our time would pursue the course of disengagement from anti-Christian structures and of counterengagement by alternative reshapings of human life, that would have a significance comparable to that which Tertullian envisioned in relation to the Roman Empire.

Church historian Kenneth Scott Latourette wrote:

> There can be no reasonable question that if the great majority of professed Christians led by the churches...were utterly and wholly to renounce war and decline to participate in it, and were positively to do those things which make for peace, reconciliation among nations could be effected, peace become the normal state of mankind, and international relations be placed on the basis of justice.[6]

Even if this be regarded as an overstatement of the case, such a massive Christian witness would have great influence and power for moving things in that direction. If even a fourth of those who profess to be Christians would take the stand Latourette points to, they would have far more impact for human well-being than all the church people who involve themselves compliantly in things as they are. Yet, if no such proportion of church people choose to live the way of Christ, God works with the much smaller remnant, scattered among the churches, that does.

Since the time of Constantine, the churches generally have been co-opted by the established power structures. What has come has been mainly deformation of church people and churches rather than decisive transformation of structures. The current achievements of the politics of leverage in bringing a just and peaceable world are pathetically limited. The worst dimensions of the projection of power by the rich countries are possible only because of the collaboration or complicity of most citizens, a great many of whom (in most of these countries) see themselves as Christians. The world is headed for catastrophe, even terminal catastrophe, because of the general failure of the churches to be what God intends.

Jesus gave what turned out to be a characterization of churches in the Constantinian collaborationist pattern: savorless salt not really different, salt that has become non-salt incapable of preserving or enhancing flavor (Mt. 5:13). That which has become the bland opposite of its reason for being is then good for nothing but to be "trodden under foot" — pressed into the conformity of the general societal mire, so far distant from hilltop visibility.

Already now Jesus is King of kings and Lord of lords. Disciples seek to make that reality known and to live out the present drama of it right under the noses of pretenders and their entourage. When disciples do that, they have high political significance as countersign. In the pluralistic mix, they are the grouping that stands out as most different from other groupings. Pretenders fear the true Sovereign. In ancient empires slaves and certain ethnic minorities were not to be counted on as soldiers or upholders of the status quo, but they needed to be reckoned with as part of the political equation. So it should be far more with Christians. In the politics of leverage the intended Christian influence becomes so diluted and co-opted that it ends up having little effect for bringing about transformation of the society. In the politics of the hilltop city, a transformation is already manifestly underway, and the status quo is confronted by total challenge and threat of overturn. It was in this manner that Jesus on earth and the apostolic church bore witness.

Disciples, looking to Jesus as Lord, dare not participate in societal structures in ways counter to that Lordship. Some posts, some employment, some involvement in those structures may be entered into, without pulling back from the primary allegiance to Christ. The shared discernment of the community is often needed for the problems and ambiguities. A disciple might even run for higher political office. But such a disciple, advocating the way of Jesus in challenge to the violence and injustice of the status quo, would have virtually no chance of being elected, given the dominant attitudes in any country and the manipulative power of the ruling elites. Ordinarily one must forsake adherence to Jesus Christ if one is to gain a position of higher managerial power. This is not to say simply that persons in those positions are not Christians. God alone searches the hearts and is Judge at the End. But it is to say that they are not where they are as Christians if the positions inherently involve unfaithfulness to Jesus Christ. This can be discerned by "the fruits" (Mt. 7:16) — the horrendous repression, violence, deception, and mindless greed proliferating from those structures and positions.

There is wide agreement in the churches and beyond that a government can be so bad that one should not become a participant in it but should instead live out resistance. Nazi Germany was seen that way in the countries allied against it. Stalinist dictatorships or the South African government enforcing apartheid have been seen in much the same way. Church people by and large agree that followers of Christ cannot be managers or functionaries aligned with the inhumanities of such regimes but should resist. In the United States and other countries, Christians need to recognize that their nation and its elites sponsor inhumanities of such magnitude that they must live out resistance rather than collaborate.

Disciples say in effect: "If you insist on structuring society largely contrary to the way of Jesus, we do not join you in that. We do not join you in wars, covert and overt, or in standing behind a vast array of implements of mass destruction. We do not join you in affluent adherence to the global economy that is ravaging the biosphere and consigning forty thousand children to die daily of hunger and preventable diseases. We do not join you in the disregard of limits, the promiscuity, the 'bread and circuses' diversions. We engage rather in our alternative endeavor as counterweight to what you are about." The issue is not perfection or freedom from wrongdoing. Disciples are hardly ever free from elements of complicity in the worst that is being perpetrated by the society. To hear the call of Jesus in its full radicality is to have some understanding again and again of how far short one falls. In affluent countries it is very difficult to move away from being rich Christians in a hungry world.[7] But the imperative is that disciples give themselves, even if falteringly, to the way of Jesus rather than to its opposite.

Discipling in the Church[8]

The politics of the hilltop city begins within the fellowship in the struggle for faithfulness to the Master with regard to political and social issues. Matthew 18:15–20 states guidelines that are critically important for that struggle. A disciple is to go to a brother or sister seen as snared in sin, first one to one. Then, as may be necessary, one is to take along additional persons or bring the matter to the assembled body of believers.

The most destructive and ominous sins of commission are for the most part social-political-economic-military in their form. Disciples need the counsel, warning, and intercession of one another for liberation from such sins. In discipling, other biblical imperatives (such as those concerning sexuality and marriage) should also be kept in view. But in our time the imperatives having to do with nonviolence and violence, peace and war, justice and injustice are the ones most of all contested and assailed by the seductive powers of destruction. There is a pathetic incongruity when a denomination issues an official statement against the nuclear arms buildup or some military action but has not one word to say to the large numbers of its own members engaged in that buildup or action.

The call to turn to Christ and his way is for everyone, but first of all for people within the churches. Personal reliance on military

power and adherence to the structures that maintain the great disparity between rich and poor in the world constitute desertion of
Jesus Christ and grave jeopardy before God. There is from Jesus so
clearly the imperative to go and plead with the brother or sister who
is in the armed forces, in an "intelligence agency," in "defense" work,
in a ruling elite, in management of an exploitative corporation, in an
organ for captivating the public mind. When the call is given to leave
military employment or other work aligned with the powers of repression and death, those inclined to heed that call should be able
to reckon with caring support and financial assistance from a fellowship of Christians. There is the imperative to help young people
understand that entering the armed forces is sin against God and
humanity and to offer them Christian alternatives. Christian young
people should be able to turn to other Christians rather than to the
military for help in getting an education, vocational training, or simply a job. Fellow church members must be warned that attitudes
supporting military buildup, imperial projection of power, and war
are betrayal of the Gospel. Disciples are to give this call to faithfulness through conversation, preaching, teaching, writing, meetings,
vigils, symbolic actions.

Church people and others cling to military "security," saying,
"Otherwise we would lose our freedom." They need to hear God's
word: "Freedom is what we have — Christ has set us free!" (Gal. 5:1
TEV). This freedom cannot be preserved by "smart" bombs, attack
helicopters, and Trident submarines. One cannot have it by killing
for it but only by living it. Jesus sets persons free to point to him as
the One who died and rose that all human beings might have life,
free to leave behind the fear that ensnares the world, free to step
out from behind Satanic weapons, free to love those who have been
designated as enemies, free to stand with the poorest of the human
family, free to call sin sin and to warn of God's impending judgment,
free to proclaim that the foolish, raging nations are about to become
the transfigured domain of the One who was freed from death. All
living out of this freedom has political impact.

On the issue of resort to violence, persons in the churches can
be asked questions such as the following. Which is prior for you,
your faith in God or your country and its need for defense? If you
accept such things as the national military posture, the nuclear arsenal, fighting the U.S.-Iraq War, what basis in Jesus Christ do you find
for doing that? How can you be in the armed forces or in the manu-
facture of weapons and be a disciple of Jesus? When the Lord of the
universe says, "Love your enemies," how do you have the audacity

to go against that? If fighting a nuclear war would be the most horribly anti-Christian action imaginable, how can you go along with preparations to fight it? Would you yourself be willing to be at the firing controls for nuclear bombs, ready to fire if commanded to do so? If you say yes, how can you square that willingness, upon command, to kill more human beings than the six million the Nazis killed in their concentration camps with what you see in Jesus Christ? Are you willing to face enemies as Jesus did? Would you be willing to risk your life in nonviolent resistance to evil?

Most powerholders in Western countries claim to be Christians. That claim should be taken seriously. When what they are doing warrants it, they can be approached in a caring "Matthew 18" way as brother or sister snared in sin. At the higher levels, such persons are typically so inaccessible that initiatives may come as no more than an unread letter or a sign held up along a presidential route. Most powerholders are members of congregations that would not follow the Matthew 18 guidelines in any matter at all — and most certainly not in such matters as the oppression or slaughter of multitudes. But disciples in shared discernment can come to see certain powerholders as pagans and tax collectors (Mt. 18:17), that is, as persons outside the faith who need to be won to it. Membership in establishment churches ordinarily insulates powerholders from such a recognition about themselves. The heart of Christian witness to powerholders is simple Spirit-led evangelism. The call is given to repent, turn from managerial participation in evils, receive forgiveness, and enter into the new life of discipleship to Jesus. Instead of collaborating in anti-Christian structures, Christians encourage persons in those structures to come out of them into the Messianic community. A warning, welcoming evangelism pervades the politics of the hilltop city.

The mesmerism or perceived awesomeness of the powerful tends to stifle such evangelism even when there would be occasion for it. Martin Niemöller told of a dream of his. He saw a dazzling light and then Adolf Hitler standing in the shadows. A voice asked, "What have you to say for yourself?" Hitler replied, "Only that no one ever told me the Gospel." Then Niemöller remembered that the one time when he, along with other church leaders, talked with Adolf Hitler, he put before him issues of church rights but not the Gospel of Jesus Christ.

In terms of the need of any human being, not every occasion is an opportune time for presenting the Gospel. So too for powerholders. To disciples seeking and asking, the Spirit gives the times and the leading. On other occasions one may simply seek to express to powerholders what might have some persuasiveness in terms of their frame of reference and professed ideals. But even then one stays near the possibility of shifting to the heart of the matter.

In Defense of Life

Jesus offered to lead in the transformation of life in Palestinian Jewish society. His offer was put down. Christians point to a derivative possibility for their time and place. Jesus and the scriptures centered in him give the outline of what that reshaping would look like. "Put away the sword" (Mt. 26:52, altered): turn from reliance on weapons, repression, and killing; meet hate with love and "overcome evil with good" (Rom. 12:21). "Swords into plowshares" (Is. 2:4): shift the resources and efforts of the society completely away from weaponry and imperial domination to education, assistance to the poor at home and abroad, health care, decent housing, protection of the environment, development of renewable energy programs and public transportation systems.[9] Cultivate all that enhances human life; reject all that degrades and destroys it: "for the Son of Man has not come to destroy the lives of human beings but to save them" (Lk. 9:56 NRSV, in some ancient texts). "Sell your possessions, and give to the poor; provide yourselves [through doing this] . . . with a treasure in the heavens that does not fail" (Lk. 12:33, altered); or in Paul's words, "as a matter of equality your abundance at the present time should supply their want, so that their abundance may supply your want, that there may be equality" (2 Cor. 8:14): Turn from amassing wealth and from all exploitation; share with such compassion that the needs of all may be met, not only within the country, but in the whole human family.[10] "You are not to be called rabbi, for you have one teacher, and you are all brethren. . . . Neither be called masters, for you have one master, the Christ. He who is greatest among you shall be your servant" (Mt. 23:8, 10–11): Aim for nonhierarchical leadership, for societal dynamics centered in servanthood rather than power-seeking, for decentralization of political and economic power into units small enough to depend mainly on face-to-face interaction. The centuries of Christendom were filled with attempts to have a Christian society but almost always without an understanding of the radically new life into which Christians have been called.

Such guidelines are not utopian. They are simply Christian and evangelical (coming from the Gospel). They are not burdensome imperatives from Jesus but rather his gracious, empowering offer for how life on this earth can be lived. Even the life of broader societies could be recast in these directions, though only through adherence to Jesus Christ and by the power of his Spirit.

The possibility remains (remote it would seem for almost any country) that the attraction of the Lordship and way of Jesus would become so strong that the various groupings within a society would agree to having it organized in accordance with that way. Disciples could be leaders in that effort. (The Quaker government of colonial Pennsylvania was to a degree an example of this sort of endeavor.) There would not need to be unanimity of Christian belief; but the faith lived out by most would determine the societal context for all. Such an ordering would not approach perfection, but the impetus and basic direction for it would be from Jesus.

Disciples in the Messianic community are not indifferent to the question of how to defend the society from being overrun by hostile forces. They point to nonviolence, peaceableness toward enemies, civilian-based defense (in their understanding of that), as alternative ways of resisting the threat or actuality of an invasion and occupation by such forces: no weapons, no violence to counter violence, but rather acts of loving resistance and noncooperation.[11] Disciples are ready to participate in modes of defending the society or of bringing down a repressive government that are consistent with the teachings and Spirit of Jesus. When there is enough common ground, they can join with those who see the effort more in terms of strategy and practicality. The revolution that overthrew the Marcos regime in the Philippines had this mix, as did the 1989 Eastern European uprisings.[12] The East German Revolution began in the churches. The Gospel impetus remained formative even as all sorts of citizens joined in. Confronted with the likelihood of massive resistance comparable to that carried out in those uprisings, a prospective invader would probably be deterred or, if not, would hardly be able to maintain control in the longer term. In August 1991 the Soviet coup leaders discovered that the huge populace was mostly unwilling to accept their rule, and they gave up. The nonviolent resistance of a relatively small population can be overwhelmed by the violence and repressive resources of a far more powerful and fully determined nation state, as happened in Czechoslovakia in 1968 (though the full takeover required seven months). Ironically, the world's foremost military power would be one of the easiest countries to defend by nonviolent resistance without weapons. A hostile power would probably not try to invade. If it did, it would have extreme difficulty holding in subjection a large population engaged unitedly in that sort of defense.

A comment of George F. Kennan speaks to the still immensely influential question about fighting Adolf Hitler: "I was stationed, as a diplomat, in Germany during part of the war, and I visited almost every Nazi-occupied country. I came away with the impression that even if Hitler had won the war, he would not have been able to maintain the empire he was trying to establish."[13] The case can be made that if there had been the popular will, countries all over Europe could have resisted nonviolently as the Norwegians and Danes did,[14] with the resulting world probably a much better place than that left by World War II.

In a further irony, the darkest American and West European fear for decades was that of a Soviet takeover ("better dead than red"); but then abruptly the Soviets could no longer retain control over their East European client states and, soon after that, lost control over the various regional ethnic minorities within the Soviet Union. Probably the Soviet leaders all along were not oriented toward trying to take over Western Europe and the United States.[15] If, hypothetically, they had been confronted by civilian-based defense rather than by the military might of NATO and had taken over Western Europe and even the United States, they could not have retained control for very long. Christians, however, should see any such pragmatic considerations as secondary to the issue of faithfulness to Jesus as Lord.

What cannot be defended without gigantic military power is the imperial exploitative dominance around the world by the United States and other rich countries. Disciples see in all these countries much structuring of power that does not deserve to be defended. But a country turning to nonviolent resistance would be on the way to becoming a society (or medley of societies) somewhat deserving of such defense.

Disciples disengage themselves from "defense" that could bring on the destruction of what is supposed to be preserved. They point to alternative defense. But especially in the United States there seems very little possibility that such alternative defense will be turned to. It is hard to think of a persuasive scenario in which a determining majority of the U.S. population would give up on military might and war. Even if that majority does emerge, it could be repressed by a military coup — the hard-liners seizing control and continuing their accustomed ways.

Unlike adherents of the military, followers of Jesus are not absorbed with how to prevent a takeover or aggression by foreign adversaries who would slaughter, repress, and crush the humaneness of life. In almost any country they are within a society that projects power in such ways. So it is that disciples transpose the hypothetical issue of nonviolent resistance to an enemy invasion into the immediate question of how to resist with creative nonviolence the inhumanities of their own government, which for a great many people is a ruthless occupying power. The victims far away or close by are mostly out of view. How do nonvictim followers of the One who stands with all victims stand with them too and resist what is being done? Could President Bush's determined course toward war in the Persian Gulf have been turned back by millions of Americans, especially Christians, taking to the streets in an uprising comparable to those in Eastern Europe? Could it have been stopped if a hundred thousand Western Christians had gone to Iraq to be with "the least" in that country in their extreme jeopardy?

Among Christians in Latin America an understanding of *accompaniment* has developed:

> Members of Latin American communities and individuals at risk realized that military repression diminished as a result of the presence of internationals with those individuals or communities.... We say that repression against people decreases when internationals are present, but this doesn't necessarily mean that the repression is thwarted. Therefore, accompaniment is also the witnessing of atrocities committed against people and the documenting and reporting of those atrocities to our home communities and churches. In this way, people of faith are able to get reliable, first-hand accounts of incidents which the U.S. media have almost always ignored. Most important of all, however, is the role which accompaniment plays in bringing to flesh what Paul spoke of in 1 Corinthians 12 — that we are *all* the body of Christ and that when one part suffers, so too does the rest of the body.[16]

Instead of the racist devaluation of human lives, the life of each accompanied person is valued to the point of readiness to sacrifice one's allegedly far more valuable life. Acts of solidarity and resistance in the rich countries provide the complement to such accompaniment in the poor countries. Over against the triumphalism of Empire, God's people "weep with those who weep" (Rom. 12:15). They pray the psalms with victims crying out. They see Jesus in the midst of every population smitten by violence and with all the poor of the earth, marginalized by the rich. Disciples intercede and enter into prayer combat against the powers of destruction. They seek to represent in contrition those who have not yet come to that.

Disciples hear the Master's call to turn back from the things that take the world toward destruction and to choose the things that make for peace. They do not decide on the basis of whether something will "work." Yet within the call itself is the promise that, seen in widest perspective, faithful discipleship serves the fulfilment of life. Jesus' phrase "the things that make for peace" (Lk. 19:42) has that promissory element. It is often and truly said that Christians are to be faithful, not necessarily to be successful, in what they undertake. But biblical faith, which issues into faithfulness, looks toward the ultimate triumph, the manifest success, of what is right. God in Jesus brought failure to victory and will bring that victory to its completion. Christian nonviolence lives out that failure and hidden victory to prefigure the consummation.

Christians can note in human life corroborative indications that rejection of the way of Jesus does not work and that living it does. The turn from violence to love of enemies has become a prerequisite for human survival. For those with eyes to see, technological and other developments in the world support a recognition that the way of Jesus is the one most promising, even in pragmatic terms. Sooner or later, continued reliance on military might will lead to cataclysm. Sooner or later, economic systems driven by greed and disregard of victims will bring on their own undoing. Capitalism, like communism, has not come to grips with the fallenness of human nature and what it leads to. The hubris of the technologically advanced nations cannot continue indefinitely. Christians know that, because God is just and God is Judge. But even apart from faith, sober longer-term analyses and projections point to collapse and catastrophe. Many thinkers have stressed that such can be avoided only by a revolutionary global reorientation. The Gospel of Jesus provides the contours for that.

Signalling Life

Paul wrote: "Show a gentle attitude [*epieikes*] toward everyone. The Lord is coming soon" (Phil. 4:5 TEV). Assured in that hope, Christians are to live out magnanimous gentleness toward all humans. This attitude is a main aspect of who Jesus Christ was and is, and it should be a leading trait of disciples (2 Cor. 10:1). Magnanimous gentleness should also be a formative component in the attitude of Christians toward rulers who act as enemies of humanity. They are blind leaders of the blind (Mt. 15:14). "Father, forgive them; for they know not what they do" (Lk. 23:34). In resistance disciples have no need to veer into the shrillness of desperation, for they understand that in the longer term they themselves are not the ones losing out. With the prophets, they may cry out against what those in power are doing. With Jesus, they may negatively characterize a ruler (Lk. 13:32). Disciples, however, do not wish the worst for rulers but rather seek their liberation from the grip of infernal powers. They can see behind the masks of power to how lost these managers of the society are, how much in need of grace and transformation. (John Schuchardt said of his bearing witness against the U.S.-Iraq War twenty feet away from President Bush in the February 17, 1991, Sunday morning service of the First Congregational Church in Kennebunkport, Maine: "That the commander-in-chief could enter a church...without somebody ministering to his needs, to his unbelievably distorted conscience, is unbelievable."[17]) Disciples seek to take in something of horrors perpetrated and yet to intimate toward perpetrators, more than the prospect of judgment, Christ's clemency offered no less to them than to those who through repentance have already received it.

In faith's calculus of power, "He who is in you is greater than he who is in the world" (1 Jn. 4:4). Greater is the One pointed to by a disciple alone in front of the White House than the one who may be the source of much in a presidential message to the nation seen and heard by most of the populace. The lone vigiler has no evident political importance but stands with the One whose movement is winning out.

Early on an Easter Sunday morning Jennifer Haines walked in all simplicity onto the forbidden territory of the Rocky Flats Nuclear Plant, holding a lily: sign of Life into the domain of death. In the darkness before an Easter morning seven friends entered the high security area of the Wurtsmith Air Force Base in Michigan, wrote on a control building, "CHRIST IS RISEN! DISARM!," and completed the Easter liturgy at gunpoint.[18] As Congress debated new missile programs, 250 Christians proceeded with a Peace Pentecost prayer service after being warned by bullhorn, "It is unlawful to pray in the Rotunda of the U.S. Capitol."[19] Three witnesses entered Ft. Benning, Georgia at night, climbed a tree near the barracks of 525 Salvadoran soldiers there for training, and with a high-powered tape player, broadcast the last speech of Oscar Romero, in which he ordered soldiers to lay down their arms and stop killing. But alongside acts such as these are innumerable others that are less dramatic: conversations, preaching, teaching, stands that lead to loss of one's job, refusal to pay the portion of taxes devoted to imperial power and transfer of those sums to life-enhancing programs. Such witness has "divine power to destroy strongholds" (2 Cor. 10:4) in persons and in societal structures. It prefigures the final casting down.

In a 1984 lecture at the National War College a high-ranking general told an audience of two hundred military leaders: "The greatest challenge to all that we do now comes from within the churches.... A whole new way of thinking is developing in the churches, and we have to know what to do with it."[20] That state of affairs continues. As Jim Wallis has concluded, "An independent biblical vision is what the present U.S. government and its religious apologists are most afraid of."[21] Forthright Christian resistance to the evils of the status quo has much more political impact than numbers alone would suggest, for it intimates the threat of the Word of God.

God's Lifting up of the Marginalized

Throughout the Hebrew scriptures God lifted up those who were weak and in distress: Joseph brought out of prison; Israel liberated from the Egyptians, the Midianites, the Philistines; David saved from Saul; Jerusalem preserved from invading armies; Daniel rescued from the lions; exiles given permission to return to Palestine. The earthly ministry of Jesus was a lifting up of the lowly: "good news to the poor... release to the captives... recovering of sight to the blind... [setting] at liberty those who are oppressed" (Lk. 4:18). Those acts of Jesus were eschatological, giving evidence of the inauguration of the Messiah's Rule and pointing to its consummation. In the Beatitudes Jesus gave definitive description of ways in which the Messianic community was being lifted up by God. Then the One who was lowest in death was raised up to be Lord over all.

Rightly seen, all liberation comes from the life, death, and rising of Jesus of Nazareth and should not be sought apart from that source. Through Christ even the coercive lethal power of those who manage this world has lost its terror. He delivers "from the hand of... enemies" (Lk. 1:74) in ways that resort to violence never can. For a new creature in Christ "old things have passed away; behold, all things are become new" (2 Cor. 5:17 AV). Demeaning power structures are no longer there in the same way. Even when a person has to yield to their outer grip (as in imprisonment for living the faith), their inner hold is gone. As subjects of a nation state, Christians can recognize its de facto authority but resist its highest claims and heinous ways of exercising power. Disciples do not so much demand that freedom be granted as live out the freedom that Jesus gives. Wherever the poor, the oppressed, the marginalized are drawn together in Christ-centered, Spirit-led, hope-filled base communities and comparable groups, the most decisive social transformation is taking place. Communities of disciples in the provinces may continue to show the way much more than those in the imperial heartland.

Those in a desperate plight who cry out to God do not resign themselves. Theirs, like the cry of the Hebrews in Egypt, is the opposite of passivity. Those who count on God are, with Hannah and Mary, exalted in their exaltation of the One who casts down and lifts up. That change of heart does not depend on actual betterment of outward circumstances but looks toward it. True lifting up is not on the world's terms but on God's. It may be a lifting up derived from the first phase of the glorification of Jesus: "and I, when I am lifted up from the earth..." (Jn. 12:32). The Christian practice of active love (nonviolence) toward enemies always has something of the weakness of God shown in Jesus' death on the cross and by small additions is completing "what is lacking in Christ's afflictions" (Col. 1:24). True lifting up has something of the hiddenness of Jesus' resurrection. Breakthroughs may or may not be achieved in terms of changing the dominant structures; but when rightly sought, breakthrough in ways of relating to those structures does come.

Mary's Magnificat does not picture the lowly being exalted to thrones — to positions of central political power. Only in the consummation are Christ's people given enthronement with their Lord. In the remarkable image of Revelation 3:21 (NRSV) Jesus promises, "To the one who conquers I will give a place with me on my throne." In this world disciples can assume no positions of power except in accord with the One who, contrary to the ways of the world, has "conquered and sat down with [his] Father on his throne."

Through the centuries since Constantine the apostolic teachings about subordination have been taken as authorization of the dominant power structures. But they cannot be that if they are understood in the light of how Jesus related to the power structures around him. In this issue most of all, to keep the epistles in the foreground and the Gospels much in the background makes for a distorted theology and an unfaithful church. Romans 13:1–7 has been lifted out of scripture and exalted as *the* basis for a Christian understanding of the state. It should, however, be understood as counterbalanced and complemented by other motifs in scripture (many of which are treated in this book).[22] The passage is to be understood, not in terms of subservience to an enduring status quo (the tragically dominant interpretation through so much of church history), but in terms of

not forcing the demise of what is about to pass away. As in the Hebrew scriptures, God lifts up and casts down, and his people deal
with the actuality of the powers that are so soon not to be. "The night
is far gone, the day is at hand" (v. 12).

Romans 13:1–7 has been used to justify killing millions of human
beings in war but would seem to forbid taking part in the nonviolent
overthrow of a repressive government. "Whoever opposes the exist-
ing authority opposes what God has ordered" (v. 2 TEV). Persons who
take the traditional understanding of these verses as the foundation
for their political ethic would do well to ask themselves how they
see this passage in relation to Christian participation in nonviolent
uprisings such as the one in the Philippines against the Marcos government and those in Eastern Europe in 1989. Can there rightly be
any sort of popular (or personal) *resistance* to even the worst abuses of
power by a government? Actually, the passage is hardly ever seen as
teaching uniform obedience to any and all governments but rather
as requiring full obedience and loyalty to one's own government
viewed very positively.

In the light of the Magnificat and much else in scripture, times
come when God's people discern that the power structures around
them are at the point of collapse, that God seems about to cast down
what deserves to be cast down, and that God is using modes of
action that they can rightly join in. However, Christians should not
suppose that participation even in such amazing revolutions is at the
center of their mission. Freedom that may be won is not the deeper
freedom in Christ. Again and again what comes after an overthrow
has been most disappointing. The way of Christ had much influence
on those East European uprisings but rather little on the restructuring
of the societies afterward. For the United States, in any case, such
nonviolent overthrow of pernicious power structures seems a remote
prospect; and collapse of those structures would probably bring with
it tides of violence because readiness to resort to violence permeates
the public.

The centrally determinative reshaping of history has been accomplished in Jesus Christ. Disciples strive to live that soon-to-
be-triumphant reshaping as challenge to all that remains defiantly
outside it. They savor already "the powers of the age to come" (Heb.
6:5). They are to be a city, a gathering of people, a countervailing
political entity, prefiguring the glorious New City that God is about
to bring into view. Those visions about swords into plowshares, lions and lambs peacefully together, a bountiful communal banquet,
have some anticipatory fulfilment in the life and ministry of Chris-

tian fellowships internationally: no more weapons, no more fighting, no more repression, but the inner and outer conversion away from all that into living out God's shalom coming to his people and to the nations in Jesus Christ.

Chapter 13

HOPE IN GOD ALONE

Biblical eschatology has an interest only for [those] who at last have discovered that no future worth having can be of their own making and who have become willing not only to hear what the Scriptures have to tell them about their future but also to receive their future, both as individuals and as a society, and above all, as a church, from God.... Eschatology is the vision of the future that gives direction to the present and confidence to take the next necessary step toward a future goal.

—James D. Smart[1]

All humans are drawn into the drive to secure the future. That drive impels much of our effort in the personal realm. It finds culminating expression in the "security" arrangements of nations. The basic rationale for military power is that of securing the collective future. Citizens suppose that their nation state must survive, and they give themselves to it.

The two opposite positions with regard to security are trust in an earthly sovereignty or trust in God's gracious sovereignty. With the Constantinian shift, the church for the most part moved from the latter trust to the former. The era of intense eschatological expectancy had dwindled away. The church placed its hope in political structures. Impatient with waiting for God to take over and set things right in the world, church people assumed that task. God's Rule was understood as absorbed and amalgamated into the supposed centrality of the earthly sovereignty. Through the centuries since then, the goal has been to shape enough of history to provide a measure of security and well-being for those who compliantly trust that collective endeavor.

The dominant outlook in the Western peace and justice movement has been within that Constantinian orientation. With all the world viewed as being in extreme jeopardy, activists generally have tended to see themselves under constraint to become the saviors and guarantors of the future. Instead of looking to military might, they see the strategies and efforts of the movement as decisive for the proposed future.

The peace and justice movement has focused much attention on having hope. When the oft-repeated song "We Shall Overcome" is followed by very little identifiable overcoming, the hope expressed in those words can become too frail to serve as a basis for continuing the struggle. Not reaching the political breakthrough they seek, large numbers of people burn out in discouragement and despair. To involve themselves in the struggle for a better future, most people must have the buoyancy of hopefulness grounded in some vision of that future. Within the movement, hope has usually been taken to mean "projecting confident images"[2] of the future rather than giving way to dark premonitions. The idea is that if enough people catch sight of these brighter images and strive to actualize them, the vision can become reality, to some extent at least. But hope understood in this way tends to be simply "the power of positive thinking"[3] and is in its essential nature hardly different from the "official optimism"[4] promoted by the managers of the society.

The Nuclear Freeze Campaign of the early 1980s in the United States can be taken as one model for hoping. The idea was to get enough people at the grassroots committed to a bilateral verifiable nuclear freeze so that the leaders at the top would have to yield to the public pressure and halt the nuclear arms race. Hope was directed toward the power of the people and reaching the wider populace in their basic decency and good sense. Hope for rescue from the rush toward destruction has been given a variety of bases: the particular movement being promoted, the combined efforts of all peace groups, peace studies, conflict resolution, an alternative presidential candidate, the United Nations, world government, the peace vibrations emanating from great numbers of meditators, and much else. What has not been sufficiently reckoned with is that the dominant elites in every country have the superior resources and means for keeping most people supportive of, or indifferent to, current policies. The hopes that were directed toward the Nuclear Freeze Campaign and the West European peace movement largely faded. Though these efforts had much impact, basic change of direction at the top did not come. Even after the collapse of communism in Eastern Europe and the Soviet Union, there has been no such change of direction. Powerholders in the rich countries have been able to pursue imperial politics with greater freedom of action.

In Whose Hands?

A main peace movement slogan for a time was "The future is in our hands." Arnold Toynbee had written in 1950, "Our fate lies in our own hands."[5] The intent of the exhortation "The future is in our hands" is partly right. What humans do is prime determinant of the future that comes upon them. In nuclear issues most strikingly societies can choose what leads toward survival or what leads toward annihilation. But the claim "The future is in our hands" puts the matter much too strongly. It implies (as does the stance of those who hold power in the society) the manageability of the future and the human capability of making things come out right. It assumes a general freedom to choose life, without recognizing the predominance of the relentless pressures toward the choice of death. That claim does not take into account the possibility that some aspects of a viable future may already be lost because of things done wrong previously, for example, in the poisoning of the environment. The momentous question remains as to the extent and depth of the global reorientation needed to avoid catastrophe and bring in a brighter human future. Nuclear disarmament will almost certainly not be carried out except as a part of general disarmament, and that in turn can come only when correlated with the relinquishment of imperial power and imperial lifestyle.

What then politically is the Christian alternative to seeing the future as humanly manageable and seeking a part in that management? In the contrasting mode of hope, disciples affirm, "The future is in God's hands." A central biblical declaration of God's word is found in Deuteronomy 30:15, 19: "See, I have set before you this day life and good, death and evil. . . . Therefore choose life that you and your descendants may live." In this passage everything is in God's hands: the choosers, the choice, the choosing, and the consequent future. People by choosing what is good do not lay hold of life, do not have it and the unfolding future in their hands. Even the right ethical choices do not, in and of themselves, bring the good future. God gives life to those who choose him as Giver of life. God's people look to him and, in deeper ways, only to him for their good (salvation) and for the good (salvation) of the world. This stance is not to be understood as inaction but rather as choosing, receiving, and living out what God gives. Those who see themselves and the future as held in God's hands are rightly positioned to have some little part in the shaping of that future.

It is commonly forgotten that in Deuteronomy 30 the choice for life consists chiefly in this: "loving the Lord your God, obeying his voice, and cleaving to him" (v. 20). This with its manifold dimensions is the only adequate reorientation. A political choice by a society or an individual may be for life and against death, simply in terms of prospective consequences. As such it can be commendable and promising to a degree. But if it is not derivative from choosing God, it remains quite delimited. The claim that any choice promoting peace, justice, and care of the earth constitutes choosing God cannot be sustained in terms of the witness of the Bible. Such choices have their natural source and basis in a committed personal relationship of loving, obeying, and cleaving to the One who is gracious living Lord. But they do not, in whatever accumulation, add up to it. They can be made in isolation from the most basic choice that is their natural source.

The vision set down in Isaiah 2:4 (and Micah 4:3) has fascinated human beings around the world:

> They shall beat their swords into plowshares,
>   and their spears into pruning hooks;
> nation shall not lift up sword against nation,
>   neither shall they learn war any more.

But usually when this imagery is quoted, alluded to, or depicted (as in the statue at the United Nations headquarters in New York), no attention is given to the context. What the prophet described is viewed as a visionary possibility, something to yearn and strive for. Seldom is it noticed that the coming of peace is pictured to be the result of other actions. All the peoples of the earth together say (v. 3),

> Come, let us go up to the mountain of the Lord,
>   to the house of the God of Jacob;
> that he may teach us his ways
>   and that we may walk in his paths.

In the prophetic vision, that worldwide human community without war emerges only when all the nations turn to God and walk in his ways. But humanly seen, the prospects of this happening seem still more remote than do those of the world turning completely from armaments and war. In spite of all the high hopes and huge outpouring of effort in the modern missionary movement, the crazy, chaotic patchwork of nations that is so unready to lay down arms seems even less ready, as a collective whole, to hear and obey the God of Israel and of Jesus.

Speaking out against the continuing nuclear arms buildup, Earl Mountbatten, Admiral of the Fleet, said in 1979, "And since the threat to humanity is the work of human beings, it is up to man to save himself from himself."[6] In view of the vastness of the threat, Mountbatten's conclusion may seem the most elementary common sense. But in the biblical understanding, "man" cannot "save himself from himself." The biblical story is about God's doing what human beings cannot do. Salvation does not arise from within history. It is given for individuals and for history as God comes in Jesus Christ from beyond.

Life has just two directions: toward God and away from God. Away from God means on one's own. Isaiah 30:15–16 lays out the contrary possibilities:

> For thus said the Lord God, the Holy One of Israel,
>   "In returning and rest you shall be saved;
>   in quietness and in trust shall be your strength."
> And you would not, but you said,
>   "No! We will speed upon horses."

With all their plans and efforts, the people of Judah were headed away from God. But the Holy One of Israel was calling them back. They were to stop their own frantic striving to save themselves. They were to be still before God, waiting for him to act, and he would most certainly rescue them from their enemies. The Hebrew word translated "strength" had as its most common meaning the valiant might of warriors; it was a military term. Isaiah's fellow citizens were trying so hard to have that kind of strength. But God declared his total No to their attempt and gave a radical redefinition of what truly constitutes national strength: In quiet expectancy they were to trust in God to bring them through.

Gerhard von Rad comments:

It is precisely at this point, the passionate elimination of all reliance on oneself, that Isaiah's zeal begins. That he saw a great act of deliverance lying in the immediate future was only one side of his message. Ahaz and the leaders in Jerusalem had to leave room for this act of God. And this is what Isaiah called faith — leaving room for God's sovereign action, desisting from self-help. Thus in Isaiah the demand for faith is actualised in an emphatically polemical and even negative sense — only do not now usurp God's place by your own political and military plans.... When Isaiah speaks in this way of being still, he is quite certainly not thinking only of an inward condition of the soul, but also of an attitude which must be expressed in a perfectly definite mode of political conduct.... The astonishing thing was therefore this: Isaiah demanded of his contemporaries that they should now make their existence rest on a future action of God.[7]

That word through Isaiah calls away from more than reliance on the military. It demands a still more difficult turning: to desist from self-help, to leave room for God's sovereign action. In the peace and justice movement too that turning is very much needed.

Whatever Christians do should be within the expectancy of what God will do at the End and in this time before the End; and that acting comes as completion of what he has already done in the incarnation, ministry, death, and rising of Jesus of Nazareth. Leaving room for God's sovereign action was what Jesus did supremely when he went to his death. In that corpse cold in a sealed tomb, more than at any other place in all of history, God was given space to act. Because God raised Jesus from the dead, disciples in quietness and trust count on him to act into the littleness of their acting and into the affairs of nations. Within their human capabilities they cannot turn the world around. They cannot overcome. But God in Jesus has overcome and is turning the world around. Disciples look to him to act beyond their own dying and that of history.

Paul wrote, "But I have this treasure in a frail vessel of earth, to show that the transcending [*hyperbole*] power belongs to God, not to myself" (2 Cor. 4:7 Moffatt, altered). In all that disciples do, they should be looking, not to the power and wherewithal that they bring to the situation, but to that extraordinariness (*hyperbole*) of God's acting from beyond. Precisely in the recognized marginality and apparent powerlessness of Christian resistance to the rebel powers the way is open for that extraordinariness.

Isaiah was not quietistic or passive. Out of his attunement in quietness before God he heard God's message and proclaimed it. Hope in God's acting is not an inactive passivity but impels into God-given acting. Hoping, the Hebrews marched around Jericho, the prophets offered God's promise, the three Jewish exiles declared their faith to Nebuchadnezzar. God says, "I am watching over my word to perform it" (Jer. 1:12). Hope is the responsive human watching under that word. To hope is to leave room, first of all in oneself, for God's acting. When the expectation that God will act shapes the depths within a person, what the person does arises out of that shaping and becomes part of what God is doing.

If I truly pray, my prayer is infused by the desire and expectancy that God will evoke and guide my praying. I look not to any inner resources of my own but to God, who can change my groping and floundering into prayer. If I talk with a distraught friend and that person is significantly helped, "it was not I, but the grace of God which is with me" (1 Cor. 15:10). The determinative content of the help was God's feeling into my perplexed empathy and speaking into my faltering words. If I talk with a non-Christian about faith, my hope must not be in the cogency and incisiveness of my words but in God, who alone can give right words and use them, along with much else, to touch that person. Such considerations do not mean that I am simply to identify what I have said and done as God's words and deeds. Inadequacy and questionableness inhere in anything I do. But at times the assurance is given that these are outweighed and overpowered by acting from beyond me. Or that acting may be there without my recognizing it. "Thy will be done" (Mt. 6:10) is in part a plea that one's acting become a medium for God's acting. God makes peace through his children as they live out his peacemaking initiatives (Mt. 5:9). In true prayer and action Christians do not lay hold of power, but God's power, love, and truth lay hold of them. "Not that we are sufficient of ourselves to claim anything as coming from us; our sufficiency is from God" (2 Cor. 3:5).

Deliverance from Death

In 2 Corinthians 1:8–10 Paul, after a recent escape from death, expresses hope for his and his companions' earthly future:

> For we do not want you to be ignorant, brethren, of the affliction we experi-
> enced in Asia; for we were so utterly, unbearably crushed that we despaired
> of life itself. Why, we felt that we had received the sentence of death; but that
> was to make us rely not on ourselves but on God who raises the dead; he
> delivered us from so deadly a peril, and he will deliver us; on him we have
> set our hope that he will deliver us again.

The record in Acts about Paul's work in Ephesus and the province of Asia does not mention events that would account for Paul's using the strongest possible phrasing here: "utterly, unbearably crushed." In 2 Corinthians 4:8 Paul could write: "We are afflicted in every way, but not crushed; perplexed, but not driven to despair." In chapter 1, however, Paul alludes to a time of extreme mental anguish. He and his companions were in despair of coming through alive. The odds against them seemed overwhelming. What had come upon them was beyond their strength to bear and must have been considerably more than the prospect of being killed. They felt pressing upon them the irresistible weight of a death sentence about to be carried out as the culmination of defeat otherwise.

For Paul and the apostolic church the climax of the Midpoint event was God's raising of Jesus from the dead. Because of that they had the assurance that God will raise up those who are his out of the abyss of physical death. But in this passage Paul focuses not on Jesus's rising and not on that final resurrection. Rather, he points to God who, in between those two supreme acts and in intimation of them, intervenes to rescue persons from almost certain death. A comparable statement is found in 2 Timothy 4:17–18: "So I was rescued from the lion's mouth. The Lord will rescue me from every evil and save me for his heavenly kingdom." This motif of deliverance from impending death is found hundreds of times in the Hebrew scriptures.

We experience in elusive and repressed ways something similar to that distress Paul endured. All that is being done against a sustainable future far outweighs all that is being done for it. Human desolation of the world could come in various ways, some of which we may hardly recognize. Collective, even global, death sentence could come upon us before private dying. The most accessible consolation with regard to death has always been the prospect of vestigial "survival" by the continuance of one's addition to the human story through descendants and contributions otherwise. Now that consolation is as jeopardized as humanity itself.

But in the midst of this, Christians can have the understanding given to Paul. That shattering time, he wrote, was "to make us rely not on ourselves but on God who raises the dead." Paul had been driven to consider what the prospects were. Within that human situation everything seemed ominously against them. Nothing was in sight that could save them. There in the anguish of defeat, with death coming upon him, he turned from any reliance on himself, his own capabilities, or conceivably promising aspects of the situation. Only God's rescue could hold off death and bring them through. All his hope was in God who intervenes to save. And so it can be for Christians. They no longer set their hope on human capabilities, movements, and political prospects or possibilities to bring humanity through. (They do not disregard or dismiss these.) They count, rather, "on God, who raises the dead." In the midst of all that presses toward doom, they look to God, who rescues from death. And all interim rescue from death, individual or collective, points to that Day when all death will be swallowed up in Christ's victory (1 Cor. 15:54).

After a shipwreck some survivors might be swimming in an expanse of ocean with neither land nor floating objects in sight. Everything in the situation would seem contrary to hope. They would hardly base hope on their ability as swimmers but might swim on in hope of some saving fluke. The alternative possibility corresponding to what Paul described is that those persons would swim on, hoping in the God who rescues. They would not stop swimming because of trust in God. Quite the contrary. But the swimming, instead of taking its rise simply from the drive for self-preservation, would come as expression of that hope. What would be hoped for and possibly given would not be a fluke but God's means of rescue. Disciples can see their efforts against the powers of destruction in the world as comparable to that swimming. They continue as would-be survivors. They take part in efforts that seem to offer so little prospect of preserving the world from disaster and look to God who delivers from death.

In any dire circumstances one should not try to generate hope as the certainty that God must and will act to rescue from impending death. Confidence about deliverance must not be a claim upon God, supposedly because of one's faith. Rightly, it can come only as special gift from God, who in the specific situation intends the rescue. Even when neither assurance nor rescue is given, God remains the One who characteristically delivers his people from deadly perils. The biblical record bears vibrant, variegated witness to that. Through the ensuing centuries biblical people have found it to be true. When God does not hold back death, when swimmers sink into the depths, a rescue that is immeasurably more than any temporal one is soon to come. That rescue issues from the raising of Jesus, who was not rescued from execution by his enemies.

Most certainly Christians are to take part in efforts for justice, peace, and the integrity of creation. When large (or small) numbers of people rise up against oppression and death, disciples thank God. They seek to help such things happen, but they do not center their hope in them. Rather, they look to God to work surprises beyond their envisioning. Disciples orient their hope, not to millions of mobilized people and the multiplication of the millions, but to God who, with few or many or none, finds his ways to bring his purposes toward fulfilment.

Herbert Butterfield wrote: "The believer in Providence can be prepared for any surprises. The Christian need put no limits to the Creator's versatility."[8] The lives of individuals and the whole of history are continually reshaped by those surprises. If large numbers of church people in imperial countries would start to live under the Lordship of Jesus with regard to the world of nations, that would open a way for amazing surprises. Disciples point to the impossible as the expected. Yet when breakthroughs do not come and the grip of the powers of destruction seems to tighten, disciples look all the more to this God of surprises. The consummation will be all surprise and unimaginable versatility.

Hope as Anchorage

In such a world Christians desperately need an inspiriting with courage. This is given by the God of encouragement, first in the witness of the Hebrew scriptures, that they "might have hope" (Rom. 15:4, 5). Finding refuge in God, they "have strong encouragement to seize the hope set before [them], anchoring the soul to it safe and secure, as it enters the inner Presence behind the veil [the heavenly Holy of Holies]" (Heb. 6:18–19 Moffatt) — there with Jesus in the place of ultimate sacrifice, which is also the throne room of the universe.

"The darkness is passing away and the true light is already shining" (1 Jn. 2:8). The central dynamic of the darkness is hate (v. 9) with all its works. Because disciples see the true Light already shining, they have a firm basis for the confidence that the world's darkness is passing away. They do not take the magnitude of the darkness as indication of its permanence. In the decades following the resurrection of Jesus, the extent of darkness in the world remained immense. But that actuality was not decisive for how early Christians viewed their present and future. Nor should the comparable contemporary situation be decisive for the outlook of present-day Christians. The One who is Light of the world has broken the sway of that darkness. It is about to vanish before the Light. In these days and in places beyond number, usually hidden from general view, the Light overcomes darkness. Whenever the powers of death are held in check or driven back, intimation is given of God's approaching triumph.

"By his great mercy we have been born anew to a living hope through the resurrection of Jesus Christ from the dead," hope in "a salvation ready to be revealed in the last time" (1 Pet. 1:3, 5). All Christian hope has its source and grounding in the resurrection of Jesus. There the living God overwhelmed death. What was defeated, though, was not, first of all, death as the common destroyer of every human life but death in its commandeering of societal structures. All in the status quo that was against life, specifically the misdirected governmental and religious structures, moved to do away with Jesus but were in their turn defeated. Because of this, disciples can stand in hope against all around them and in them that moves against life. They hope simply in the One who at the Midpoint met all the onslaught of evil and everywhere through history meets it. Other fully decisive, enduring defeat of those powers is not to be found in history. Disciples hope for no other. The completion (*telos*) of Jesus' triumph is the "salvation ready to be revealed in the last time."

"Set your hope fully upon the grace that is coming to you at the revelation [*apokalypsis*] of Jesus Christ" (1 Pet. 1:13). Hope is to have its center, breadth, and depth in the consummate marvel of what God is about to give in this apocalypse. In their personal lives and for the world Christians have their lesser hopes. But hope for the consummation is to have such determining intensity within them that the lesser hopes become its adjuncts. I may be hoping that a child of mine succeeds in a particular endeavor. But far more than this, I hope the child will be so drawn into life with Jesus Christ that grace now may open into the grace that is coming. I may be hoping that a friend wrongly held on death row will not be executed on the scheduled date. But this Christian friend is included within my far more encompassing hope in God's mercy and faithfulness on the Day of manifest vindication of the One who was executed, though he had done no wrong at all. I hope for an end to the madness of the escalating militarization of the planet. But that, if it does come, will be constraint mainly upon one dimension of human folly. My wider hope is that God will end all madness and heal the creation. Hope for the consummation is not an addition or a complement to other hoping. It is the keystone; all other hopes should lean toward it. No other hope, cause, or movement, however important for the human future, is to be given that central place.

Paul wrote to the Christian community in Philippi, "And I am sure that he who began a good work in you will bring it to completion at the day of Jesus Christ" (Phil. 1:6). Any hope for another person is truncated unless it is oriented beyond this earthly life. Whatever fulfilments of lesser hopes may come, these decline and pass away. But ultimate hope looks to God, who draws up out of transitoriness and death. Lesser Christian hopes for persons, for humanity, and for all the earth seek smaller developments that may be taken up into the consummation.

Admittedly, absorption with biblical prophecies, the end of the world, and heaven often coincides with acceptance of things as they are. Many who are adept at gaining the rewards of this world think themselves assured of gaining the rewards of the next life. But multitudes deprived of earthly necessities are provided with tantalizing information about the future and end of the world and are given the consolation of a better life in heaven. If God is to set things right before long, church people, whether in the overclass or the underclass, can consider themselves relieved of that task. Much fundamentalist missionary work in the Third World has that slant, typically with the enthusiastic approval of the lords of the status quo.

Such waiting for heaven which inhibits concern and action for a better world on earth has of course been widely and rightly deplored. The standard pie-in-the-sky, opium-of-the-people objection is that if people hope mainly for what God will do beyond this life, they are inclined to sit on their hands for the present, at least with regard to seeking needed social changes. But biblical faith centered in Jesus Christ is very different from what is objected to. In this faith one discerns the collapsing, intolerable wrongness of the old over against the New that is breaking in. Because one glimpses the justice and shalom that God will bring to pass, one knows that God is presently engaged in that task around the world and draws his people into it. To align oneself with anti-Christian aspects of the status quo runs counter to the hope that they are about to be overcome. But in that hope one becomes a participant in their being overcome. Robert Jay Lifton writes, "Since all action depends upon images, rebels of any kind must have the capacity to imagine the overturning of their immediate world."[9] More than in any other stance, biblical faith gives that capacity, with images nurturing it.

Hope's Past

The Hebrews, singing the psalms, again and again recounted what God had done in their past, corporate and individual. All the past was congealed, irretrievably behind and inaccessible. Yet it was not fully so because with praise they were meeting Yahweh, whose gracious deeds were at the heart of it. In adverse circumstances they could celebrate what God had done earlier and thus form and ground their expectation of what he was about to do. Those songs of praise in the midst of trial were themselves a mystery of God's acting.

One can approach the basis of hope by looking at marriage. In any marriage times come when the present is dull and lifeless or strained and grating. Such a time seems to offer nothing for sustaining the marriage. In contemporary society such times, when prolonged, often result in marital collapse. But even when things have gone wrong in a marriage, there is often a past constituted in considerable measure by unobtrusive marvels of shared life and loving. So much has been good in discovering and receiving, in bringing children into the world and caring for them, in coming through hard times together, in the renewals of love. Divorce ordinarily comes by losing touch with and dismissing the amazing depth and extent of that past. A constricted present closes it off.

Couples in their marriage can do something comparable to what the Hebrews did in the psalms: look back over the drama and celebrate the call into covenant and God's unfolding acts of creation, pardon, and rescue. Their past is in the keeping of the One who gave the days and years and much of what filled them. Albums, diaries, letters, keepsakes, and other contents of a home represent that past. Children incarnate it, yet manifest most notably change away from it. By praising God for the fullness of what has been given in the marriage, couples help open the future for God's further gracious acting in the drama. Such praise should arise for every dimension of life. Like the psalmists Christians are to have eyes wide open to behold God's providential acting, not only in the biblical story, but in the world around them and in their own lives. All such discernment evokes expectancy.

Before describing hope (Rom. 5:2–5), Paul states its basis: "Therefore, since we are justified by faith, we have peace with God through our Lord Jesus Christ" (v. 1). In the words of T. F. Torrance, "That is the deepest reason for our hope, that God has overcome our alienation and reconciled us to Himself."[10] With all the social, political, economic, technological, military, and environmental problems that beset the world, one too easily loses sight of the central and most radical (root) problem, human estrangement from God. This problem, as hidden as God is, can be more convincingly denied than the derivative problems. Yet those provide vast evidence for the magnitude of the primary one. Because Christians find that God draws them back into relationship with him in spite of all that is wrong with them, they can rely on him for the lesser problems. Only the God of biblical faith who seeks wholeness of relationship with each human being is able to deal with all the forces that work against the wholeness of the world. God, who "was in Christ reconciling the world to himself" (2 Cor. 5:19), effects reconciliation, shalom, within the world.

Jesus broke down the barrier humans had erected between them and God. In drawing together the Messianic community, Jesus has broken down the dividing walls of enmity between the factions of humanity (Eph. 2:14). What he does already, he will soon bring to completion. Disciples live in ways that anticipate the consummate unity. To stand behind any dividing walls, as in racism, ethno-centrism, machismo, military preparations, or war, is to reject the fullness of Jesus' reconciling work — what he has done and is doing. However, to recognize the urgency of reconciliation only for relations between creatures (but not for the relation to God) is also a rejection of that fullness. This latter departure from the Gospel and its "message of reconciliation" (2 Cor. 5:19) has characterized the main range of peace and justice efforts in the churches.

Churches and individual Christians have so often taken up one or more aspects of hope and dropped others, thus adopting for themselves a fractional gospel. They may hope for God's forgiveness but hardly for God's transforming grace. They may have hope for a transformation of the society but hardly for God's saving action in individual lives. They may hope for an apocalyptic consummation but not for earthly triumphs of creative love over hate and violence. They may hope for personal healing but not for the healing of society. Or in each case hope may be oriented to the other side. But God's promises in their roundedness draw his people toward wholeness of hope.

Disciples recognize the church's responsibility and their own for the prevalence of false hopes in the world and the scarcity of true hope. Hoping all too sporadically against everything that dims hope, disciples take on themselves the burdens of those who have not yet come to know or no longer know "the God of hope" (Rom. 15:13). Christians hope representatively on behalf of all who struggle without hope.[11] Christians too are confronted much of the time with the seeming inadequacy of what God can be discerned as doing in history, in the church, and in their lives. Only in Jesus Christ do they see the adequacy of God's acting, which moves behind all that apparent inadequacy.

Within the churches a remnant, a confessing church, becomes a sign of hope. (In Hebrew *remnant* referred originally to the survivors of a campaign aimed at their destruction. Any present-day remnant is a gathering of those who in faithfulness come through campaigns of seduction or persecution aimed at eliminating them.) As persons and groups in that remnant live out their faith and hope, they become for others signs of hope, pointing to the future intended by God and to God's actions bringing it to reality.

"And this hope does not put us to shame, for God's love has been poured out in our hearts through the Holy Spirit who has been given to us" (Rom. 5:5). God is taking over human lives and human life together in the church, and all this is anticipatory of his completed takeover. Disciples "exult in hope of the glory of God" (5:2)[12] which is to fill that consummation, as intimations of that glory infuse their living.

Disciples hope in God who is incomparably gracious, but reckon with "a fearful prospect of judgment, and a fury of fire" (Heb. 10:27) — the cataclysmic harvest of what has been sown. They do not, however, resign themselves to any supposed inevitability of nuclear annihilation or other global disaster. God may yet be able to bring about *in time* a turning back from worldwide destruction. The most amazing surprise of the twentieth century was the overthrow of the East European communist governments by nonviolent popular uprisings in 1989. Any who discern the grace that was in those events will hardly insist that there can be no shift to far more peaceful relations among the peoples of the world. But even if such a shift comes, the emergent era could at any time relapse into the old. The opportunity, epochal in its possibilities, given the nations by the close of 1989, was largely shattered by the potentates of the old order and strewn across the desert sands.

Still, in spite of whatever may come, disciples seek to live what P. T. Forsyth described: "Faith is more than an individual calm; it is the Church's collective confidence on the scale of the world for the destiny of the world. The evil world will not win at last, because it failed to win at the only time it ever could."[13] Disciples are not bound by repressed despair. There is for the human family a future under the Rule of God. Jesus calls his community to live within that Rule as beginning of that future.

Chapter 14

PROMISE AND PAROUSIA

We must come under the guidance of a mind which is in entirely immediate and undisturbed communion with the creative Spirit of God, who
consequently has been initiated into all God's plans and who can say
about Himself: "No one knows the Father except the Son and any one to
whom the Son chooses to reveal him" (Mt. XI.27). That is to say we either
stop at the darkness of an impenetrable future and reject all the words of
Jesus dealing with the future of the world as concepts belonging to His
time and as Jewish dreams; or we entrust ourselves for our way into the
future to the One who makes this lofty claim for Himself. Then we cease
once and for all to make our own conjectures as regards the destiny of the
world. We trust absolutely that what this One tells us regarding the end
of the world is no human fancy but is based on a real knowledge of God's
plan, and that He made this knowledge, which is of infinite importance
for His Church, so clear to His disciples that we are perfectly justified in
believing the reports of the first witnesses.

—Karl Heim[1]

In the last decade of the eighteenth century, Immanuel Kant wrote
a treatise titled *Whether the Human Race Is Continually Advancing
towards the Better*. He saw three main possibilities for the future:
continual ascent, continual decline, or continuance on more or less
the same level. Josef Pieper presents Kant's thinking on the second
prospect:

To be sure "retrogression to the worse" (as he expresses it) is a theoretic possibility, but *in concreto* it does not exist; to Kant it is inconceivable. Why? His
statement on the matter runs as follows: "Deterioration cannot continue indefinitely in the human race; for when the process reached a certain pitch
the race would annihilate itself." In the Kantian view the self-destruction of
the human species cannot even be considered by a realistic historical thinker;
such a thing cannot happen.[2]

So limited was Kant's understanding of human nature and history. Yet, in spite of all that overshadows the world, a similar unreasoned dismissal of that supremely irrational prospect is strong within each of us.

A comparable listing of possible futures from our present vantage point would be: progressive transformation of human life to such an extent that a persuasive redemption of history will be achieved; enough of a shift away from destructive patterns of behavior to life-enhancing ones so that humanity can survive in a sustainable world (similar to Kant's same-level possibility); decline into global catastrophe, even extinction; the end of history through natural changes in the physical world such as the cooling of the sun. In terms simply of the last prospect, it may seem probable that history will continue for a very long time (if not "forever"). This could go with either of the first two prospects. To proceed in currently dominant patterns of human behavior must result, not in a plateau for the human condition, but in disastrous decline. Even Kant's same-level prospect is possible only through revolutionary changes in human attitudes and behavior.

There can be no well-grounded assurance that history will continue without end. The seemingly quite remote possibility of a termination resulting from changes in the physical world apart from human activity will always remain. That possibility has significant implications for how one views humanity and history. But quite obviously, human choices are not determinative for whether there will be an end of history brought on by slow or sudden natural changes in the physical world. What can be faced and dealt with are the human threats to survival.

Human nature is fundamentally the same everywhere. It seems to have remained much the same throughout recorded history. At present this human nature, which is the mold of each of us, inclines corporately toward catastrophe. Even if the human race achieves the most urgently needed improvements in attitudes and policies, the dark proclivities individually and collectively would still lurk. With the technological means available, the relapse of even a segment of humanity could bring the destruction of the whole. Only if human nature is basically freed from the inclinations in it that go against life will there be a human redemption of history with some dependability for the longer-term future. For humans to bring this off would be marvelous beyond measure, but the human past and present provide virtually no basis for such hope. Even if such a liberation within human nature could be achieved in the relatively distant future, until then survival and sustainability would hinge on human nature as we know it, that is, on what currently drives the world toward destruction.

Furthermore, any such liberation would not resolve the problem of death. Even in a utopian world individuals would die, would at that point lose everything, and would be left out of the future. An individual contributes to the shaping of the future but after death has no part *as person* in that future.

The objection can be raised that the Christian Gospel offers transformation of human personality away from destructiveness toward life. It is argued that when such transformation (even if in secularized form) becomes largely determinative of the global situation, humanity will be reaching a redemption of history. To be sure, multitudes through the centuries have experienced a measure of individual and group transformation by conversion and the work of the Spirit. But this reality is always something that is partial, jeopardized, and awaiting completion by God. One cannot hope for an adequate redemption of humanity within history through transformation understood in terms of the Gospel because the Gospel itself goes against any such hope. The Gospel portrays human beings as in critical need of initial and continuing conversion from the deformities of sin. The witness of Jesus and of all the apostolic scriptures knows nothing of a redemption of humanity within history away from that need. It sees rather the sure beginnings, always contested, of what God will bring to consummation beyond history's collapse. Only apart from Christian faith biblically understood can one engage in wishful dreaming about such a redemption. Human beings direct their hope for the future of humanity primarily toward humans or toward God. Biblical hope has to do most basically not with what humans can actualize in relation to God but with what God will fully actualize in relation to humans.

Terminal Questioning and Biblical Affirmations

In what seems to be a terminal illness, an individual may be confronted with ultimate questions much more than before. Is there One who rescues out of death (before and after) to give life? Is death final extinction? Is there a dynamic within one's personality that brings it through death into continued existence? Such questions are so important because they have to do with *future or no future* for each person.

In our time the question about God seems most pressing in relation to the threat of the imminent death of history and to the yearning
that there be a humane future for humanity. Can God really be
counted on for the rescue of history from death or out of death?
Is God seen as One who can overcome the worst that human beings
might do? Or can the "God" that is looked to be conclusively defeated? Can the powers of destruction win out *finally* — at least on
earth? Would God as understood in a particular theology or philosophy survive human extinction? And, if so, what significance would
that have for humanity?

History has been filled with the cry for salvation, for things to
be set right, for shalom. In our time this yearning has become more
intense and widespread than that for personal survival after death.
In response various offers of salvation to be achieved by humanity
have been brought forward. Some theologies have promoted such
offers. Reinhold Niebuhr could characterize the dominant modern
conception of history as "the belief that historical development is a
redemptive process."[3]

If, as in many theologies, God is not seen as sovereign, the problem of how there can be both evil *and* God's Rule is eliminated. But
then the "God" looked to is not the God of Israel and of Jesus, whose
initial proclamation focused on the inauguration of God's Rule.
"God" who is not sovereign, purposeful, all-knowing, all-loving
Thou cannot rescue. Neither can "God" understood as life-giving
effervescence contained within the cosmos. If "God" is seen as desig-
nation for the highest human potentialities and ideals or as reservoir
of goodness, love, and creativity, *everything* depends on the tapping
of those resources. But preponderant evidence around the world
weighs heavily against hope that depends simply on humanity by
itself or on the human utilization of "God." A prevailing global altruism has not emerged in periods when the international situation was
relatively conducive to that. If, as seems likely, overall conditions in
the world become much worse through such things as global warming, destruction of the ozone layer, and rapid population growth,
what is already "the age of triage"[4] will very probably become that
far more.

If humanity is divinized, such a "God" can die more fully than
have so many others, for not even a recollection would remain.
Human beings cannot have sure hope in any such "God"; for a divinity not really in control can be as thoroughly vanquished and
undone (at least on earth) as humanity itself. If "God" is viewed as
something like a magnetic field of goodness through the cosmos,

the human species and much other life can, nonetheless, disappear permanently and quite soon from that field. If (as is widely claimed) "God" is not yet but becoming, that becoming can be cut off — at least for humanity and any human connection to it. Even if "God" continues or emerges elsewhere in the cosmos, that remains without substantive significance for a vanished species at this point in the cosmos. Any "God" seen as other than all-comprehending Thou is by nature unresponsive to human dilemmas or less responsive than humans may be. A reservoir or a magnetic field does not feel with children dying of hunger. But a nonsovereign "God" who is simply co-sufferer cannot be looked to for rescue. Any of these views offer slender basis for hope. Either God is ultimate Thou, mightier than what destroys life, or humans are basically on their own, faced with the immensity of evil.

Judgment comes upon philosophies and theologies as well as upon nation states and peoples. "In the time of their trouble" adherents of false gods call out, "Arise and save us!" (Jer. 2:27). Idols of wood and stone cannot arise. Neither can the contrived gods of philosophy, theology, or ideology. A common denominator of such gods is their inability to arise in sovereign redemptive action. Those gods have failed to bring decisive progress toward such redemption as they promise. Now they show themselves powerless to hold back the rush to global destruction. One can cling to the delusive hopes proffered in such divinities or turn from them. Any hope apart from the God of Israel and of Jesus Christ totters toward debacle with history itself. In the vision given to prophets and psalmists, all creatures are to shout for joy before God. But now humanity faces the contrary prospect that the earthly creation will cry out in anguish. What could be a more comprehensive judgment by God than the manifest collapse of the human project of self-redemption?

In the Christian understanding, the redemption of the world has been accomplished and will be completed, not by human beings as such and not by the realization of immanent potentialities. It was brought about by the One who came as God's initiative from beyond the flow of history. The story of Israel as narrow developmental line within that flow provided the preparation for his coming. That One took human life and all the preparation to himself; but who he was and what he did were not, in the deepest dimensions, a product of history. "And the Word became flesh and dwelt among us" (Jn. 1:14). "God was in Christ reconciling the world to himself" (2 Cor. 5:19). Humanity needed far more than the law and strict adherence to it, far more than ethical instruction, insight about living, and spirited encouragement. So extreme was the human predicament that the One who came from God had to die on a Roman cross. God limited his own sovereignty when he created humankind. But the extremity of that delimiting in the execution of Jesus brought the central disclosure of how God rules the world. Most of all because of Jesus' rising, Christians know that God is in control.

So too the redemptive fulfilment of history will not emerge from within the flow of history. The One who came before will appear again as God's consummating initiative from beyond. All this will be God's doing, simply and conclusively — grace, not human works. In the beginning God created the world. At the Midpoint God redeemed the world. In the End God will bring humanity, history, and the cosmos to consummation. But moment by moment through time, everything that has come from that Midpoint moves in struggle toward the End. And disciples pray, "*Maranatha!* Our Lord, come!" (1 Cor. 16:22).

One is inclined to search for rescue and Rescuer from sin only if one recognizes deformity and guilt within oneself as extreme problems. One is inclined to seek the Rescuer and rescue of history only if one recognizes that the proliferating evil within history is taking it toward catastrophe. Clearly, the extremity of need in either dimension does not prove that there is a Savior and salvation. But the Gospel offers these for the individual and for history. Any who see the dire need do well to examine what is offered.

Do I really believe that Jesus' life, death, and rising are stronger than the amassed evil in this world? For these to be stronger than one's own sin and guilt may seem a relatively easy matter. But are they stronger than all the powers of destruction in history? The witness of the apostolic scriptures, climaxing in the book of Revelation, affirms that they are. During and after Jesus' crucifixion, the dominance of evil in the world overwhelmed his disciples. But then they were shown who truly has dominion.

True to His Promise

Biblical hope is directed toward promise, that is, toward One who has promised and is able to fulfill his promise. All other hope is at bottom wishful thinking. In Christian faith what is decisive is not projections about the future that humans come up with but rather God's promises about the good future he brings in. The many pictures of that future given in scripture are to be seen, not as visions born of human longing, but as expressions of the utterly trustworthy promise of God. Paul S. Minear writes: "Every genuine promise comes from God. He alone is absolutely dependable in doing what he says he will do.... This is why his promise is the only sure basis of hope."[5]

"Let us hold fast the confession of our hope without wavering, for he who promised is faithful" (Heb. 10:23). As "father of us all" (Rom. 4:16), Abraham was "fully convinced that God was able to do what he had promised" (Rom. 4:21). A most decisive frontier between theologies comes at this point: whether or not God is understood as the One who can promise and fulfil what has been promised. Any "God" that is not Thou and not sovereign could not make the biblical promises.

Issues of eschatology go back to issues of christology. If Jesus was no more than a great, even the greatest, ethical teacher, shaman, or exemplar, one can pick and choose which of his ideas one happens to like. His teachings come before the tribunal of one's selective reasoning formed by the contemporary thought-world. One may find vitally important ethical insights but reject much of his understanding about God and eschatology as products of naive Jewish conceptions of his time.

But Christians see Jesus as the One most of all in touch with the Mystery vaguely sensed throughout the human story, because he came into the human midst from the heart of that Mystery. They turn to him as the One from whom to learn all that matters most. The overall impression made by Jesus on his first and closest friends was such that they could not consider him simply as superlative human being. In accord with Jesus' self-understanding, which he disclosed to them, they concluded that he had come from beyond, from God, and that he was living out and proclaiming God's truth — was indeed himself God's Word become flesh — in a way axial for all history. Out of that conclusion the Christian movement emerged. The impression Jesus made can still be examined in the recorded witness of those friends and can lead persons to the same conclusion. If it does, Jesus becomes their Lord. That means *Lord,* not only of acting, but of thinking, of how they see God, other humans, this age, and the coming age. Disciples have one Teacher, one Master (Mt. 23:8, 10); they seek to have all their thinking formed by him. They take to themselves those promises and pictures, such as that of dazzling clouds surrounding One upon whom all eyes around this planet are gazing. They "wait for the revealing [*apokalypsis*] of [the] Lord Jesus Christ" (1 Cor. 1:7).

Those within or outside the churches who follow the lead of a thinker or movement with conceptions of God, humanity, and history quite different from what Jesus taught depend on the thinker or movement as more reliable guide with a truer apprehension of ultimate reality. Those who come up with their own do-it-yourself theology designate themselves as persons nearer to the truth about God than Jesus was. Continuing partly in modes of traditional homage to Jesus while rejecting his basic understanding of God and humanity makes no sense. Disciples believe that Jesus is a more reliable teacher about God and the human future than is the latest meteoric theologian. Whether Jesus is looked to as Lord (of thinking) is the central issue for how theology is to be done.

The alternatives can be examined in a different aspect. If the "resurrection" of Jesus was the resilient continuance of his teachings, example, and "spirit," much like what remains from any beloved person who has died, that remainder is there for others to draw from. They have the say in relation to it. But if Jesus is risen indeed, humans are confronted by a Person, the supreme Person, who comes to have the say. They do not have at their disposal what was left over from him. Rather, they are to be at his disposal.

Twentieth-century theology and biblical scholarship have been much preoccupied with eschatology. There is wide agreement that Jesus had a strongly apocalyptic outlook and expected the catastrophic ending of the world and the glorious establishment of God's Kingdom on earth. "All His words presuppose the fact of an imminent day of judgment for the world."[6] "All the appeals and parables of warning taken together show that Jesus is not thinking of the inevitable death of the individual as the impending danger, but of the approaching eschatological catastrophe, and the coming Judgement."[7] Jesus "required no evidence from anyone about human nature; well did he know what was in human nature" (Jn. 2:25 Moffatt). Knowing his own people and God's way with the world, he foresaw the coming destruction of Jerusalem. Knowing the make-up of all humanity and discerning the purpose of God, Jesus foresaw the catastrophic ending of history. "The whole thinking of Jesus is permeated by ideas of *parousia*. This is true in all strata of the Synoptic tradition."[8]

The Hebrew scriptures were filled with promises. In promise God communicated his purpose to his people. Jesus saw himself, and was seen, as the fulfilment of God's earlier promises. "It is in him that all God's promises are affirmed as true" (2 Cor. 1:20).[9] But Jesus also stated promises for the future, recasting those in the Hebrew scriptures. The Beatitudes are promise. In spite of all contrary indications, the humble before God shall inherit the earth. Promise underlies the Lord's Prayer. Jesus taught that the Kingdom prayed for would fully come. Disciples were to pray ardently for what he promised — for God's consummate takeover of the world, completing all steps toward that.

James and John came to Jesus with the request, "Grant us to sit, one at your right hand and one at your left, in your glory" (Mk. 10:37). Scholars recognize that the early church would not have invented this incident with Jesus' rebuke of two of its leaders. Jesus rejected the self-seeking of the two but not their expectation of a coming Kingdom; he clearly shared it. As Karl Heim points out, "If we possessed only this one piece of most ancient tradition it would be sufficient proof that the expectation of a coming Realm of Glory is not a later doctrine of the Church but belongs to the most ancient tradition of Christ's words."[10]

Mark 14:61–62 records a remarkable exchange: "Again the high priest asked him, 'Are you the Christ, the Son of the Blessed?' And Jesus said, 'I am; and you will see the Son of man sitting at the right hand of Power, and coming with the clouds of heaven.'" That answer was almost certainly not an imaginative creation of the early church but Jesus' climactic witness to himself, which was taken as the most decisive evidence for sentencing him to death. That statement was challenge to those who supposedly represented the entire heritage of Israel. It can be taken as the most momentous assertion Jesus ever made. Either he spoke the truth or he was pathetically mistaken, mistaken about his parousia, about his expectation of sharing in God's sovereignty, and therefore about being God's eschatological agent understood in such ways. But if he was mistaken, he was a false prophet as the Hebrews understood this. He was making claims for himself and the future that were untrue. Within that understanding he deserved to die (Deut. 18:20–22).

It will not do to say that Jesus is Lord and suppose that he was mistaken in his understanding of humanity's future. It will not do to dismiss Jesus' eschatology with the comment that he took over Jewish ideas of his time, now quaint and outdated. Any who believe that Jesus was mistaken on such supremely important matters assume for themselves the favored position of being right where he was wrong. At stake is not simply eschatological ideas held by Jesus but his promise to his people.

In his living and his dying Jesus set his hope on God. For his own vindication and for God's, "he trusted to him who judges justly"

(1 Pet. 2:23). He taught and passed on an ethic that centers in such trust. The Gospels tell of his hoping and of how that shaped his life. Jesus' disciples were drawn into his hoping. At present also disciples not only hope in Jesus but hope with him. Jesus promised his first disciples that he would rise after being executed and return to them. They experienced his fulfilment of that promise. They saw his resurrection as God's validation of his threefold claim before the Sanhedrin: "The God of our fathers raised Jesus whom you killed by hanging him on a tree. God exalted him at his right hand as Leader and Savior.... Repent ... that he may send the Christ appointed for you, Jesus, whom heaven must receive until the time for establishing all that God spoke by the mouth of his holy prophets from of old" (Acts 5:30–31; 3:19–21). If Jesus rose, as the apostolic witness proclaims, he is Lord, sharing in the Rule of the universe, and the manifest glory of that Rule is soon to envelop the earth.[11]

If humanity lives before the God of Israel and of Jesus, it is intolerable that his gracious purposes for humanity be unendingly thwarted on earth. If Jesus in his death and rising triumphed over the powers of destruction, it is intolerable that this triumph never be brought to completion. If it was impossible for Jesus to be held in the grip of death (Acts 2:24), so is it too for the human story to be held perpetually in that grip. If Jesus is Lord of the universe behind the curtain of the seen, the moment must come when "every eye will see him" (Rev. 1:7). As surely as the unseen electromagnetic charge in a cloud builds up to the flash of lightning, so must that Coming shine forth from east to west.

Jesus took up the task of God's chief agent on earth — "good news to the poor ... release to the captives ... recovering of sight to the blind ... liberty [for] those who are oppressed" (Lk. 4:18 from Is. 61:1). He passed on that task to those in his movement. Jesus carried out the beginnings of that work, but those who remained unhelped were far more numerous than those he was able to help. This is still the case as his followers, with all their failings, continue the task. Jesus did not become the messiah that so many of his fellow Jews were longing for — a military leader who would seize power and, with spectacular success, set things right for Jews and for humankind. The immensity of all that has not been set right in the world is still taken as grounds for making decisions totally contrary to the decision Jesus made. But if Jesus was God's chief agent in history and decided in accord with God's purpose, the course of action he chose must receive its manifest vindication. That which was inaugurated in Jesus, that which is still so partial, incognito, and ever imperiled, must come to all-embracing sway. God will most certainly set things right in all the world.

The promise of God in the Hebrew scriptures and the promise of Jesus echoed by his first followers is that God will bring his purposes for humanity to fulfilment. History will come out right. Christians hold to that promise, "not shifting from the hope of the gospel which [they] heard" (Col. 1:23). Jesus believed that history would collapse but then be transfigured as God's glorious Rule sweeps over it. The apostolic church took up his belief. This outlook has been profoundly unacceptable to modes of thought dominant in the modern world. It continues to constitute a humiliating affront to human pride in spite of the global developments that tend to support its negative aspect. Beyond the affront, however, the Gospel with this view as part of it provides the only well-grounded affirmation of the worth of human beings over against all that looms to negate that worth. The incalculable worth of each individual and of all humanity is grounded in God's valuation, which shows itself in his promise to transfigure these creatures on the New Earth.

In the ancient Mediterranean world, people generally believed in a realm beyond this one perceived by the senses. Those who died were thought to pass into that realm of shades and shadows. Most cultures and religions have had some such outlook. Similarly, the Hebrew scriptures nearly always view any continuation of human life beyond death as little more than a hovering in the shadowy realm. Our most robust perceptions are those of material entities around us. We are inclined to suppose that these perceptions point us to substance and that anything beyond them is shadow at best. Even in the experience of Christians much of the time, God has far less intensity of existence than that which they perceive for themselves and for persons and things around them. If "God is spirit" (Jn. 4:24), "spirit" may seem quite insubstantial and vacuous. Such an ordering of existence leads naturally to disbelief or agnosticism with regard to the Parousia of Jesus. One may believe in a departure into another far less substantial dimension but hardly in another dimension's sweeping over the world in superlative reality.

When the risen Jesus first appeared to his disciples, they thought they were seeing a ghost returning from the shadowy realm. But Jesus helped them to recognize that he was no pallid phantom. Life in such intensity so confronted the disciples that everything else seemed pale and partial by comparison. The risen Lord continually seeks to reverse the perception of disciples and others. Theirs is the world of shadow; he and his Realm are substance. His is the incomparably greater density, concreteness, and resilience. The One who holds the cosmos up into existence must be far more real than that which is held up. The hidden sovereignty of Jesus seated at the right hand of God has immeasurably greater intensity than that exercised by imperial leaders dominating the world media. John on Patmos "saw a great white throne and him who sat upon it; from his presence earth and sky fled away, and no place was found for them" (Rev. 20:11). The less real shrinks away from the full coming of the ultimately Real.

To live in hope of the glorious Appearing of Jesus should not at all lead to giving up on the present world, filled as it is with illness, starvation, pollution, violence, armaments, repression, and official lying. The One who will vanquish the powers of darkness at the End is moving in might against them now. The Pentagon, the White House, the Capitol, all their counterparts, and the death dances within them are relatively insubstantial and are about to shrink away before the manifest reality of the coming One. The Servant, who will bring "justice to victory" (Mt. 12:20) in the consummation, is doing that proleptically in these days. Under this Servant Lord, Christians have stronger reasons than others to live for humaneness of life and against the powers of death.

The "Delay" of the Parousia

"When you see these things taking place, you know that he is near, at the very gates" (Mk. 13:29). If a lion escaped from a circus nearby and one heard a roar outside the house, one would do well, even without seeing the lion, to assume that it was close. To John on Patmos Jesus was portrayed as "the Lion of the tribe of Judah" (Rev. 5:5). The Lion is right outside the gates, just behind the curtain of the seen. Disciples do not know how soon he will come through the gates, how soon the curtain will be flung to the side, but they know that he is near.[12]

Disciples understand that God's timing is none of their business ("It is not for you to know times or seasons which the Father has fixed by his own authority"); but they are to be witnesses (Acts 1:7–8). Earlier Jesus had emphasized that no one could know the time of the End. One implication of this was that the End could come at any time. But another was that his followers could not be sure that the End would come within any given period of time (such as the lifetime of the apostles). Disciples were to be on the watch like servants left in charge of a house, whose master might at any time return. The apostolic church lived in that watchful expectancy: The Lord might at any moment appear.

Jesus' statement, "this generation will not pass away before all these things take place" (Mk. 13:30), can hardly have been a prediction that the generation then living would not all die before the glorious Coming of the Son of man; for it would then stand in blatant opposition to the warning given in the following verses against trying to know the time. It would be comparable to the prediction of some pop apocalyptists that the Second Coming will take place within a generation (reckoned as about forty years) from the founding of the State of Israel in 1948. Some scholars have pointed out that this saying originally may have been part of Jesus' answer to the disciples' question about when the destruction of Jerusalem would come (Mk. 13:2). Similar considerations apply to Jesus' prophecy, "Truly, I say to you, there are some standing here who will not taste death before they see the kingdom of God come with power" (Mk. 9:1). Whatever the meaning (reference perhaps to the day of Pentecost), it was not intended to meet human curiosity about the timing of the Parousia (cf. Jn. 21:23–24).

The centuries passed and the church struggled with the problem of "the delay of the Parousia." No passage in the apostolic scriptures suggests the prospect that history might continue for nearly two thousand years or more. Yet no passage need be understood as clear forecast that it could not continue this long.

The following considerations can be weighed in relation to the lapse of time.

A number of comments in the teaching of Jesus seem intended to prepare his followers for prolonged waiting and watching. In several parables the master of the house delays his return. Disciples were told, "Now after a long time the master of those servants came and settled accounts with them" (Mt. 25:19). In the parable of the wise and foolish maidens, "the bridegroom was delayed" (Mt. 25:5). To reach all ethnic groups in the world with the Good News before the End (Mt. 24:14) would take considerable time.

In the understanding of the apostolic church, Jesus triumphed over the colossal wickedness of the world. All evil has already received its death blow and is about to be totally vanquished by the revealed might of the One who "is called The Word of God" (Rev. 13:3; 19:11–16). Disciples do not need to know the timing of the consummation. It is enough that they look to the One who has conquered and will conquer.

Christians believe that the End may come soon in the common understanding of *soon* but realize that God's *soon* in passages of scripture about the consummation is quite different from that human understanding. The author of Hebrews quotes from Habakkuk 2:3 Septuagint (the ancient Greek translation of the Hebrew scriptures): "For yet 'in a very little while, / the one who is coming will come and will not delay' " (10:37 NRSV). That author must have been aware that these words (key ones in the Jewish messianic expectation of the time) were written more than a half a millennium earlier. He did not quote them like a pop apocalyptist who would take them to mean that after such a long delay the calendrical time still remaining before the final event had almost run out. Rather, that promise was for him as valid as it had been hundreds of years earlier because the Coming that God would surely bring to pass loomed all along as imminent and awesomely near.

In Isaiah 54:7–8 God's word is given:

> For a brief moment I forsook you,
>> but with great compassion I will gather you.
> In overflowing wrath for a moment
>> I hid my face from you,
> but with everlasting love I will have compassion on you,
>> says the Lord, your Redeemer.

For Jews the time of the Babylonian destruction of Jerusalem and the seventy years of exile must have seemed excruciatingly long. But in God's perspective it was "a brief moment." God gave the promise of redemption for the exiled Jews in terms of his perception of time rather than an ordinary human perception. Paul was drawn into God's perspective when he wrote about "this slight momentary affliction" (2 Cor. 4:17). Disciples are drawn somewhat into that perception of time. They understand the *soon* in such passages as Revelation 1:1; 22:6, 7, 12, 20 in terms of the impinging intensity of the Reality that could at any time burst over the earth.

"For a thousand years in thy sight / are but as yesterday when it is past, / or as a watch in the night" (Ps. 90:4). "With the Lord one day is as a thousand years, and a thousand years as one day" (2 Pet. 3:8). In an era when human beings have been able to measure the incomprehensible length of time since the beginning of the universe, it is ironical that many, even in the churches, should consider a period of about two thousand years disproof of the eschatological hope stated by Jesus and his first followers. Three hours, the time it takes to watch a longer movie, has about the same proportionate relation to two thousand years as the two thousand years has to thirteen billion years, a lower estimate of the age of the universe. The One who determines the Day of the Parousia is the Creator of the cosmos.

"When the fullness [*pleroma*] of time had come, God sent his Son" (Gal. 4:4 NRSV). As a pregnancy comes to its completed allotment of time within the ordering of God, so does the swelling flow of history. The period beginning with Abraham and fulfilled in that coming of Jesus was almost as long as the period since. "A hardening has come upon part of Israel, until the full number [*pleroma*] of the Gentiles come in" (Rom. 11:25). The martyr host under the altar in heaven are told to wait a little longer until the full number of those to be martyred is complete (Rev. 6:11). "The times of the Gentiles" are to be fulfilled (Lk. 21:24). History's *pleroma* for the Parousia has not quite been reached: multitudes of Gentile Christians, but not the full number; so many martyrs, especially in the twentieth century, but not the completed count; the still more inflated hubris of Gentile world dominion, but not yet its culmination.

For conclusion of the parable of the doorkeeper, Jesus said, "Watch therefore — for you do not know when the master of the house will come, in the evening, or at midnight, or at cockcrow, or in the morning — lest he come suddenly and find you asleep" (Mk. 13:35–36). The bridegroom comes at midnight (Mt. 25:6). Today or tonight or tomorrow may bring the world's last hour. Disciples live as those to whom God gives the fullness of one day after another. Concurrently they live as those who have little time left for living Christ's cause in a world that (even humanly seen) may have little time left.

In the usual way of thinking, the most certain aspect of the future is that each of us will die. Yet that way of thinking is contrary to the revelation centered in Jesus. Paul wrote, "We shall not all sleep [that is, die], but we shall all be changed, in a moment, in the twinkling of an eye, at the last trumpet" (1 Cor. 15:51–52). Each living person moves steadily toward the end of his or her earthly life. In the consensus of human experience, that end is the coming of death. That end may, however, be the Appearing of Jesus. Any living person may have as much time still to live as history has for the completion of its course.

Smaller tremors usually come as a forewarning before a great earthquake. Before Mt. St. Helen's erupted, there were many indications that this was about to happen. Disciples feel the tremors before the final shaking of earth and heaven (Heb. 12:26). Endtime signs spoken of by Jesus, such as upheavals in history and nature, should evoke intensified watchfulness. They should not be taken as a basis for calculations or conclusions about the timing of the Parousia. These signs are given throughout the time ("the latter days") from Jesus' resurrection until the End. Beyond all such signs is what Karl Heim points to in the metaphor of seeing the lightning, then waiting for the thunder: Jesus' resurrection was the lightning, and since then disciples have been awaiting the sure thunder of the Parousia.[13]

Images of the End

In prophetic passages such as Isaiah 13, Ezekiel 7, Mark 13, and Matthew 24, and in Revelation, the culminating upsurge of rebellion against God precedes the End. That perennial insurgency reaches its ghastly climax. According to biblical teaching, history will die before its resurrection. That death is not to come as human extinction but as the terminal exhaustion of human possibilities. (According to biblical prophecy human beings will be alive on earth at the moment of the Parousia.) The story and course of all humanity will end but will then be lifted up out of its ruin and transformed on the New Earth.

In pop apocalyptism the end of the world comes when the insuperable Good Guy wipes out the bad guys — by violence, in the nick of time, for rescue of the innocent, almost as in all those television dramas. A facile reading of certain passages, especially Revelation 19:11–21, may give apparent support to that picture.

Such an understanding divorces the Parousia from the cross. The Parousia, however, will be the unveiling of the resurrection, the Appearing of the Lamb that was slain. In raising Jesus from death, the might of God's gracious love triumphed over all that was set against it. Still largely hidden, that victory will burst into view in the Parousia, and his love will have its way. The glory of the Parousia will be the glory of that life and that death — the glory of God's coming to suffer with and for humankind. All human beings, all the creation, will be face to face with Jesus. When the veil that hides the splendor of the Risen One is drawn aside, that apocalypse will cast away "the mourning veil covering all peoples, / and the shroud enwrapping all nations, / he will destroy death forever" (Is. 25:7–8 JB).

Jesus, crucified and risen, will appear as Lord of all. Beyond any other conceivable possibility, this will constitute a totality of judgment upon the nations and what they have been. "The nations shall see and be ashamed / of all their might" (Mic. 7:16). The Coming of Jesus will effect fullness of reversal: "many that are first will be last, and the last first" (Mk. 10:31). The largely hidden underside of history will be lifted up, and so too the underside of the church. Cultural glories of the nations will be brought into the New City (Rev. 21:26). But much that went unrecognized and unpraised before will shine in reflected splendor, and much that was wrongly exalted will fade. The dominant elites have almost always managed the writing of history. But then, in most awesome transposition, history as God has appraised it will be open to retrospective survey. The horrors of the inhuman past will not be entirely out of view but will be intimated in the still visible wounds of the One who has triumphed. Whoever and whatever from all the human story yield to that resplendent enveloping sway will come forth into its full disclosure.

Christians should not be taken in by the ethereal (and unbiblical) individualizing of the Christian hope: A person dies, and the consolation is that this life somehow continues with God in heaven. Rather, they are to hold fast to those Hebrew prophecies about vines and fig trees, lions and lambs, and to the plea Jesus entrusted to the Messianic community, "Thy kingdom come, thy will be done on earth as it is in heaven." God will bring shalom on earth, the earth recreated. What draws near will not be the multiplication of a narrow private happening but a cosmic event embracing all God's people. With the New Earth will come the perfected wholeness and harmony of all that does not hold out unendingly against God.

"Behold, he is coming with the clouds, and every eye will see him, every one who pierced him; and all tribes of the earth will wail on account of him" (Rev. 1:7). But this (at least in its major strains) will be no wail of despairing consternation. The allusion is to Zechariah 12:10: "When they look on him whom they have pierced, they shall mourn for him, as one mourns for an only child, and weep bitterly over him, as one weeps over a first-born." All peoples will see the unfathomable marvel of who Jesus was and is, and take in the all-embracing pathos of what was done to him. They shall mourn for him as the One dearest and most beloved, mourn for what all have inflicted on him and on all others; and they that mourn shall be comforted by this One who was pierced to death and is first-born from the dead.

In the recurring Hebrew vision, taken up in John's Apocalypse, all the nations unite in praising Yahweh. "All nations shall come and worship thee, / for thy judgments have been revealed" (Rev. 15:4). Ethnic distinctions no longer count except in manifesting the remarkable variegation of that praise. The praise of each Christian and of each fellowship around the world enters already into global prefiguration of that coming symphony of Iranians, Iraqis, Russians, Americans, Salvadorans, Tibetans, Israelis, Turks, Japanese, Zunis, Yakuts, Bantus, Maoris, Basques, Aucas, and all the rest in that "great multitude which no one could number, from all tribes and peoples and tongues" (Rev. 7:9). Christians see that every person and every ethnic and national grouping is meant for that inclusive unity of adoration. They dare not join in any delimited grouping set against another. More encompassing still is "the hope...that creation as well as humanity will one day be freed from its thraldom to decay and gain the glorious freedom of God's children" (Rom. 8:21 Moffatt, altered), joining without impediments in the universal chorus.

The prospect that humans may devastate the planet and even terminate human history can be seen as the climactic threat to the sovereignty of the living God. President Harry Truman, hearing of the Hiroshima blast, was right in a certain infernal sense when he called the bomb "the greatest thing in history."[14] Seemingly, global nuclear holocaust or desolation of the earth brought on in other technological ways would be the most determinative action in history. It would appear to be immeasurably more decisive than anything else that can be pointed to, including biblical events; for it could erase (or go far toward erasing) everything in life — thus, the results of anything earlier. A president, a maverick missile commander, or a malfunctioning computer system might initiate the nuclear fury and in one day become more determinative of the human situation (it would seem) than God's revelation centered in Jesus of Nazareth. What does that mean for the sovereignty of God over the course of history?

The crucifixion of Jesus brings some explication. There most of all, humans were permitted the power and "freedom" to move against God, to crush the inauguration of God's Rule in Jesus, to do away with God who had come so near. That move did not impose the insurgent human will upon God but was taken up by God's incomparably more determinative countermove of atonement and resurrection. What human defiance of God imposed, God in Jesus took freely to himself for the rescue of all. That countermove remains more determinative of the human future than any possible insurgency, even that of human self-destruction, because God is bringing it toward consummation in the unveiling of the One still hidden. Only the rising of Jesus of Nazareth has more power and momentum than the sway of death that is tightening so perceptibly around our planet. God who remained graciously sovereign when the corpse of the incarnate Son was entombed would be equally omnipotent even in the aftermath of the ultimate war or other terminal madness and near the full revealing of his power. "The Lord is risen indeed!" Death's dominion is at an end. The fullness of God's Rule is breaking in. What God has begun on earth he will complete.

NOTES

PREFACE

1. To avoid identifying as Christian (coming from Jesus Christ) what is not Christian, the terms *church people* and *church folk* are used when unfaithfulness to Christ is being considered. This is done with the recognition that every Christian is partly characterized by unfaithfulness.

2. Stanley Hauerwas, *Against the Nations: War and Survival in a Liberal Society* (Minneapolis: Winston Press, 1985), 28.

3. See G. B. Caird, *Saint Luke* (Harmondsworth, Middlesex: Penguin Books, 1963), 169.

4. G. C. Berkouwer, *The Providence of God* (Grand Rapids: William B. Eerdmans Publishing Company, 1952), 165.

5. In spite of its serious defects and in the absence of any accepted alternative, the term *American(s)* is used in this book with its common meaning.

Chapter 1
GOD'S WORD AND POLITICAL DISCERNMENT

1. George Hunsinger, "Barth, Barmen, and the Confessing Church Today," *Katallagete* (Summer 1985): 26–27, drawing from and quoting Karl Barth, *The Church and War* (New York: Macmillan Company, 1944), 12.

2. Langdon Gilkey, *Reaping the Whirlwind: A Christian Interpretation of History* (New York: Seabury Press, 1976), 242.

3. *Herbert Butterfield: Writings on Christianity and History*, ed. C. T. McIntire (New York: Oxford University Press, 1979), 4.

4. Emil Brunner summarizes: "And this is the essence of paganism, old and new — either the pantheistic deification of the world (God is the universe) or the deification of the human self (God is mind)." "Is Jesus Coming?" *The Christian Century* (December 23, 1931): 1622,

5. Emil Brunner, *Christianity and Civilization, First Part: Foundations* (New York: Charles Scribner's Sons, 1947). As Karl Heim has put it: "All things ... have no power in themselves to endure from this moment into the next. Left to themselves, they would without God fall back into their non-existence. God, who *alone* has immortality, is able to hold temporal beings like ourselves over the

Void, and carry us over from one moment to the next" (*The Transformation of the Scientific World View* [New York: Harper & Brothers Publishers, 1953], 29–30).

6. Karl Heim, *Christian Faith and Natural Science* (New York: Harper & Brothers Publishers, 1953), 74ff.

7. Karl Heim, *The Transformation of the Scientific World View*, 214ff.

8. Simone Weil proposed, "so one must learn to feel in all things, first and almost solely, the obedience of the universe to God" (*Waiting for God* [London: Routledge and Kegan Paul, 1951], 74; *Waiting for God* [New York: Capricorn Books, 1951], 131).

9. Paul S. Minear, *Christian Hope and the Second Coming* (Philadelphia: Westminster Press, 1954), 149.

10. Gerhard von Rad, *Old Testament Theology*, 2 vols. (Edinburgh: Oliver and Boyd, 1962–65), 2 (1965): 43.

11. On the problem of the Hebrew scriptures and war, see Millard C. Lind, *Yahweh Is a Warrior: The Theology of Warfare in Ancient Israel* (Scottdale, Pa.: Herald Press, 1980); Willard M. Swartley, *Slavery, Sabbath, War, and Women: Case Issues in Biblical Interpretation* (Scottdale, Pa.: Herald Press, 1983), 96–118, 138–49; John H. Yoder, *The Original Revolution: Essays on Christian Pacifism* (Scottdale, Pa.: Herald Press, 1971), 91–111; Lois Barrett, *The Way God Fights* (Scottdale, Pa.: Herald Press, 1987).

12. As Mathias Rissi expresses this: "The task accepted by John in his vocation to be a prophet (1.9ff.) consists essentially in the *interpretation of history*, more precisely the interpretation of present and future history.... It is important to notice that John does not predict specific historical events, as is the case with Jewish apocalypticism. He rather interprets the true meaning and nature of the history with which he is concerned in terms of a traditional imagery long since known and taken over particularly from the Old Testament and also from Jewish concepts"(*The Future of the World: An Exegetical Study of Revelation 19.11–22.15* [London: SCM Press, 1972], 6–7).

13. The term *End* (of history) is capitalized when it is viewed in faith with this fullness of meaning and not capitalized when it is seen apart from faith as a terminal cutting off.

14. Ludwig Köhler, *Old Testament Theology* (Philadelphia: Westminster Press, 1957), 78.

15. Fyodor Dostoyevsky, *The Brothers Karamazov*, part 2, bk. 5, chap. 5.

16. Claus Westermann, *Isaiah 40–66: A Commentary* (Philadelphia: Westminster Press, 1969), 86.

17. Karl Barth, *Church Dogmatics* (Edinburgh: T. & T. Clark, 1960), III/3: 34.

18. This translation is supported by Artur Weiser, *The Psalms: A Commentary* (Philadelphia: Westminster Press, 1962), 373.

Chapter 2
THE IMMINENCE OF THE END

1. G. C. Berkouwer, *The Providence of God* (Grand Rapids: William B. Eerdmans Publishing Company, 1952), 12.

2. Karl Heim, *The New Divine Order* (London: Student Christian Movement Press, 1930), 87.

3. Psychiatrist Robert Jay Lifton has concluded: "We are haunted by the image of exterminating ourselves as a species by means of our own technology" (*The Broken Connection* [New York: Simon and Schuster, 1979], 5).

4. George Wald, quoted in Ted Peters, *Fear, Faith, and the Future: Affirming Christian Hope in the Face of Doomsday Prophecies* (Minneapolis: Augsburg Publishing House, 1980), 21.

5. See R. P. Turco, O. B. Toon, T. P. Ackerman, J. B. Pollack, Carl Sagan, "Nuclear Winter: Global Consequences of Multiple Nuclear Explosions," and Paul R. Ehrlich et al., "Long-Term Biological Consequences of Nuclear War," *Science* 23 (December 1983): 1283–1300.

6. See my *Darkening Valley: A Biblical Perspective on Nuclear War* (New York: Seabury Press, 1981; reprinted by Herald Press, Scottdale, Pa., 1989).

7. A U.S. study cited in Helmut Gollwitzer, *Frieden 2000: Fragen nach Sicherheit und Glauben* (Munich: Chr. Kaiser Verlag, 1982), 38.

8. Albert Einstein, cited in Alfred Kazin, "A Jew at Seventy-five," *The Progressive* (July 1990): 12.

9. Jonathan Schell, *The Fate of the Earth* (New York: Alfred A. Knopf, 1982), 118.

10. Klaus Koch has noted: "Apocalyptic is one of the few theological terms which has been absorbed into the jargon of the mass media" (*The Rediscovery of Apocalyptic* [London: SCM Press, 1972], 119).

11. Hans Schwarz, *On the Way to the Future* (Minneapolis: Augsburg Publishing House, 1972), 127.

12. Hans Walter Wolff, *Confrontations with Prophets* (Philadelphia: Fortress Press, 1983), 35.

13. This statement assumes that the peaceable visions of Hebrew prophets are to be understood in relation to the End of history as pictured in prophetic visions with a darker side and in the apostolic scriptures.

14. W. I. Thompson, *At the Edge of History* (New York: Harper & Row, 1971), 159.

15. Rudolf Bultmann, "New Testament and Mythology," in Hans Werner Bartsch, ed., *Kerygma and Myth: A Theological Debate* (London: SPCK, 1953 [German 1948]), 1:5 [German, 18].

16. Ruth Leger Sivard, *World Military and Social Expenditures 1991* (Washington, D.C.: World Priorities, 1991), 11.

17. The translation follows that given in Ernst Jenni and Claus Westermann, eds., *Theologisches Handwörterbuch zum Alten Testament*, 2 vols. (Munich: Chr. Kaiser Verlag, 1984), 2:662.

18. C. E. B. Cranfield, *The Gospel according to Saint Mark* (London: Cambridge University Press, 1959), 388, 390, 404, 405. Christopher Dawson, also commenting on Jesus' teaching in Mark 13, writes: "To the Christian the world is always ending, and every historical crisis is, as it were, a rehearsal for the real thing" (*The Dynamics of World History* [New York: Mentor Omega Books, 1962], 264).

Chapter 3
COUNTERFEITS FOR THE RULE OF GOD

1. Hans J. Morgenthau, *Scientific Man Versus Power Politics* (Chicago: University of Chicago Press, 1946), 200.

2. Claus Westermann, *Isaiah 40-66: A Commentary* (Philadelphia: Westminster Press, 1969), 83.

3. At the close of the U.S.-Iraq War Ken Sehested pointed out: "This war, as with all wars and other acts of violence, is at bottom a theological issue ... a conflict over who, finally, is in control; over the nature of true power in the universe; over the question of whether or not there is indeed One who promises and is able to bring final redemption, or if we are finally left to our own strength, cunning and prowess, abandoned to a monumental and deadly serious game of 'king of the mountain' where the winner takes all" ("Yet Will I Rejoice," *PeaceWork*, Baptist Peace Fellowship of North America, no. 2, [1991]: 1).

4. Quoted in Robert Jewett, *The Captain America Complex: The Dilemma of Zealous Nationalism* (Philadelphia: Westminster Press, 1973), 148.

5. An unidentified member of Congress as reported on National Public Radio, February 28, 1991.

6. Disarmament and peace-conversion specialist Seymour Melman commented in an interview: "The Gulf war fits into the ways of the military economy, whose chief executive officer is George Bush. The United States is now a military form of state capitalism in which the top managers of the military forces and their economy have dominant power — economic, political, and military. George Bush is now the CEO of that system, with the tacit and active agreement of the two main political parties" (Sherwood Ross, "Seymour Melman," *The Progressive* [February 1992]: 36).

7. As Michael T. Klare explains: "It was not only Iraq's military infrastructure that the United States sought to destroy. It was also the very idea of a major Third World power not under U.S. control" ("One, Two, Many Iraqs," *The Progressive* [April 20, 1991]: 22).

8. Russ W. Baker, "CIA Out of Control," *The Village Voice*, September 10, 1991.

9. Martin Hengel, *Christ and Power* (Belfast, Dublin: Christian Journals, 1977), 8.

10. Ed Gerlock, "Philippine National Dignity," *The Catholic Worker* (October–November 1991): 1.

11. "The Year of Dangerous Reporting: Indonesia Bloodbath, New York Times Whitewash," *Extra!* FAIR — Fairness & Accuracy In Reporting (July/August 1990): 16.

12. Andrew and Leslie Cockburn, *Dangerous Liaison: The Inside Story of the U.S.-Israeli Covert Relationship* (New York: HarperCollins Publishers, 1991), 110–11, 113–20.

13. See Martha Gellhorn, "Leben und Sterben in Panama,"*Die Zeit*, July 20, 1990, 9–13.

14. See Hunsinger, "Barth, Barmen, and the Confessing Church Today," *Katallagete* (Summer 1985): 16, which lists a number of documented studies.

15. Ibid., 18, citing Amory B. Lovins et al., "Nuclear Power and Nuclear Bombs," *Foreign Affairs* 58 (Summer 1980): 1175.

16. For these as well as other haunting photographs and commentary, see Thomas Y. Canby, photographs by Steve McCurry, "After the Storm," *National Geographic*, August 1991, 2–33.

17. Charles Kimball, "The Soldiers Are Leaving, but the Issues Remain," *Baptist Peacemaker*, Baptist Peace Fellowship of North America (Summer 1991): 3.

18. For book-length studies of undercover U.S. involvement in drug trafficking see Leslie Cockburn, *Out of Control: The Story of the Reagan Administration's Secret War in Nicaragua, the Illegal Arms Pipeline, and the Contra Drug Connection* (New York: Atlantic Monthly Press, 1987), and Alfred W. McCoy, *The Politics of Heroin: CIA Complicity in the Global Drug Trade* (New York: Lawrence Hill Books, 1991).

19. "UNICEF, Hoping to Prevent Deaths of Millions of Children, Calls for Sept. Summit," *The Sun* (Baltimore), December 13, 1989, 4A.

20. U.S. military spending amounts to about $450 billion yearly when one includes hidden components such as veterans benefits and interest on that part of the national debt resulting from military expenditures.

21. The figures, except the first, are taken from the statement "US Fellowship of Reconciliation Condemns the Widening War in the Persian Gulf" (1991).

22. Sylvia Ann Hewlett, "The Cost of Neglect of America's Children," *The Sun* (Baltimore), July 7, 1991, 1N.

23. *Fighting Crime in America: An Agenda for the 1990's*, A Majority Staff Report, Committee on the Judiciary, United States Senate, 1991, 1–8.

24. A study by the National Centers for Disease Control cited in "Firearms Blamed for Many Deaths of Young Men," *The Sun* (Baltimore), March 15, 1991, 16A.

25. TRB, "In Defense of the Exclusionary Rule," *The Sun* (Baltimore), April 18, 1991, 19A.

26. In a speech of the high priest Ananus as given in Josephus, *Wars of the Jews*, IV. iii. 10.

27. Ibid., VI. vi. l.

28. See Hendrikus Berkhof's discussion of 2 Thessalonians 2:3–12 in *Christ the Meaning of History* (Richmond, Va.: John Knox Press: 1966), 114–18. He writes: "Here the question tends to rise whether the antichrist is a person or a group, a tendency or a spirit of the age. Whenever this is viewed as an 'either-or,' we are trying to force biblical thought into a Western alternative. Christ is a person, and at the same time he is the head of a body (moreover, he himself is this body, 1 Cor. 12:12) who with his Spirit moves triumphantly through the world; the antichrist is similar to all this.... He is more than a group; he is the object of this group's worship, and that can only be a person.... The Word could work only, and was able to conquer and influence only, after it had become flesh (for only the person can bear power). In the same manner the demonic power will become flesh and person" (117).

29. In 1 Corinthians 3:16–17, 2 Corinthians 6:16, and Ephesians 2:21 Paul calls the church the temple of God.

Chapter 4
FALSE PROPHECY

1. John Bright, trans., *Jeremiah* (Garden City, N.Y.: Doubleday & Co., 1964), 44–45.

2. Hans Walter Wolff, *Confrontations with Prophets* (Philadelphia: Fortress Press, 1983), 76.

3. R. Musil, quoted in Jürgen Moltmann, *Theology of Hope* (New York: Harper & Row, 1967), 23.

4. *New York Times*, March 24, 1983, 20A.

5. October 21, 1984.

6. "Hucksters for Capitalism," a taped radio program from The Great Atlantic Radio Conspiracy, Baltimore.

7. Gustavo Gutiérrez, *A Theology of Liberation* (Maryknoll, N.Y.: Orbis Books, 1973), 235.

8. Mark Crispin Miller, "TV's Ironic Age," *Harper's Magazine*, November 1986, 32.

9. John Pairman Brown gives the definition: "This monolithic political-industrial-military-intellectual-propagandist complex is what I call an Establishment" (*The Liberated Zone: A Guide to Christian Resistance* [Richmond, Va.: John Knox Press, 1969], 40).

10. I am indebted to a conference comment by John Howard Yoder, later elaborated in "The Christian Case for Democracy," *The Priestly Kingdom: Social Ethics as Gospel* (Notre Dame: University of Notre Dame Press, 1984), 151–71.

11. Herbert Marcuse, *An Essay on Liberation* (Boston: Beacon Press, 1969), 65.

12. Noam Chomsky, "The Bounds of Thinkable Thought," *The Progressive* (October 1985): 30. For analyses of propaganda in the media, see Edward S. Herman and Noam Chomsky, *Manufacturing Consent: The Political Economy of the Mass Media* (New York: Pantheon Books, 1988), and Martin A. Lee and Norman Solomon, *Unreliable Sources: A Guide to Detecting Bias in News Media* (New York: Carol Publishing Group, 1990).

13. This motif, though now heightened, has had a long American past. During the Normandy invasion, June 6, 1944, President Franklin Roosevelt asked his fellow Americans to join him in a long prayer: "Almighty God: Our sons, pride of our nation, this day have set upon a mighty endeavor, a struggle to preserve our Republic, our religion and our civilization, and to set free a suffering humanity.... With Thy blessing, we shall prevail over the unholy forces of our enemy. Help us to conquer the apostles of greed and racial arrogances. Lead us to the saving of our country, and with our sister nations into a world unity that will spell a sure peace — a peace invulnerable to the schemings of unworthy men. And a peace that will let all men live in freedom, reaping the just rewards of their honest toil. Thy will be done, Almighty God. Amen" (*New York Times*, June 7, 1944, 1).

14. Ulrich Wilckens, "*hypokrinomai*," *Theological Dictionary of the New Testament*, 8:567.

15. *The Peloponnesian War*, 3.82–83, quoted in Robert Jay Lifton and Nicholas

Humphrey, eds., *In a Dark Time* (Cambridge, Mass.: Harvard University Press, 1984), 11.

16. Christopher Lasch, "Paranoid Presidency," *The Center Magazine* (March–April 1974): 31.

17. Gordon Zahn, *In Solitary Witness: The Life and Death of Franz Jägerstätter* (Collegeville, Minn.: Liturgical Press, 1964), 111–13.

18. National Public Radio broadcast, May 16, 1989.

19. Garry Wills, "Ready on the Right," *The Sun* (Baltimore), February 7, 1991, 15A.

20. A Sunday evening broadcast on February 17, 1991, referred to by Joyce Hollyday, "Grounded in Hope," *Sojourners* (April 1991): 33.

21. Vernon Grounds, "The Purpose of Prophecy,"*ESA Parley*, Evangelicals for Social Action (July 1987): 5–6. Grounds pictures the superabundance of such materials: "Visit a typical Christian bookstore, and you find shelf upon shelf stocked with all kinds of publications purporting to explain what Scripture reveals concerning the future. And you may be appalled as you realize that books like these are shaping the mind-set and influencing the political outlook of millions ... of devout, well-meaning Christians" ("Eschatology: Cutting the Nerve of Christian Social Concern," *ESA Parley* [January 1987]: 1).

22. P. T. Forsyth, *The Person and Place of Jesus Christ* (London: Independent Press, 1909), 220.

23. Jacques Ellul, *Apocalypse: The Book of Revelation* (New York: Seabury Press, 1977), 96. See also Ellul's classic study, *Propaganda: The Formation of Men's Attitudes* (New York: Alfred A. Knopf, 1965).

24. Gerhard von Rad, *Old Testament Theology* (Edinburgh: Oliver and Boyd, 1962–65), 2:210.

25. "Witness to Hope against a Demonic World," *Sojourners* (August–September 1991): 23.

26. But certainly disciples should hold also to the vision and purpose of transformation of the society and world, beginning in the Christian community and, however extensively actualized, still proleptic to God's consummation of history.

Chapter 5
PUBLIC ENEMIES

1. Herbert H. Farmer, *God and Men* (New York, Nashville: Abingdon-Cokesbury Press, 1947), 188–89.

2. Quoted in Jack Nelson-Pallmeyer, *War against the Poor: Low-Intensity Conflict and Christian Faith* (Maryknoll, N.Y.: Orbis Books, 1989), 18.

3. "A Call to Reflection, Resistance, and Reconciliation: The Fellowship of Reconciliation's Statement on the Gulf War," March 8, 1991.

4. Quoted in William L. Shirer, *The Rise and Fall of the Third Reich: A History of Nazi Germany* (New York: Simon & Schuster, 1959), 26, from Adolf Hitler, *Mein Kampf* (Boston, 1943), 56.

5. Paul F. Walker and Eric Stambler, "...And the Dirty Little Weapons," *Bulletin of the Atomic Scientists* (May 1991): 22, 24. The discussion of the use of cluster bombs concludes: "The 28 B-52s which reportedly dropped 470 tons of explosives on Iraqi ground forces on one day, January 30, could have obliterated 1,600 square miles, an area one-third the size of Connecticut." David Noble in "Professors of Terror: Meet the Scholars Who Burned Iraq," *The Progressive* (September 1991): 32, writes that fuel-air explosives "are sufficiently similar to nuclear weapons that they are routinely used in experimental settings to simulate nuclear explosions. Though they contain no nuclear material, they create mushroom clouds, just like the real thing. FAEs disperse a cloud of highly volatile fuel which is detonated to produce a massive explosion, sucking up oxygen and creating firestorm-like conditions. Human beings caught in the target area thus suffer first the shock of the concussion, then suffocation, and finally incineration." Of the 88,500 tons of bombs dropped during the war, only 6,520 tons — 7.4 percent — were "precision-guided" weapons.

6. Quoted in "Fellowship of Reconciliation Calls for an End to Non-Military Sanctions against Iraq," *Civilian Casualty Fund, F.O.R.*, Summer 1991.

7. "U.N. Aid Available, U.S. Says, If Iraq Has Shortages of Food," *The Sun* (Baltimore), October 23, 1991, 2A. The heading and content frame of the brief news article were such as to outweigh points mentioned from the report, financed by UNICEF and several private foundations.

8. See "Incubating an Atrocity Tale," *Extra!* FAIR — Fairness and Accuracy in Reporting (March 1992): 5. Outstanding among the coached "witnesses" was (as later came out) the fifteen-year-old daughter of the Kuwaiti ambassador to the United States.

9. Figured in 1987 dollars. See Ruth Leger Sivard, *World Military and Social Expenditures 1991*, 11.

10. Joseph Sittler, "Moral Discourse in a Nuclear Age," *The Christian Century* (March 6, 1985): 243.

11. Part of this and the preceding paragraph appeared in my article, "The Execution of Ronnie Dunkins," *The Christian Century* (August 30–September 6, 1989): 783–85.

12. Joachim Jeremias has shown that "many" means "all" in Isaiah 53 and in Jesus' echoing of it during the Last Supper in the phrase "poured out for many" (Mk. 14:24; Mt. 26:28). See *The Eucharistic Words of Jesus* (Philadelphia: Fortress Press, 1977), 226–31.

13. C. F. D. Moule, "The Judgment Theme in the Sacraments," *The Background of the New Testament and Its Eschatology*, ed. W. D. Davies and D. Daube (Cambridge: Cambridge University Press, 1956), 475.

14. Richard Shaull writes: "A high percentage of the men, women, and children being slaughtered in Central America by groups and governments the United States supports are Christians, leaders and members of the base communities" (*Heralds of a New Reformation: The Poor of South and North America* [Maryknoll, N.Y.: Orbis Books, 1984], xi).

15. See Hendrikus Berkhof, *Christ the Meaning of History* (Richmond, Va.: John Knox Press: 1966), 103.

16. Stanley Hauerwas draws this conclusion about Reinhold Niebuhr: "Fi-

nally, in spite of all the trenchant criticism he directed at America, America was his church" (*Against the Nations: War and Survival in a Liberal Society* [Minneapolis: Winston Press, 1985], 47).

17. Jean Lasserre, *War and the Gospel* (Scottdale, Pa.: Herald Press, 1962), 112.

18. *Sojourners* (January 1990): 28; *Kairos: Three Prophetic Challenges to the Church*, ed. Robert McAfee Brown (Grand Rapids: William B. Eerdmans Publishing Company, 1990), 129, 137.

19. See Vicki Kemper, "In the Name of Relief: A Look at Private U.S. Aid in *Contra* Territory," *Sojourners* (October 1985): 12–20.

20. Stephen Neill declares: "I will maintain against all comers that my God, deserted, bruised, bleeding, dying, is greater than any other that has ever been thought or imagined or worshipped by man; that this God is, in fact, that than which nothing greater can be conceived" (*Christian Faith Today* [Harmondsworth, Middlesex: Penguin Books, 1955], 262).

21. Fyodor Dostoyevsky, *The Brothers Karamazov*, part 2, book 4, chap. 4.

22. Remarkably, the term *Yad Vashem* ("a monument and a name") is taken from a passage in Isaiah 56 in which God declared his purpose of drawing in those who were seen as outside of Israel (foreigners, eunuchs) and gathering the outcasts of Israel and yet others besides (a purpose that Jesus echoed in John 10:16); that is, to those excluded on the outside God gives a monument and a name.

23. Quoted in Eberhard Bethge, *Dietrich Bonhoeffer* (New York: Harper & Row, 1970), 512.

Chapter 6
MASADA AND GOLGOTHA

1. Karl Barth, *Church Dogmatics* (Edinburgh: T. & T. Clark, 1960), II/2: 470, 213.

2. Hendrikus Berkhof, *Christ the Meaning of History* (Richmond, Va.: John Knox Press: 1966), 152–53.

3. See Mark Gaffney, *Dimona: The Story Behind the Vanunu Revelation* (Brattleboro, Vt.: Amana Books, 1989).

4. For a survey of support for Israel by the religious right, see Grace Halsell, *Prophecy and Politics* (Westport, Conn.: Lawrence Hill & Company, 1986).

5. Ronald J. Sider, "A Pilgrimage to the Holy Land," *ESA Advocate* (July/August 1990): 1–2. With regard to anti-Semitism C. E. B. Cranfield has written: "The supreme privilege and dignity of the Jews is the fact that [Jesus] is, so far as His human nature is concerned, a member of their race.... To despise them is to despise and dishonour Him.... The Jewishness of Jesus of Nazareth is the final and irrevocable condemnation of every form of antisemitism" ("Light from St. Paul on Christian-Jewish Relations," *The Bible and Christian Life* [Edinburgh: T. & T. Clark, 1985], 40).

6. RSV margin. In his commentary *Genesis* (Philadelphia: Westminster Press, 1961), 155–56, Gerhard von Rad makes a strong case for this traditional translation.

7. Wolfhart Pannenberg has expressed this caution: "The election of Israel was aimed at the blessing of all mankind, and this vocation continues. When Jesus chose twelve disciples to follow him, they were to represent the twelve tribes of Israel, an eschatologically renewed Israel that would be faithful to its calling. This indicates the continuity between the chosen people of Israel and the Christian church. The church is not the 'new Israel' as if the old one were no longer God's elected people. The church is an extension of the election of Israel, including within its community members from all nations" (*Human Nature, Election, and History* [Philadelphia: Westminster Press, 1977], 30).

8. There could have been further Jewish resettlement in Palestine without the establishment of the State of Israel. There could have been a binational development, with the two peoples living together in the land.

9. In *Blood Brothers* (Old Tappan, N.J.: Fleming H. Revell Company, 1984), Palestinian priest Elias Chacour gives a moving and conciliatory account of what it has been like to live under Israeli oppression.

10. For depiction of life under Israeli occupation see Gloria Emerson, *Gaza: A Year in the Intifada: A Personal Account from an Occupied Land* (New York: Atlantic Monthly Press, 1991), and the BBC documentary video, *Children of Fire* (available from Americans for Middle East Understanding, Inc., Room 241, 475 Riverside Drive, New York, NY 10115).

11. Rabbi I. Amital, cited in "Messianic Trends in Modern Israel" (Jerusalem: Melitz Center for Jewish-Christian Encounter, n.d.), 3. Resurrection is also a primary image. Pinchas Lapide has written: "In the collective soul of present-day Jewry ... Auschwitz and Jerusalem — the mass crucifixion and the national resurrection of Israel — have the same relation to each other that Good Friday and Easter Sunday have in the heart of a believing Christian" (*Am Scheitern hoffen lernen: Erfahrungen jüdischen Glaubens für heutige Christen* [Gütersloh: Gütersloher Verlagshaus Gerd Mohn, 1985], 20). In the words of Abraham Heschel: "This is part of our exultation: to witness the resurrection of the land of the Bible; a land that was dead for nearly two thousand years is now a land that sings.... The wonder of the risen Israel and the gratitude of Him who has raised martyred Israel from the dead belong together. We are witnesses of the resurrection" (*Israel: An Echo of Eternity* [New York: Farrar, Straus and Giroux, 1969], 122, 220).

12. In any society there may be foreshadowings of the future redemption. What is being stated is not that such foreshadowings are lacking in Israel but that they do not predominantly shape and distinguish the nation.

13. Amital, cited in "Messianic Trends in Modern Israel," 4.

14. "A Briefing on Israel's $10 Billion Request," *Breaking the Siege*, The Middle East Justice Network (August–September 1991): 5.

15. "Human Rights Activists from East and West on the Middle East Crisis," *New Outlook* (November–December 1988): 26.

16. Josephus, *Wars of the Jews*, VII. viii, ix.

17. The meaning of "meek" given in Floyd V. Filson, *The Gospel according to St. Matthew* (London: Adam & Charles Black, 1960), 77.

18. Friedrich Hauck and Siegfried Schulz, *"praus," Theological Dictionary of the New Testament*, 4:649.

19. Colin Chapman, *Whose Promised Land?* (Tring, Herts., England: Lion,

1983), 142–43. See W. D. Davies, *The Gospel and the Land* (Los Angeles: University of California Press, 1974) and Walter Brueggemann, *The Land* (Philadelphia: Fortress Press, 1977).

20. Richard Falk, "From Dispossession to Palestinian Statehood," *Palestine Human Rights Newsletter* (January/February 1989): 9.

21. See Joachim Jeremias, *The Eucharistic Words of Jesus* (Philadelphia: Fortress Press, 1977), 256–62, for commentary on the use of this cry of acclamation from Psalm 118:26.

Chapter 7
"FALLEN IS BABYLON!"

1. Karl Heim, *The Transformation of the Scientific World View* (New York: Harper & Brothers Publishers, 1953), 21.

2. Jacques Ellul, *Apocalypse: The Book of Revelation* (New York: Seabury Press, 1977), 193.

Chapter 8
"THE JUDGMENT OF THIS WORLD"

1. R. Lejeune, *Christoph Blumhardt and His Message* (Rifton, N.Y.: Plough Publishing House, 1963 [German 1938]), 84.

2. G. C. Berkouwer, *The Providence of God* (Grand Rapids: William B. Eerdmans Publishing Company, 1952), 27.

3. See *Now Is the Time: Final Document and Other Texts: World Convocation on Justice, Peace and the Integrity of Creation, Seoul 1990* (Geneva, Switzerland: World Council of Churches, 1990).

4. Albrecht Oepke, "*apokalypto*," *Theological Dictionary of the New Testament*, 3:580.

5. P. T. Forsyth, *The Person and Place of Jesus Christ* (London: Independent Press, 1909), 73–74.

6. For a survey of times Jesus was angry, see Gustav Stählin, "*orge*," *Theological Dictionary of the New Testament*, 5:427–29.

7. Jean Danielou, *The Lord of History: Reflections on the Inner Meaning of History* (Chicago: Henry Regnery, 1958), 155.

8. Artur Weiser, *The Psalms: A Commentary* (Philadelphia: Westminster Press, 1962), 528.

9. Walther Zimmerli, *Old Testament Theology in Outline* (Edinburgh: T. & T. Clark, 1978), 171.

10. Walther Zimmerli has delineated a motif that emerges in the Hebrew scriptures: "Yahweh himself suffers when he brings judgment upon Israel.... Behind all the incomprehensible suffering of the world [is] the ultimate depth that constitutes the background of this suffering: Yahweh himself suffers in the judgment that he must execute upon his people. In the suffering of the prophet

is reflected the suffering of God for his people. Thus the prophet's suffering becomes a part of his message" (ibid., 206–7).

11. *Christ and the Powers* (Scottdale, Pa.: Herald Press, 1962). For that book the author's name is given as Hendrik Berkhof.

12. John Howard Yoder, *The Politics of Jesus* (Grand Rapids: William B. Eerdmans Publishing Company, 1972), 135–62. See also Jacques Ellul, *The Ethics of Freedom* (Grand Rapids: William B. Eerdmans Publishing Company, 1976), 144–60.

13. In *When War Is Unjust: Being Honest in Just-War Thinking* (Minneapolis: Augsburg Publishing House, 1984), 18, John Howard Yoder gives the following list of "just-war" criteria:

1. The authority waging the war must be legitimate.

2. The cause being fought for must be just.

3. The ultimate goal ("intention") must be peace.

4. The subjective motivation ("intention") must not be hatred or vengefulness.

5. War must be the last resort.

6. Success must be probable.

7. The means used must be indispensable to achieve the end.

8. The means used must be discriminating, both

   (a) quantitatively, in order not to do more harm than the harm they prevent ("proportionality"), and

   (b) qualitatively, to avoid use against the innocent ("immunity").

9. The means used must respect the provisions of international law.

14. "Confronting Threats to Peace and Survival," *Gathered for Life: Official Report, VI Assembly of the World Council of Churches, Vancouver, Canada, 24 July–10 August, 1983,* ed. David Gill (Geneva: World Council of Churches; Grand Rapids: William B. Eerdmans Publishing Company, 1983), 75. This is part of a report approved in substance by the assembly and commended to the churches for study and appropriate action.

15. Marcus J. Borg points out: "'Love your enemies' thus meant 'Love your non-compatriots,' i.e., non-Jews. What would this have meant in teaching directed to Israel in the late twenties of the first century? It had an inescapable and identifiable political implication: the non-Jewish enemy was, above all, Rome. To say 'Love your enemy' would have meant, 'Love the Romans — do not join the resistance movement,' whatever other implications it might also have had" (*Conflict, Holiness & Politics in the Teachings of Jesus* [New York and Toronto: Edwin Mellen Press, 1984], 130).

16. Otto Weber, *Foundations of Dogmatics* (Grand Rapids: William B. Eerdmans Publishing Company, 1983 [German 1962]), 2:673.

Chapter 9
FATE AND FAITH

1. Gerhard von Rad, *Old Testament Theology* (Edinburgh: Oliver and Boyd, 1962–65), 2:153.

2. Gabriel Marcel, *Homo Viator: Introduction to a Metaphysic of Hope* (Chicago: Henry Regnery, 1951), 37.

3. There is much evidence for the view delineated by Philip Agee in "Producing the Proper Crisis," *Z Magazine* (November 1990): 54–56, that the Bush administration intentionally let Saddam Hussein think it would accept his invading Kuwait so as to have, with that invasion, the grounds for proceeding as it then did. U.S. intelligence certainly knew of the Iraqi buildup for the invasion, but, rather strangely, no clear warning was given to Saddam Hussein not to proceed. On the contrary, certain statements by U.S. officials gave him strong reason to believe that he could get away with an invasion of Kuwait. As became widely known, the U.S. ambassador April Glaspie told him on July 25, 1990: "I have direct instructions from the President to seek better relations with Iraq....We have no opinion on the Arab-Arab conflicts, like your border disagreement with Kuwait."

4. Langdon Gilkey, *Reaping the Whirlwind: A Christian Interpretation of History* (New York: Seabury Press, 1976), 49, 50, 51.

5. G. B. Caird, *St. Luke* (Harmondsworth, Middlesex: Penguin Books, 1963), 104.

6. Reinhold Niebuhr, *The World Crisis and American Responsibility*, ed. Ernest W. Lefever (New York: Association Press, 1958), 34, 35.

7. As Rachel H. King has pointed out: "If Jesus were living in a period of total war only three lines of action would be open to him: he could be some form of combatant, he could be some form of conscientious objector, or he could commit suicide....If all of the possible choices necessarily involve sin, Jesus would be a sinner if he lived today. To say that is to deny that he is an adequate saviour of men, for it is to deny that he 'was in all points tempted like as we are, yet without sin' " (*God's Boycott of Sin* [New York: Fellowship, 1946], 71).

8. George F. Kennan, *The Nuclear Delusion: Soviet-American Relations in the Atomic Age* (New York: Pantheon, 1982), 176.

9. Richard J. Barnet, "Losing Moral Ground," *Sojourners* (March 1985): 28.

10. See E. Würthwein and J. Behm, *"metanoeo, metanoia," Theological Dictionary of the New Testament*, 4:985–86, 1003.

11. *The Challenge of Peace: God's Promise and Our Response, A Pastoral Letter on War and Peace* (Washington, D.C.: National Conference of Catholic Bishops, 1983), 58–59.

Chapter 10
"ARISE, O LORD!"

1. The translation of v. 10 (the last quoted) is that given in Artur Weiser, *The Psalms: A Commentary* (Philadelphia: Westminster Press, 1962), 505.

2. William Shakespeare, *Julius Caesar*, Act I, Sc. 2, Line 134.

3. Weiser, *The Psalms*, 512. Weiser writes of this passage: "Nowhere else in the Old Testament is the power of faith in God to master life so profoundly grasped in such purity and strength, nowhere so forcefully formulated, as in the 'nevertheless,' uttered by faith, by which the poet of Psalm 73 commits himself to God" (515).

4. Arnold J. Toynbee, *A Study of History*, abridgment of vols. 1–4 by D. C. Somervell (New York: Oxford University Press, 1947), 379–80.

5. John K. Stoner and Lois Barrett, *Letters to American Christians* (Scottdale, Pa.: Herald Press, 1989), 19.

6. George Mendenhall, "The 'Vengeance' of Yahweh," *The Tenth Generation: The Origins of the Biblical Tradition* (Baltimore: Johns Hopkins University Press, 1973), 78, 83, 89, 83, 100.

7. Ibid., 84.

8. James D. Smart, *The Old Testament in Dialogue with Modern Man* (Philadelphia: Westminster Press, 1964), 38.

9. Mendenhall, "The 'Vengeance' of Yahweh," 100. Cf. Millard C. Lind, *Yahweh Is a Warrior: The Theology of Warfare in Ancient Israel* (Scottdale, Pa.: Herald Press, 1980), 52: "Outside Israel the experience of divinity in history was god *and* king. Within Israel the experience of divinity in history was Yahweh *versus* king."

10. "Altered" indicates a change of wording in a quotation from the Revised Standard Version or from another translation.

11. In *Love of Enemies: The Way to Peace* (Philadelphia: Fortress Press, 1984), 120, William Klassen makes a point that is seldom understood: "Paul does not assume, any more than did the writer of the proverb, that you simply hand your enemy some food and offer him/her a drink. Rather, in the Orient one eats and drinks with the one who receives the food."

12. C. E. B. Cranfield, *The Epistle to the Romans*, 2 vols. (Edinburgh: T. & T. Clark, 1979), 2:647–48.

13. Robert Lowry in the hymn "Low in the Grave He Lay."

Chapter 11
ARMAGEDDON MIRAGE

1. The most influential proponent of this view has been Hal Lindsey, whose *The Late Great Planet Earth* (Grand Rapids: Zondervan, 1970) was the best-selling book in the United States during the 1970s.

2. Ibid., 51–55.

3. It would be interesting to study what effect the collapse of the Soviet Union as the world's second superpower has on the speculations of pop apocalyptists. Given the world situation after the breakup of the Soviet Union, a Russian invasion of Palestine in the foreseeable future is extremely unlikely. It was very unlikely even at the height of Soviet power. On the basis of "prophecy" one can ignore the power relations involved. Or one can say that at some later time this Russian threat will again become great and will be carried out. But in such a view "the battle of Armageddon" can hardly be so near in terms of calendrical time as feverish popularizers have been claiming.

4. Grace Halsell, *Prophecy and Politics: Militant Evangelists on the Road to Nuclear War* (Westport, Conn.: Lawrence Hill & Company, 1986), 47.

5. Ibid., 50, quoting James Mills, formerly president pro tem of the California State Senate during a part of the time that Ronald Reagan was governor of the state.

6. Gerhard von Rad, *Old Testament Theology* (Edinburgh: Oliver and Boyd, 1962–65), 2:156.

7. Jacques Ellul, *Apocalypse: The Book of Revelation* (New York: Seabury Press, 1977), 32.

8. Joachim Jeremias, *"Ar Magedon," Theological Dictionary of the New Testament*, 1:468.

9. Hans Walter Wolff, *Confrontations with Prophets* (Philadelphia: Fortress Press, 1983), 38.

10. This is the overall tenor of the passages. Zechariah 12:6–9 and Micah 4:11–13 could be taken as exceptions. In the former passage Yahweh is to make "the clans of Judah...a flaming torch among sheaves; and they shall devour to the right and to the left all the peoples round about." In the latter passage the nations assemble against Zion, but through that Yahweh gathers them "as sheaves to the threshing floor." The command, "Arise and thresh... / you shall beat in pieces many peoples" (v. 13), and the imagery of booty seem to suggest Jewish military involvement in Yahweh's harvesting, defeat, and despoiling of the nations. These late echoes of the Hebrew holy-war motif are to be understood as transformed, along with the motif itself, once and for all in Jesus Christ. His disciples have gone under a new command into the harvest fields.

11. Though many popular interpreters date this battle as a thousand years later than Armageddon, the reference to Gog and Magog clearly identifies it as a recasting of Ezekiel 38–39, which the same interpreters generally see as describing Armageddon. Scenes in Revelation are often coordinate; an aspect of history is pictured in one way, then in another and still another.

12. Joachim Jeremias in *"pule," Theological Dictionary of the New Testament*, 6:927, supports this translation and interpretation of the saying.

Chapter 12
THE POLITICS OF THE HILLTOP CITY

1. Helmut Gollwitzer, *An Introduction to Protestant Theology* (Philadelphia: Westminster Press, 1982 [German, 1978]), 105. Emil Brunner has written: "The

criterion of all genuine theology is this — does it lead to the cry, 'God, be merciful to me a sinner,' and beyond it to the exclamation: 'Thanks be to God, who giveth us the victory through Jesus Christ our Lord' " (*Eternal Hope* [Philadelphia: Westminster Press, 1954], 183). The two statements can be seen as complementary.

2. See André Trocmé, *Jesus and the Nonviolent Revolution* (Scottdale, Pa.: Herald Press, 1973), 19–66.

3. Joachim Jeremias, *The Sermon on the Mount* (London: University of London, Athlone Press, 1961), 30.

4. See Gerhard von Rad, "Die Stadt auf dem Berge," *Gesammelte Studien zum Alten Testament* (Munich: Christian Kaiser Verlag, 1958), 214–24.

5. Quoted in Martin Hengel, *Christ and Power* (Philadelphia: Fortress Press, 1977), 47, from *Apology* 37.4 ff. (Loeb edition).

6. Quoted in John Nevin Sayre, "Today's Word for the Church Is No," *Reconciliation Quarterly*, British Fellowship of Reconciliation (Autumn 1962): 293.

7. See Ronald J. Sider, *Rich Christians in an Age of Hunger*, rev. ed. (Downers Grove, Ill.: Inter-Varsity Press, 1984).

8. See Marlin Jeschke, *Discipling in the Church: Recovering a Ministry of the Gospel* (Scottdale, Pa.: Herald Press, 1988).

9. See Seymour Melman, *The Demilitarized Society: Disarmament and Conversion* (Montreal: Harvest House, 1988).

10. Helmut Gollwitzer writes: "The whole system of production should serve the whole of society, in order to give equitably to all its members what they materially need for the maintenance of their lives" (*Frieden 2000: Fragen nach Sicherheit und Glauben* [Munich: Chr. Kaiser Verlag, 1982], 201).

11. See Ronald J. Sider , *Nonviolence: The Invincible Weapon?* (Dallas: Word Publishing, 1989); Duane K. Friesen, *Christian Peacemaking and International Conflict* (Scottdale, Pa.: Herald Press, 1986); Adam Roberts, ed., *The Strategy of Civilian Defence: Non-violent Resistance to Aggression* (London: Faber and Faber, 1967); Anders Boserup and Andrew Mack, *War without Weapons: Non-Violence in National Defense* (New York: Schocken, 1975); Gene Sharp, *Politics of Nonviolent Action* (Boston: Porter Sargent, 1973).

12. Pavel Stolar, a friend of mine, wrote from Prague: "My wife and I took part in many demonstrations. In the biggest one there were nearly one million people, who wanted to change the history of their country. The most important moment in this demonstration I shall never forget: that the people were ready to forgive three policemen for what they had done in a police action some days earlier. After that all the people present in the demonstration, Christians and atheists, prayed the Lord's Prayer. The words, 'Forgive us our debts, as we also have forgiven our debtors,' are our motto in these present days."

13. George F. Kennan, *The Nuclear Delusion: Soviet-American Relations in the Atomic Age* (New York: Pantheon, 1982), 61.

14. See Magne Skodvin, "Norwegian Nonviolent Resistance During the German Occupation," and Jeremy Bennett, "The Resistance Against the German Occupation of Denmark 1940–45," in Roberts, ed., *The Strategy of Civilian Defence*, 136–53, 154–72.

15. What George F. Kennan in the *The Nuclear Delusion*, 100–101, wrote about

the Soviet leadership in 1977 applies to a much longer period: "It faces serious internal problems, which constitute its main preoccupation. As this leadership looks abroad, it sees more dangers than inviting opportunities. Its reactions and purposes are therefore much more defensive than aggressive. It has no desire for any major war, least of all for a nuclear one. It fears and respects American military power even as it tries to match it, and hopes to avoid a conflict with it. Plotting an attack on Western Europe would be, in the circumstances, the last thing that would come into its head."

16. Jeff Schoonover-Higgins, "View from El Salvador," *Brethren Peace Fellowship Newsletter*, Mid-Atlantic District (March–April 1990): 1. For an account of efforts along these lines during the Contra war in Nicaragua see Ed Griffin-Nolan, *Witness for Peace: A Story of Resistance* (Louisville, Ky.: Westminster/John Knox Press, 1991).

17. Quoted in Todd Moore, "Bearing Witness: John Schuchardt Attends the Church of His Choice," *Zephyr*, Galesburg, Ill., February 28, 1991.

18. Bill Wylie Kellermann, *Seasons of Faith and Conscience: Kairos, Confession, Liturgy* (Maryknoll, N.Y.: Orbis Books, 1991), xix–xxiv.

19. Joyce Hollyday, "Bathed in the Spirit," *Sojourners* (August 1983): 24–28.

20. Quoted in Jim Wallis, "The Rise of Christian Conscience," *Sojourners* (January 1985): 12.

21. Jim Wallis, "A Wolf in Sheep's Clothing," *Sojourners* (May 1986): 22.

22. For a fuller treatment of Romans 13:1–7 and the view of government that it supposedly gives the basis for, see my *Darkening Valley: A Biblical Perspective on Nuclear War* (New York: Seabury Press, 1981; reprinted by Herald Press, Scottdale, Pa., 1989), 92–99. Martin Hengel writes of Romans 13:1–7: "Under no circumstances should this passage be misunderstood as an eternally valid prescription for an attitude of reverence toward the state. Probably Paul formulated this excursus with one eye on the special situation of the Christian community of Rome" (*Victory over Violence: Jesus and the Revolutionaries* [Philadelphia: Fortress Press, 1973], 63). On Paul's view of the Roman state see Klaus Wengst, *Pax Romana and the Peace of Jesus Christ* (Minneapolis: Fortress Press, 1987), 72–89, where Romans 13:1–7 as an "isolated statement" (138) is considered in the context of other relevant passages.

Chapter 13
HOPE IN GOD ALONE

1. James D. Smart, *The Old Testament in Dialogue with Modern Man* (Philadelphia: Westminster Press, 1964), 106. Smart states a prior guideline: "The test, then, of any modern interpretation of Scripture is whether in it the same word from God that once sounded into an ancient world is actually to be heard in the modern world" (24).

2. G. Clarke Chapman, *Facing the Nuclear Heresy: A Call to Reformation* (Elgin, Ill.: Brethren Press, 1986), 190.

3. Norman Vincent Peale, *The Power of Positive Thinking* (Englewood Cliffs, N.J.: Prentice-Hall, 1954).

4. G. Clarke Chapman, "Faith as Official Optimism," *Facing the Nuclear Heresy*, 175–91.

5. Arnold Toynbee, *War and Civilization* (New York: Oxford University Press, 1950), xii.

6. Quoted in Robert Jay Lifton and Nicholas Humphrey, eds. *In a Dark Time*, (Cambridge, Mass.: Harvard University Press, 1984), 138.

7. Gerhard von Rad, *Old Testament Theology*, (Edinburgh: Oliver and Boyd, 1962–65), 2:160, 161.

8. *Herbert Butterfield: Writings on Christianity and History*, ed. C. T. McIntire (New York: Oxford University Press, 1979), 159.

9. Robert J. Lifton, *History and Human Survival* (New York: Random House, 1970), 203.

10. T. F. Torrance, *When Christ Comes and Comes Again* (Grand Rapids: William B. Eerdmans Publishing Company, 1957), 153.

11. See Karl Barth, *Church Dogmatics* (Edinburgh: T. & T. Clark, 1960), IV/1: 119.

12. Both quotations are from the translation given in C. E. B. Cranfield, *The Epistle to the Romans* (Edinburgh: T. & T. Clark, 1979), 1:256.

13. P. T. Forsyth, *The Justification of God* (New York: Charles Scribner's Sons, 1917), 232.

Chapter 14
PROMISE AND PAROUSIA

1. Karl Heim, *Jesus the World's Perfecter: The Atonement and the Renewal of the World* (Edinburgh and London: Oliver and Boyd, 1959), 155–56.

2. Josef Pieper, *Hope and History* (New York: Herder and Herder, 1969), 14.

3. Quoted in Roger Lincoln Shinn, *Christianity and the Problem of History* (New York: Charles Scribner's Sons, 1953), 201.

4. Richard L. Rubenstein, *The Age of Triage: Fear and Hope in an Overcrowded World* (Boston: Beacon Press, 1983).

5. Paul S. Minear, *Christian Hope and the Second Coming* (Philadelphia: Westminster Press, 1954), 37.

6. Karl Heim, *The New Divine Order* (London: Student Christian Movement Press, 1930), 105.

7. Joachim Jeremias, *The Parables of Jesus*, rev. ed. (London: SCM Press, 1963), 165.

8. Albrecht Oepke, *"parousia," Theological Dictionary of the New Testament*, 5:866.

9. Paraphrase by Paul S. Minear, "Promise," *The Interpreter's Dictionary of the Bible* (New York, Nashville: Abingdon Press, 1962), 3:894.

10. Karl Heim, *Jesus the World's Perfecter: The Atonement and the Renewal of the World* (Edinburgh and London: Oliver and Boyd, 1959), 130.

11. T. F. Torrance brings out a crucial aspect in all this: "No, we do not worship some inhuman ghost, we worship and adore Jesus — and that is of the very

essence of our hope: that Jesus Christ wearing our humanity, Jesus bone of our bone and flesh of our flesh, is at the right hand of God, and is exalted as Lord and King of all. Because it is our humanity that Jesus wears, you and I are anchored to Him within the veil" (*When Christ Comes and Comes Again* [Grand Rapids: William B. Eerdmans Publishing Company, 1957], 154).

12. Or in another image applied by James Orr to Hebrew prophecy: "To the prophet's faith and expectancy ... [the consummation] seemed always near; as a high mountain on the verge of the horizon always seems at hand, so this event loomed up behind whatever phase of Providence was immediately in view" (*Sidelights on Christian Doctrine* [New York: A. C. Armstrong & Son, 1909], 169).

13. Karl Heim, *Jesus the World's Perfecter*, 146–47. The passage reads: "The act of atonement and the new creation belong as inseparably together ... as lightning and the ensuing rolling thunder. The Church therefore, which has experienced the power of the redemption of the world, is waiting for the change of the world with the same tension as after we have seen the lightning we expect the rumbling of the thunder. For lightning and thunder are merely two effects of the same electrical discharge. The interval is caused only because the waves of sound take longer to cover the distance than the rays of light. But the sound must come. Once there has been lightning the thunder cannot fail to come."

14. Quoted in Fletcher Knebel and Charles W. Bailey II, *No High Ground* (New York: Harper & Bros., 1960), 177.

INDEX

NEW TESTAMENT